Mandarin Brazil

ASIAN AMERICA

A series edited by Gordon H. Chang

The increasing size and diversity of the Asian American population, its growing significance in American society and culture, and the expanded appreciation, both popular and scholarly, of the importance of Asian Americans in the country's present and past—all these developments have converged to stimulate wide interest in scholarly work on topics related to the Asian American experience. The general recognition of the pivotal role that race and ethnicity have played in American life, and in relations between the United States and other countries, has also fostered the heightened attention.

Although Asian Americans were a subject of serious inquiry in the late nineteenth and early twentieth centuries, they were subsequently ignored by the mainstream scholarly community for several decades. In recent years, however, this neglect has ended, with an increasing number of writers examining a good many aspects of Asian American life and culture. Moreover, many students of American society are recognizing that the study of issues related to Asian America speak to, and may be essential for, many current discussions on the part of the informed public and various scholarly communities.

The Stanford series on Asian America seeks to address these interests. The series will include works from the humanities and social sciences, including history, anthropology, political science, American studies, law, literary criticism, sociology and interdisciplinary and policy studies.

A full list of titles in the Asian America series can be found online at www.sup.org/asianamerica

Mandarin Brazil
Race, Representation, and Memory

Ana Paulina Lee

STANFORD UNIVERSITY PRESS

STANFORD, CALIFORNIA

Stanford University Press
Stanford, California

Printed in the United States of America on acid-free,
archival-quality paper

Library of Congress Cataloging-in-Publication Data

Names: Lee, Ana Paulina, author.
Title: Mandarin Brazil : race, representation, and memory / Ana Paulina
    Lee.
Description: Stanford, California : Stanford University Press, 2018. |
Series: Asian America | Includes bibliographical references and index. |
Identifiers: LCCN 2017054936 (print) | LCCN 2018019828 (ebook) |
    ISBN 9781503606029 | ISBN 9781503605046 (cloth : alk. paper) |
    ISBN 9781503606012 (pbk. : alk. paper)
Subjects: LCSH: Chinese—Brazil—History. | Chinese in popular
    culture—Brazil. | National characteristics, Brazilian. | Brazil—Race
    relations—History. | Racism—Brazil—History.
Classification: LCC F2659.C5 (ebook) | LCC F2659.C5 L44 2018 (print) |
    DDC 305.800981—dc23
LC record available at https://lccn.loc.gov/2017054936

Cover design: Rob Ehle
Cover illustration: *Chinese Tea Plantation in the Rio de Janeiro Botanical
Garden*, engraved by Leon Jean Baptiste Sabatier, after Johann Moritz
Rugendas. Bridgeman Images.

For my parents, Tony and Paula, in loving memory
Yen Lin Show Jein

Contents

Acknowledgments

It gives me immense joy to express my gratitude to the numerous people who have supported this project. Many thanks to Margo Irvin at Stanford University Press (SUP) for her enthusiasm for the project and guidance throughout the editorial process. I thank Gordon H. Chang for including this book in SUP's Asian America series, which I have admired for a long time. It is a thrill to see this title among so many that have informed this work. Thanks to Nora Spiegel and the staff at SUP for their outstanding editorial support. I thank Tim Roberts, production editor, and Stephanie Adams, marketing manager, for their attention to detail.

I am indebted to many friends and interlocutors who have commented on and improved this book: Macarena Gómez-Barris, Dominic Cheung, Jerry Dávila, Evelyn Hu-Dehart, Roberto Ignacio Díaz, Christopher Dunn, Eugenia Lean, Jeffrey Lesser, and Erin Graff Zivin. I thank Mae Ngai and Charles Armstrong for organizing the Asian Migrations in Pacific World symposium and all the attendees for their critical feedback: Sascha Auerbach, Gordan H. Chang, Kornel Chang, Genevieve Clutario, Peter Hamilton, Davide Maldarella, and Andy Urban. Marianne Hirsch and Andreas Huyssen provided opportunities for me to present ideas from this book at the Cultural Memory Seminars. I thank Eileen Gillooly, the Heyman Center for the Humanities at Columbia University, and the Heyman Center Fellows for their invaluable comments, Chris Chang, Brent Edwards, Rob Goodman, Matthew Hart, Joseph Howley, Mark Mazower, Celia Naylor, Sean O'Neil, Dennis Tenen, Robert Gooding-Williams, and especially Rachel Adams, who served as discussant and read multiple drafts of the manu-script. My research assistant, Wang Siwei, provided crucial help with the late Qing documents. The work benefited greatly from Erika Stevens's sharp and crucial editing. Colleen Jankovic made insightful edits and did skillful indexing. I thank Beverly Miller for her careful copyediting. I am grateful to my anonymous readers for their meticulous readings and precious feedback.

Jesús Rodríguez-Velasco and Alberto Medina have been extraordi-nary chairs for the Department of Latin American and Iberian Cultures (LAIC) at Columbia University. I appreciate their generous guidance and consistent support during the completion of this project. I am grateful to Karen Benezra for organizing LAIC's works-in-progress series and to Gra-ciela Montaldo, Alberto Medina, and Eunice Rodríguez-Ferguson for their invaluable comments and suggestions. I feel very fortunate for the con-versations with friends and colleagues that have been invaluable as well: Lee Abraham, Alexander Alberro, Carlos Alonso, Esteban Andrade, Gus-tavo Azenha, Zainab Bahrani, Orlando Bentancor, Zach Blas, Dare Braw-ley, Bruno Bosteels, Ronald Briggs, Tina Campt, Carlos Castor, Mariana Castor, Ana Fernández-Cebrian, Nadine Chan, Laura Ciolkowski, Kency Cornejo, Rafael Cesár da Cruz, Patricia Dailey, Jean Dangler, Hernán Díaz, Daniella Diniz, Patricia Grieve, Miranda Featherstone, Luís Carlos Fernández, Ronald Findlay, Gustavo Pérez Firmat, Wadda Ríos-Font, Ana Ochoa Gautier, Isabel Gómez, Jack Halberstam, Saidiya Hartman, Feng-Mei Heberer, Ellie Hisama, Maja Horn, Jean Howard, Ana Cristina Joa-quim, Jennifer Reynolds-Kaye, Gloria Keum, Seth Kimmel, Laura Kurgan, Bia Leonel, Lila Abu-Lughod, Robson Malacarne, Adam McKeown, Anna More, Sarita Mota, José Moya, Kaitlin McNally Murphy, Frances Negrón Mutaneer, Premilla Nadasen, Alondra Nelson, João Nemi Neto, Gary Oki-hiro, Gabriel Rocha, Jashaun Sadler, Sócrates Silva, Thomas Trebat, José Antonio Castellanos-Pazos, Deborah Paredez, Lila Piccozzi, Kosmas Pis-sakos, Alex Posnen, Alessandra Russo, Lindsay Nelson-Santos, Ana Teles da Silva, Dalva Maria Soares, Melissa Teixeira, Neferti X. M. Tadiar, Zeb Tortorici, Van Tran, and Jasmina Tumbas.

Sharon Marcus has been an extraordinary dean of humanities. I am grateful for the many interdisciplinary opportunities she spearheaded, in-cluding the Brazil as Global Crossroads symposium in collaboration with the Instituto Moreira Salles where I had many important exchanges. I thank Anupama Rao for inviting me to participate in the Concept Histories of the

Urban conference, where I had the opportunity to share my research with a truly interdisciplinary group of scholars in the humanities, social sciences, and art and architecture. A Lenfest Junior Faculty Development Grant provided subvention funds for reproducing the images for the book. The Junior Faculty Diversity Grant Award and the Institute for Latin American Studies at Columbia University provided writing time and research support. The Provost's Tsunoda Senior Fellowship Program at Waseda University in Tokyo, Japan, gave me the chance to fine-tune my thinking about difficult problems regarding Sino-Japanese history. I thank Shigeko Mato for our exchanges while I was in Tokyo. I also express gratitude to Shuhei Yamamoto and Mayu Okamura at Waseda's International Office for their incredible hospitality and kindness during my stay. I thank Roosevelt Montas and the Core Curriculum, and the core chairs: Julie Crawford, Matthew Jones, and Patricia Kitcher. I am grateful to my students in my three graduate seminars on Asia and the Americas who gave me the chance to think through challenging questions.

At Tulane University, the Mellon Postdoctoral Fellowship gave me the opportunity to write and teach in New Orleans, an experience that profoundly shaped my thinking about race, performance, and memory. I am especially grateful for the warm welcome from Tulane's Spanish and Portuguese Department and the Roger Thayer Stone Center for Latin American Studies. I thank Christopher Dunn for inviting me to present this work at the Stone Center and for the fruitful dialogue that emerged. At the Latin American Library at Tulane, I thank Hortensia Calvo and Christine Hernández. At the University of Southern California (USC), the Comparative Studies in Literature and Culture Department provided me with a vibrant and rigorous intellectual atmosphere. I feel lucky to have spent a summer exploring Hong Kong and Macau with Roberto Ignacio Díaz and Dominic Cheung, and the Problems-without-Passports undergraduate class of 2013, in which we sailed on sampans and explored Portuguese architectural ruins as just another day of class. Sunyoung Lee, editor-in-chief of Kaya Press, gave me an editorial perspective on the issues surrounding Asian diasporic literatures. Panivong Norindr and Peggy Kamuf served as department chair and director of graduate studies during my time at USC. I am grateful for their dedication to the department and generosity as mentors. Sriram Dasu invited me to present my work at the Marshall School on many occasions, where I began thinking about the liberal economic theories relevant to this research. The Andrew W. Mellon Foundation John E. Sawyer Seminar, Critical Mixed-Race Studies: A Transpacific Approach, led by Duncan Williams and Brian Bernards, and the Center for Transpacific Studies, directed by Viet Thanh Nguyen and Janet Hoskins, fostered rich dialogues that helped me think comparatively about core issues in this book. The Center for Law, History, and Culture, directed by Ariela Gross, Hilary Schor, and Nomi Stolzenberg, pushed me to think about citizenship and the legal dimensions of race, performance, and representation. The Visual Studies Research Institute, steered by Daniela Bleichmar, Kate Flint, Akira Lippit, Alexander Marr, Tara McPherson, and Vanessa Schwartz, was foundational to my thinking about visual and print culture. The Dean Joan Metcalf Schaefer Scholarship provided multiple years of research funding that allowed me to develop the foundation of this project. The William J. Fulbright and Fundação Luso-Americana funded archival research in Lisbon, Portugal. Nuno Senos and the Centro de História de Além-Mar at the Universidade Nova de Lisboa were excellent hosts. In Lisbon, many thanks to the staff and archivists at the Biblioteca Nacional; the Arquivo-Histórico Diplomático; the Museu Nacional de Etnologia, and the Biblioteca da Ajuda. In São Paulo, I thank the Instituto de Estudos Brasileiros at the Universidade de São Paulo and the Biblioteca Mário de Andrade. In Rio de Janeiro, I express gratitude to the Museu Nacional de Belas Artes; the Biblioteca Nacional, and the Instituto Moreira Salles.

The Asians in the Americas Symposia and the Asia and the Americas section at the Latin American Studies Association have been incredible spaces for building this field and creating new collaborations. I am grateful to colleagues for many conversations that have helped me to think further about Asia and the Americas, especially Hsiao-Ping Hu Biehl, Grace Peña Delgado, Ignacio López-Calvo, Ana Maria Candela, Jason Oliver Chang, Andre Deckrow, Monica DeHart, Debbie Lee-DiStefano, Tao Leigh Goffe, Koichi Hagimoto, Junyoung Verónica Kim, Chisu Teresa Ko, Kathleen Lopéz, Alejandro Lee, Erika Lee, Anne-Marie Lee-Loy, Jordon Lynton, Luisa Ossa, Zelideth María Rivas, Naoki Sakai, Rosanne Sia, Araceli Tinajero, and Lisa Yun.

My sincerest appreciation must be given to João Adolfo Hansen for first exposing me to the presence of chinoiserie in colonial Brazilian architecture and then for encouraging me to spend time at the Universidade Federal de Ouro Preto to research baroque art and culture. Diana Taylor, Marcial

Godoy-Anativia, Marlène Ramírez-Cancio, Alexei Taylor, Greg James at Satisfixation, and all the people who make up the Hemispheric Institute of Performance and Politics, the hemisexuals, who tirelessly create and sustain platforms for new dialogues to emerge. In particular, at the Hemi Encuentros, Performing Asian/Americas, a permanent working group, has been the site of much exploration and fruitful debate. I express my gratitude to the working group's organizers Alexandra Chang, Beatrice Glow, Alice Ming Wai Jim, Jill Lane, Lok Siu, Anna Kazumi Stahl, and John Kuo Wei Tchen. I thank Danielle Roper for inviting me to present at the Racial Impersonation in Latin America and the Caribbean Symposium at New York University. This work benefited greatly from conversations at the Tepoztlán Institute for the Transnational History of the Americas; I thank Ben Cowan, Reiko Hillyer, María Elena Martínez, Jossianna Arroyo-Martínez, Yolanda Martínez-San Miguel, Micol Siegel, and Elliott Young.

My family provided much care and support during the completion of this project. Yen Taixing, Anny Yen, and the rest of my family in São Paulo showered me with love and delicious nourishment during the long duration of this work. Fernando Lee, Hitomi Lee, and Andreia Davies showed great enthusiasm for this project from its inception. I thank them for reading sections of the manuscript and providing their insights. Aaron David Smith has accompanied this project from its inception as an idea to its book form. I am deeply grateful to him for filling my days with tremendous creativity and love. Eileen and Vitoria are an eternal spring of inspiration and joy for me. Finally, this project could not have been possible without the unconditional love, encouragement, and wisdom of my parents, Tony and Paula. This dedication is a meager token of the immense gratitude I have for their sacrifices that opened the universe as many roads for traveling souls.

Preface: Liberty's Other Histories

São Paulo, Brazil, is home to the largest Japantown in the world, Liberdade. Prior to gaining this fame, during the colonial period, Liberdade was known as Campo da Forca (Field of the Gallows), a site where slave owners openly exerted their absolute power by encouraging the spectacle of public punishment and murder. The Brazilian government abolished hanging executions in 1870, and the location was renamed Praça da Liberdade (Liberty Plaza), a name it still holds today. Located on the corner of Praça da Liberdade, discreet and often unnoticed by local residents, sits the Igreja Santa Cruz das Almas dos Enforcados (Holy Cross Church of Hanged Souls), a place where abolitionists prayed for the souls of the enslaved people who had been publicly executed at that site.[1] As visitors enter the small chapel, they notice saints with black or brown skin. Downstairs from the main sanctuary is a room illuminated with candles and prayers. Next to the chapel is a small candle shop, Velas Santa Rita, which also sells Umbanda and Candomblé religious objects. The historical church is centrally located, yet it goes unnoticed by most passersby in the way that marginal histories powerfully shape the present even while they occupy the wings of national or collective memory.

An important figure linked to the history of this area is Francisco José das Chagas (Chaguinhas), the patron saint of Liberdade. Although the Catholic Church does not officially recognize Saint Chaguinhas, scholars have acknowledged his historical significance to the neighborhood's name, and to São Paulo's memory more broadly. Accused of leading a rebellion in Santos to demand unpaid wages, Chaguinhas was condemned to hang. However, there were complications with the hanging—the rope broke in the first two attempts, though he died on the third.[2] In popular legend, he escapes the third attempt; thus, he symbolically defies a punishment system designed to suppress insubordination and demands for justice. In the mythologized version, his own strength sets him free while the crowd chants "LI-BER-DA-DE."

Today, *torī* (Japanese gates) mark the Liberdade neighborhood in São Paulo, where Japanese immigrants began to settle in the early twentieth century. Red and white paper lantern-shaped streetlamps are interspersed among palm trees, filling Liberdade's visual landscape. A pebble's throw from the torī is the Jardim Oriental, a Japanese garden accented with bamboo-lined paths and stone steps that cross a colorful koi-filled pond. While torī are ubiquitous in Japan and are used to mark the sacred space of Shinto shrines, they serve a number of secular functions in São Paulo. A plaque secured to a torī pillar pays homage to Randolfo Marques Lobato, memorialized on the plaque as the creator of "The Oriental Neighborhood of Liberdade." Lobato, along with a group of Nipo-Brazilian community organizers, coordinated the construction of Liberdade's torī in 1974, as part of a larger project to build a Japantown in São Paulo similar to the Chinatowns of New York and San Francisco.[3] Liberdade has the look and feel of a little Japan in Brazil for both tourists and locals, who frequent the neighborhood now known as a destination for delicious restaurants. I often go to the Sunday fairs there, and in the odd times when the lines are not too long, I treat myself to one of the many selections of savory or sweet Japanese street foods. Liberdade is also home to a number of specialty supermarkets that offer products that are not commonly carried in major Brazilian supermarket chains, like rice wine vinegar, jasmine tea, chili paste, shiitake mushrooms, and concord grapes, which one shopkeeper once described to me as "Japanese grapes from the hinterlands of São Paulo."

Liberdade is an important commercial center for Japanese business networks that connect not only urban and rural economies but also international markets between Japan and Brazil. Liberdade signifies more than one century of alliance between Japan and Brazil. This alliance has given rise to the yearly Japan Festival, held at the Expo Exhibition and Convention Center on the outskirts of São Paulo. The main road that leads to the convention center is appropriately named Rodovia dos Imigrantes (immigrants' highway). At the festival, Japanese businesses and organizations table their goods. Culinary offerings from all forty-seven Japanese prefectures fill the air with mouthwatering aromas, with so many options that it is regrettably impossible to sample everything. The festival further commemorates the alliance between Brazil and Japan with yearly themes. In 2015, the theme was Celebrating 120 Years of Friendship. In 2016, it was Celebrate Sports, Culture, and a Healthy Life.[4] Liberdade and the Japan Festival convey a national narrative of integration and immigrant success. This narrative is also present at the Japanese Immigration Museum in Liberdade, which contains exhibits and archives of the century-long history of Japanese immigration to Brazil, detailing Japanese immigrants' and descendants' (Nikkei) contributions to Brazilian society. Liberdade is now considered symbolic of Brazil's Nikkei population, the largest in the world, but this association veils a number of other histories, including, for example, the Meiji Japanese annexation and colonization of Ryukyu/Okinawa in 1879, the US military occupation of Okinawa following World War II, and attendant forms of discriminatory colonial discourse against Okinawans. Political tensions continue in Brazil and may even produce new factions, observable in events such as the annual yet separate Japan and Okinawa Festivals in São Paulo.

Liberdade is, arguably, Brazil's most diverse neighborhood. Throughout the twentieth century, different waves of Chinese, Taiwanese, Korean, and Vietnamese immigrants also began to open shops and work in Liberdade alongside or replacing Japanese-owned businesses. Today it is a hub for purchasing inexpensive commercial goods from Asia, and it serves as a critical node that joins migrant networks and markets in Latin America and Asia. Liberdade is also home to a number of Chinese cultural and civic centers that represent diverse understandings of Chineseness.

People who self-identity as ethnically Hakka Chinese founded the Hakka Association of Brazil in 1989, located a block from the Japanese Immigration Museum. The Hakka Association's mirrored building makes it easy to miss, since the mirrors reflect and camouflage their surroundings. The building disappears if one does not know to look for it. But inside is a world of activity, with a large event hall, a library, a Buddhist sanctuary, and a beautiful collection of dynastic clothing from different eras of Chinese history. Not far away are the General Association of Cantonese in Brazil, the Chinese Association of Brazil, and the Colégio de São Bento, a Benedictine school located in the city center that maintains ties with the People's Republic of China (PRC). The Cultural Center of Taipei and the Chinese Social Center of São Paulo, for their part, maintain close relations with Taiwan.[5] The plethora of these associations that represent different, and even factious, political, ethnic, economic, and religious connections to China attest to the particularity of São Paulo's Liberdade as a point of convergence for myriad histories of migration and settlement, where local organizing among diverse waves of immigrants has created unique cultural collisions, and ties to national origin may be stronger in both cultural memory and cultural production than in actual functional connections to nation-states.

In 1964, a group of wealthy Shanghainese Catholic merchants founded the Chinese Catholic Missionary in Vila Olímpia, a neighborhood in São Paulo that today is home to multinational companies such as Google and Microsoft. Since the church's founding in the second half of the twentieth century, it has played an important role for Chinese and Taiwanese immigrants. As a religious, educational, sports, and cultural center, it offers meeting space for diasporic Chinese and Taiwanese people, helping them integrate into Brazilian society while strengthening cultural and linguistic ties to a vast Chinese and Taiwanese diasporic network. Mandarin-language classes have been a staple. While in previous decades Mandarin-language teachers mainly taught second- and third-generation Chinese and Taiwanese students, their classes have become popular to a wider public over the past decade.

The church also has a library and special collections archive that houses books and documents donated from the personal libraries of different waves of Chinese and Taiwanese immigrants, including rare materials from the Ming dynasty period and other items from the private collections of the wealthy Chinese businesspeople who left Shanghai before the formation of the PRC. While the original owners of these materials have since passed away or moved elsewhere, they have left to posterity an abundant material-cultural inheritance, safeguarded in climate-controlled glass cases and cared for by a team of volunteer stewards of cultural memory.

On any given Sunday, Taiwanese vendors stand outside the church selling tofu, egg tarts, *baozi* (buns composed of vegetables or meat), and *yezi* (a portable meal usually consisting of rice, vegetables, beans, and sausage wrapped in banana leaf), among other delicacies. Following Sunday Mass and lunch, elders gather for their ritual of karaoke, a custom whose origins are contested as either Japanese or Filipino. Singing and oral histories live vibrantly within and outside these walls that open onto multiple sociohistorical worlds and cultural memories. Their exquisite intricacies and contradictions collapse the possibility of any single narrative.

Despite all of this diversity, a common misconception in Brazil is that Asians writ large are Japanese, and that they live in Liberdade. In the Brazilian national imaginary, the Japanese are confined to a particular *Paulistano* (residents of São Paulo) regional identity. When I worked for a drought relief organization in Pernambuco in northeastern Brazil, people frequently asked me if I was a Japanese person from São Paulo, and they assumed that I lived in Liberdade. In a conversation I once had, a woman from Rio Grande do Sul (the southernmost state of Brazil, bordering Uruguay and Argentina) said, "Liberdade is your neighborhood." That I have never lived in Liberdade, and do not have Japanese ancestry, is immaterial. When I correct people by telling them I am of Chinese descent, a common answer is that it is difficult to tell the difference among Asians. In one particularly memorable exchange, my kung fu teacher, of Italian and Portuguese descent, who often and proudly claimed that his family's kung fu school was the first one to open in Brazil, asked me if I was Japanese. When I responded that I was Chinese, he asked me if I ate dog. This was on my first day of class, right after I had told everyone my name. These kinds of repeating interactions and clichéd questions transport me, and any other racialized body, into a form of yellowness that exists in Brazilian cultural memories about whiteness and blackness.

Historically, Paulistano identity privileged whiteness as symbolic of modernity, progress, and regional exceptionalism, implicitly reproducing pejorative constructions of blackness and African diasporic cultures to mobilize regional differences to advance a unified racial-nationalist narrative of modernity.[6] These ideas about race influenced the reception of Chinese and Japanese immigrants when they began arriving in Brazil in the late nineteenth and early twentieth centuries, respectively. While Japanese immigrant success stories are powerfully narrated in the streets of São Paulo, they elide the complex history of discrimination and racism against Nikkei that exists in Brazil and Japan. Prior to the official arrival of the first wave of Japanese immigrants to Brazil in 1908, late nineteenth-century newspapers and mass media portrayed the Japanese in ways that resembled the anti-Chinese sentiment that had been circulating around the globe in the form of the "Chinese question," which debated Chinese immigrants' suitability for joining white liberal societies. The racialization of Chinese people that developed in Brazil occurred in direct connection with the racialization of Africans, which emerged as a result of transatlantic slavery. These racialization practices overlapped with those applied to Japanese settlers in Brazil.[7] The Japanese were racialized according to preexisting ideas about the Chinese, who, on the one hand, were depicted as docile and efficient laborers and, on the other hand, were said to pose a racial and political threat, giving rise to terms such as *perigo japonês* (Japanese peril), an epithet closely linked to ideas regarding the "Yellow Peril"—the threat of Asian invasion and domination over the West.[8] This book explores the function of overlapping layers of racialization with a focus on Chinese racialization. It brings memory studies into conversation with critical theories of race and representation to explore the dynamic that political and cultural memory have in activating racialized national categories. Here we disentangle how discussions about race, free labor, liberty, and struggles toward republicanism became coterminous in defining Brazilian national identity as an aspect of an emerging global national consciousness.

Mandarin Brazil

Circumoceanic Memory

Chinese Racialization in Brazilian Perspective

Walking through Macau's main Senate Square today, one can see the vast remnants of Portuguese history in China. Middle-class Chinese consumers stroll along streets lined with Portuguese colonial architecture, whose bright pastel-colored building exteriors seem to have been freshly painted. Ocean wave-inspired Portuguese pavement recreates the exotic feel of shopping in Lisbon or Rio de Janeiro's haute bourgeois neighborhoods such as Copacabana or Ipanema, even though storefronts advertise Chinese retail chains. Macau's dual Portuguese and Cantonese heritage can be found everywhere on the small peninsula. The Loyal Senate Building bears a name bestowed on it in 1809 by Dom João VI to proclaim colonial Macau's loyalty to Portugal. In 1999, following the handover of Macau to China, the PRC quickly changed the name of the building to the "Civic and Municipal Affairs Bureau." However, the building is still widely called by Dom João VI's loyal title. On a quiet side street, facing the back of the Loyal Senate Building, is a street sign with the Portuguese words *Rua dos Cules* (Coolie Street) secured to the concrete walls of an old building (Figure I.1). Curious as to why this street was named after a racial slur used against Chinese laborers in the nineteenth century, I decided to enter the old building to learn the origins of the placard secured to its wall. At the gunmetal-gray doors, I found a man seated, surrounded by newspapers, boxes, hardware, and other items that contributed to the mildewy smell that had settled in those walls over the centuries. "May I come in?" I asked him. The man barely looked at me from behind his newspaper but nodded permission. I expected to find clues about the coolie trade, the Chinese labor migration activities wherein Chinese migrants

signed deceptive contracts that sent hundreds of thousands of men into indentured servitude and slave labor throughout the world during the nineteenth
century. However, nothing in the room supported the claims of the placard
posted outside. Probed about Coolie Street's history, the man disinterestedly
responded, "That is from a long time ago."

Coolie Street has two names that have nothing to do with each other, but
they have everything to do with the conflicting memories that may exist about
a place. In Macau, streets have two names: one is Portuguese and the other is
Chinese. These bicultural and bilingual street names symbolize the current political and economic alliance between China and Portugal. While they imply a
harmonious and long history of Portuguese settlement in China, they also do
the important imaginative work of portraying China as a vast, multicultural
geographical territory where even Portuguese is among the official languages. In
this sense, the bilingual signs are more symbolic than practical, since the Portuguese names have nothing in common with the Chinese ones. Indeed, less than
1 percent of Macau's population speaks Portuguese, and most people, including
taxi drivers, know only the Chinese names of streets. Portuguese speakers must
learn the Chinese street names to get around.

Rather than providing a direct translation of Coolie Street (Rua dos Cules),
the Chinese characters instead state *Tian tong jie,* meaning "heaven through
street." Since the character "Tian" can mean heaven, day, and sky depending on
the context, another translation might render the phrase as "passage to the heavenly skies" or "passage to heaven." The street is widely referred to by the Chinese
name, which elides the history of the coolie trade, even if it explicitly marks a
coolie trade logistics history in Portuguese.[1] The placard on Coolie Street may
at first seem that it makes for linguistic cacophony, but the convergence of Rua
dos Cules and Tian tong jie demonstrates the layers of memory that gather in a
place where the promise of heaven and the trade routes of coolie labor occupy
the same memoryscape.[2] The Passage to Heaven does not erase the coolie trade,
but transforms it into another thing, showing the collision of competing Portuguese and Chinese cultural memories that converge in a place.[3]

On the front of the old building that sits on the corner of Coolie Street are
Portuguese words and Chinese characters that declare that this building had
once been the Siyi Association of Macau, a benevolent society that provided
social services for people from Guangdong province's "Four Counties" (*Siyi* in
Mandarin or *Szeyup* in Cantonese): Taishan, Kaiping, Xinhui, and Enping. The
majority of the first "Overseas Chinese" were from Taishan. By 1901, Madeline

FIGURE I.I. Front view of Rua dos Cules, Macau, June 10, 2013. Source: Photograph by the author.

Hsu observes, Taishan had become dependent on the "export of labor," and roughly 25 percent of the county's population lived abroad.[4] Following the end of African slavery, the turn to Asian laborers funneled thousands of (mainly) Chinese and Indian people into indentured servitude or slavelike labor in European colonies, in the Americas, and around the rest of the world.[5] These laborers toiled alongside enslaved and free people of color and thus were suddenly labeled with racial categories that had emerged out of hemispheric American histories of colonialism and enslavement. In the Americas, they became racialized through derogatory names like *coolie*. This expression ran parallel to precedents set within the rhetoric of the transatlantic African slave trade history. Asian immigrant labor and productivity would likewise support the networks of global capitalism and build the wealth of nations going forward.

The coolie trade transformed southern Chinese port towns like Macau, Hong Kong, and Shanghai into sites of kidnapped and coerced labor. By 1871, the verb *to shanghai* had emerged and meant "to put aboard a ship by force often with the help of liquor or a drug," and "to put by trickery into an undesirable position."[6] In China, internal wars and desperate economic conditions motivated young men to sign the labor contracts, usually presented by deceptive means, that would take them to unknown lands whether seeking riches and adventure. Most of the men would never return to their villages, leaving behind family and neighbors who would never know what had happened to those who had departed on ships that disappeared on the sea's horizon. Many died on the oceanic voyages, and those who survived the wretched journey learned that their contracts bonded them to indentured servitude. Evelyn Hu-Dehart's pioneering studies of the Chinese diaspora to the Americas, including of the coolie trade to Peru and Cuba, discovered that only 1,887 of 100,000 contracted laborers ultimately returned to China.[7] By 1874, when the coolie trade officially ended, 275,511 people had already left for Latin America.[8] The vast majority of them had departed from Macau.[9] To be sure, not all Chinese laborers were indentured servants; however, regardless of their financial and contractual situations, upon arrival in the Americas, they were steadily homogenized, lumped together as "yellow laborers" or a "coolie race."[10]

Until recently, it was widely thought that the word *coolie* originated from Tamil to indicate "menial laborers from Madras."[11] But Mae Ngai traces *coolie* to a Portuguese neologism first used in the sixteenth century to describe a common laborer.[12] In 1510, Portuguese conquistador Afonso de Albuquerque, known for his piety and long beard, took possession of Goa and established Portuguese rule in India. By the end of the sixteenth century, Goa had become the thriving capital of the Portuguese empire in Asia. Portuguese merchants engaged in the lucrative trade in spices, ivory, and common (coolie) labor. Their prosperous commerce led to the expansion of trade routes and connected once-distant places like India, China, Portugal, and Brazil. Global trade propelled the worldwide movement of people, goods, and concepts like *coolie*. In the Mandarin dialect, *coolie* sounds like the characters for "bitter strength." While laborers to the Americas never self-identified as coolies, it became a homogenizing moniker for all unskilled and indentured laborers from India and China.[13] The label *coolie* marked racial difference onto the division of labor. The term never referred to the historical or cultural significance of actual people. It was always a product of the colonial imagination, which powered new rubrics of nationalism and racialized national identities in the modern state-building projects that developed alongside the formation of a global system of nation-states.

Similar to other societies transitioning out of slave labor, the conceptualization of the coolie played a complex role in Brazil's shift to wage labor.[14] Moon-Ho Jung shows that discourses about coolies (coolieism) formed an integral part in US congressional debates over nation, race, and citizenship during Recon-

struction. Those who were lumped together as coolies were neither free nor enslaved; rather, they "bridged [a] legal and cultural gap" during and after gradual
emancipation.[15] In Cuba, Lisa Yun observes, the institution of slavery influenced that of contractual labor. Coolies became a figuration of transition—as
physical, social, and economic intermediaries—through which to negotiate the
passage from slavery to wage labor.[16] The boundaries between one system and
the other were not always clear; indeed, upon arrival in the Americas, Asian
contract laborers faced slave codes that influenced the terms of contract labor.[17]
In Brazil, Chinese labor was a critical topic in discussions about the turn to
wage labor and republicanism. Advocates for and opponents of Chinese laborers considered them to be either "paragons of virtue" or "demons of depravity."[18]
The racialization of Chinese laborers contained these contradictory views because the Chinese were not considered free or enslaved; rather, they were considered "unfree," and they would join Brazil's already too big unfree labor class.

The actual lives of Chinese laborers upon arrival and settlement in Brazil
generated few historical records, and, according to the evidence we have, Chinese labor migration to Brazil occurred on a much smaller scale than the efforts
in Cuba and Peru. However, Chinese slaves were sent to Brazil in a small but
steady stream throughout the colonial period.[19] Efforts at introducing Chinese
laborers to Brazil increased during the nineteenth century when Dom João VI
wanted a foothold in the international tea market. In 1810, one year after he
named the Loyal Senate Building, he began an experiment in tea farming in
Rio de Janeiro's botanical garden, which led to the arrival of 750 Chinese tea
cultivators between 1810 and 1812.[20] In 1835, German artist Johann Rugendas
(1802–1858) depicted the earliest known visual representation of Chinese settlers in Brazil (Figure I.2). The Cantonese agriculturalists, who had arrived from
the Portuguese colony in Macau, confronted exploitative labor conditions in
Brazil. They were confined to the botanical gardens, and those who attempted
to escape the grounds were hunted down with horses and dogs.[21] Rio de Janeiro's black tea variety did not suit the taste of the international tea market, and
after a few decades, the tea experiment was abandoned.[22] The costly price of the
voyage back to China made the return trip prohibitive for the men. Those who
stayed became cooks and peddlers, and they also sought political representation.[23] In 1819, a group of more than fifty Chinese men signed a petition to
formally request that one of the workers, who used the Brazilian name Domin-
gos Manuel Antônio, act as interpreter and representative of their interests.[24]
The document was written in Portuguese in Rio de Janeiro, dated September

FIGURE 1.2. Johann Moritz Rugendas. "Plantation chinoise de thé dans le Jardin Botanique de Rio-Janeiro" (Chinese Tea Plantation in the Royal Botanical Garden of Rio de Janeiro). *Malerische Reise in Brasilein von Moritz Rugendas.* Illustration. Paris: Engelmann, 1835. Source: Biblioteca Nacional, Rio de Janeiro, Brazil.

6, 1819, and signed by the organizers in Chinese characters and Portuguese sobriquets.

In 1855, the Brazilian government began negotiations with Edward Price, an engineer from England, to begin a railroad project, Companhia de Estrada de Ferro Dom Pedro II, that was to connect Rio de Janeiro to São Paulo and Minas Gerais.[25] The 30 mile stretch would directly enable the expansion of the coffee economy.[26] On February 9, 1855, 303 Chinese laborers arrived in Rio aboard the US bark the *Elisa Anna*. During this year, the government also contracted 2,000 laborers from the Boston Company Sampson and Tappan.[27] The men were assigned to build the railroads that would invigorate the coffee industry. Their labor would connect downtown Rio de Janeiro Estação do Campos to the municipality known today as Queimados. During the construction of the railroad, malaria and cholera plagued the entire region, and hundreds of Chinese laborers died as a result. Their bodies were burned in such numbers that people began to refer to the route as *estrada dos queimados* (road of the burning people).

Eventually the municipality became known as Queimados.[28] This origin story of the municipality's name, whether mythical or historical, is a lasting memorial for the people made to serve as the necessary and normal collateral for Brazil's project of modernization and economic growth based on slave labor.

During the second half of the nineteenth century, gradual emancipation laws began Brazil's transition out of being a slave-based economy. The Free Womb Law, a gradual emancipation law that liberated the children born to enslaved women, passed in 1871. Debates over the law generated much concern over the labor shortage anticipated by the inevitable end of slavery. Racial theories influenced political and economic policies once abolition was deemed certain.[29] Politicians and seigneurs once again began looking to China as a solution. In July 1870, the government established the Sociedade Importadora de Trabalhadores Asiáticos to implement long-term Chinese agricultural contract labor.[30] Within two years, the Brazilian census of 1872 included Chinese immigrants and listed 436 Chinese in the country.[31] Advocates for Chinese laborers saw them as a temporary solution to the labor problem. The Chinese would provide a transition to free labor.[32] However, abolitionists like Joaquim Nabuco claimed they could never be permanent settlers since they threatened to "yellow" or "mongolize" the racial and cultural make-up of Brazil.[33] He created a commonality between Chinese labor and African slavery, stating that the Chinese would monogolize Brazil in the way it was "Africanized when Salvador Correa de Sá brought over the first slaves."[34]

This story begins at Coolie Street, an important logistics site for Chinese labor migration activities, but I am deliberately not looking at a migration history, which is predominantly a Japanese story in Brazil. I am interested in a minor story, an Other history that surfaces in brief encounters in institutional archives; in narratives that include fiction, poetry, and short stories; in performances of yellowface; in images; and in places such as Coolie Street. This is a story about how Chinese migrants became seen as a "yellow race" or a "coolie race" and the ways in which cultural constructions of Chineseness structured a symbolic national coherence.

Discourses of Chineseness, as Andrea Louie observes, are insufficiently understood within frameworks that seek a continuum between homeland and diasporic populations. State-sponsored projects of cultural citizenship naturalize "racial, national, and territorial" notions of Chineseness, but these concepts come apart in the face of transnational migration, severed state ties, and conflicting national projects that often result in "unfamiliar ways of being Chinese."[35] Using Louie's dynamic and relational concept of Chineseness as a point of departure, this book explores interdependent relations, global circuits, and a network of cultural expressions that defined Chineseness as a critical discourse within debates about Brazilian national identity. Brazilian cultural production about Chineseness fabricated a form of yellowness within a relational history of race, labor, and nationality.

Throughout the latter half of the nineteenth century, Chinese migrants were increasingly recognized around the world as a coolie race or a yellow race. So what caused these associations to transfer from the idea of race to the figure of a person? The more I tried to pin down what this relationship might mean, the more these forms and matters began to unravel, in the same way as when I say my name too many times and cannot recognize it anymore. I found myself chasing these elusive ideas across many national borders. Race-related ideas, images, and words about Chineseness took different turns across the uneven economic landscapes trodden by imperialist and capitalist expansion. My obsessive chase led me on a journey into subways, streetcars, monorails, planes, bullet trains, automobiles, junk ships, auto rickshaws, and sampans. These transportation lines took me down dead ends but also on infinite-seeming paths. Some lines reconstructed a global trade history that linked Macau to Lisbon; Lisbon to Rio de Janeiro; Rio de Janeiro to Havana; and Havana to San Francisco.

I started compiling an archive composed of fragments and scattered representations of Chineseness. I kept seeing repeating images that depicted the Chinese as primates, ants, shrimp peddlers, Qing dynasty officials (mandarins), and other intriguing but dehumanizing stereotypes. My collection began as a strange hobby at first—it made me into both the insect collector and the insect. Eventually I had a collection that spanned over a century. What to make of this archive that included the writings of celebrated authors, prominent politicians, and beloved artists and musicians? The same stereotypes of the Chinese persisted regardless of the creator. There were slight variations, but they were not random; they had a design that followed a formula. These representations, words, and concepts pointed to a common language that circulated and acquired new uses, much in the way regional vocabularies develop. For example, in parts of southern Brazil, the word *china* refers to a young prostitute, while in other areas, it references the country China.[36] Different individuals over the course of one hundred years repeated the same race-related ideas about the Chinese. Concepts, images, and words appeared often enough that a detectable pattern emerged and pointed to a shared language that was bound to a collective memory about slavery's racial regimes.[37]

In the late nineteenth century, social Darwinist thought developed the concept that human physiology naturally divided human beings into hierarchically ranked races. Racist twentieth-century Nazi and Ku Klux Klan ideologies are representative models of this kind of thinking.[38] My main concern is not with the science-fiction notion of "human races"; I am interested in the semantic structures and embodied acts that caused the Chinese, and anyone else, to be interpreted as a race and in the persistence of these ongoing ideas.[39] Paul Taylor offers a useful way to think about race as analogous to language, suggesting that race-related concepts, words, and images are systematic.[40] Once I began detecting patterns in the rhetoric of these repeating representations, words, and images, they all began to fit together like puzzle pieces, but it was like putting together a puzzle without the picture—and whose pieces were scattered across the globe. Eventually a world map of emerging national imaginaries started to appear, but to interpret it, I had to turn to the global history of slavery and, specifically, the transitional period to abolition. That connecting piece showed me that the symbols and tropes of Chineseness that constitute this book's archive belong to the racial project that developed out of slavery's racial regimes. The transatlantic slave trade made slavery synonymous with blackness.[41] The logic of slavery's racial regimes continues to shape the modern idea of race. With abolition in 1888 and Brazil's transition to a republican state in 1889, racial ideologies intertwined with liberal ideals of liberty and wage labor. Their entanglements shaped an emerging Brazilian national consciousness as an aspect of a globally racialized national consciousness.

Circumoceanic Memory

The slave trade and the forms of immigration labor that occurred in reaction to the labor shortage anticipated by abolition produced a global idea of race that persists today, especially in postslavery societies and renders clear the idea that one's relation to racialized exploitative labor determines one's access to the rights of citizenship and recognition within the ethical boundaries of the state.[42] The coolie trade, the global movement of racialized disposable laborers, was contingent on the centuries-long transatlantic slave trade routes that linked Europe, Africa, and the Americas. Joseph Roach, building on the writings of Paul Gilroy, proposes a framework he calls circum-Atlantic memory to describe the collective and institutional memories that connect the distant oceanic networks of the slave trade that constituted the cultures of modernity. Circum-Atlantic memory traces the creative processes through which the culture of modernity invents itself in the act of transmission. Key to Roach's formulation is his proposal that cultural transmission is a mode of deferred memory wherein memory functions as substitution. While the past is never gone, it may be rendered forgotten, ineffable, or transformed into something else altogether in the collective memory.[43] I am indebted to Roach's dialogic understanding of cultural memory as invention and substitution in my exploration of the cultural constructions of Chineseness.

My use of the term *circumoceanic memory* extends Roach's configuration to include transpacific passages that connect the histories of once distant places through the shared experience of racialized exploitative labor and the networked cultural processes that produce racial subaltern subjects. These routes included ports in Asia located on transpacific passageways that also carried goods, ideas, and people, including, and especially, the Chinese laborers who voyaged on the seamless currents of the world's oceans during the gradual process of emancipation and after the abolition of African slavery. Considering circumoceanic routes enables us to examine the global idea of race that developed in the making of a global national consciousness. This includes the worldwide movement of racialized, exploitable laborers that formed as colonial racialized hierarchies and contingently developed into racialized national identities. These hierarchies continue to determine the full rights of citizenship for some, but as Denise Ferreira da Silva observes, the law wholly collapses for racial subaltern subjects because racial difference names the Other as representation, as the "always-already" named threat to the state's survival.[44] Racial difference functions not only to exclude certain people from accessing the full rights to citizenship but also determines the ethical limits of the state.[45] The state legitimizes race-based violence and the deaths of racialized others, including its own citizens, as an act of self-preservation.[46] The "ever-threatening" racial Other is the grounds on which the state legitimizes its authority and establishes the limits of its ethical responsibility.[47]

Cultural constructions of Chineseness embued Chinese migrants with racial difference, designating Asians as a yellow race, which also constructed "a racial opposition to whiteness."[48] In the United States, US cultural expressions powerfully determined Asians and Latinos to be "alien citizens," persons who had US citizenship but were permanent foreigners.[49] These notions carried economic and political meaning indicating that many considered their bodily presence as a threat to the republican ideals of free white labor.[50] Narratives and representational practices—along the lines of what Edlie Wong calls the "archive of Chinese exclusion"—were critical for mediating US national identity and shaping the experience of Chinese immigrants.[51] These narratives that constructed the idea of a yellow race made possible the psychological and cultural landscape that paved the way for race-based restrictions and exclusions that were then applied to Chinese people throughout the Americas and around the rest of the globe.[52] Discourses of Chineseness did the cultural work of defining the exclusionary logic of racialized nationalisms that determines not only access to full citizenship rights but also recognition within the state's ethical responsibility to life.

While studies about Chinese racialization often focus on the United States or Canada—on North American histories of Sinophobia—my examination of Chinese racialization as it occurred within the context of a Brazilian historiography is also an exploration of how processes of racialization overlap in synchronous states of modernity/coloniality, in the making of the modern world that was inseparable from the making of the colonial order.[53]

The First Brazilian Federal Republic, established in 1889, was home to radically incompatible ideologies that shared characteristics with other plantation economies transitioning into liberal democratic nations, in which advocates for economic liberalism were also proponents of enslaved and unfree labor.[54] Entangled racial, eugenic, and liberal ideologies—and the enactment of these ideologies into policy—were at the core of Brazil's nation-building project, itself an aspect of an emerging global racialized national consciousness that took its own unique turns in Brazil's transition from postcolonial empire to republican state.

Brazil is exceptional for being the only place in the hemispheric Americas where a European empire settled in its own colony, which is related to why Brazil was the last place in the hemispheric Americas to abolish slavery at the dawn of the twentieth century. The Brazilian colony transformed into the center of the Portuguese empire in 1808 when fifteen thousand members of the Portuguese court relocated to Rio de Janeiro to escape the Napoleonic invasion of Portugal. Dom João VI himself oversaw the transfer of the Portuguese government to Brazil. He lifted imperially mandated prohibitions against the creation of universities and other civic institutions, and thus allowed an era of intellectual, artistic, and cultural production to exist in a way that had been forbidden before. Manufacture expanded, factories opened, and, most significant, Dom João VI opened Brazil's ports, making possible free trade with Portuguese colonies around the world, including Macau; previously, by Portuguese imperial command, Brazil was allowed to trade only with Portugal. The Portuguese empire in the tropics founded important institutions, including the Banco do Brasil (Bank of Brazil), Real Biblioteca (Royal Library), the *Gazeta do Rio de Janeiro* (Brazil's first newspaper), opera houses, museums, a medical school, and the Royal Botanical Garden, a 350 acre laboratory where agriculturalists cultivated and acclimated valuable spice trade items such as vanilla, cinnamon, and peppers, as well as exotic flora—including the failed tea experiment that had brought 750 Chinese tea planters to Brazil.[55] The founding of these civic institutions in Brazil, however, did not spur automatic or rapid social change toward building a civil society; rather, they cemented the socioeconomic divide between aristocratic and enslaved classes. Access to educational, cultural, and economic institutions was restricted to the elite minority who coexisted with a colonized, enslaved majority.

Meanwhile, back in Portugal, fed up with French occupation and the devastated Portuguese economy, Portuguese revolutionaries successfully carried out revolts against the French troops, beginning with the Porto Revolution in 1820. On April 25, 1821, Dom João VI returned to Portugal and left Brazil under a regency government. Within five months of his return, he sent orders to the regency and Dom Pedro to transition Brazil back to colonial rule. João VI also ordered Pedro to return to Portugal. However, his rebellious son had more ambitious plans. On September 7, 1822, Dom Pedro declared independence from Portugal and established the First Empire of Brazil, under the rule of Dom Pedro I, the First Emperor of Brazil.

The Brazilian empire witnessed an era of oligarchic liberalism that depended heavily on enslaved labor to support the agro-export economy.[56] Within this society, an elite, landed, slave-holding class relied on a large enslaved class to maintain its wealth and power. Brazil's mode of liberalism was more ornamental than functional; its laws tipped in favor of the slaveholders.[57] Alfredo Bosi explains that the kind of liberalism that took shape in Brazil was dependent on slavery and thus had a dialectical relation to the dispossession of freedom.[58] For the elite ruling class, liberalism meant that a small group of *citoyens* (landed citizens) maintained the right to political self-representation, which included preserving the freedom to "bring the enslaved worker to submission through legal coercion" and the right to "acquire new lands in open competition."[59] The

Brazilian ruling class fought as fiercely for economic liberalization as for their rights to maintain property and slaves.[60]

Critical events in 1868 sparked a transformation from earlier oligarchic liberal ideology and gave lifeblood to what Bosi calls a "civilizing idea of free labor."[61] Whereas the slave-holding oligarchy fought fiercely to preserve their rights to property and slaves, which included indemnity claims against the loss of property or slaves, the end of the US Civil War and creation of the Fourteenth Amendment became a model for abolitionists who were pushing for liberal reform and free labor in Brazil. Brazil's gradual transition to emancipation took shape in experiments with immigration contract labor. Thus, in 1870, the government introduced a ten-year labor plan to bring Chinese contract laborers to Brazil. Abolitionists did not believe they would bring with them ideas of free labor and thought that they instead would join the already substantial unfree labor class. Proslavery advocates favored Chinese labor for precisely the same reasons. Brazilian colonial relationships fell into three classes: slave, landed slaveholder, and the free man who was in many ways unfree because he lived in a completely dependent condition that relied on gaining the favors, however volatile of a wealthy patron.[62] The free man was often caricaturized to express the deadlock between liberal ideas and slavery.[63] This dependent condition created a social economy based on a system of favors in which personal relationships had more power than personal merit.[64] Brazilian oligarchic liberalism coexisted with slavery, and the liberal reformism that occurred after 1868 coexisted with the gradual transition of emancipation to unfree labor.

The Brazilian empire and the presence of the aristocratic class added new layers to the existing colonial racial caste hierarchy. In 1841, Dom Pedro II came of age and assumed the throne, becoming the first Brazilian-born ruler of the Brazilian empire. During the colonial period, the racial category of *mazombo* had negatively referred to Portuguese descendants who were born in Brazil.[65] But Pedro II's royal birth on Brazilian territory fused a noble class to existing colonial racial caste categories. The *sistema de casta* (caste system) fabricated a genealogical rubric about racial caste hierarchies.[66] Visual narratives can demonstrate entrenched value judgments about race as well as suggest ways to "solve" the problem. The artistic oeuvre of sistema de casta portraits clearly exemplifies the colonial ideology of a relational and hierarchical social organization as determined by racial distinction. A famous example, permanently on display at Rio de Janeiro's Museu Nacional de Belas Artes, is the 1895 painting *A redenção de Cam* (Ham's Redemption) by Modesto Brocos (Figure I.3). While the painting may seem to be celebrating a multiracial family, if we interpret it as an example of caste system portraits, it in fact produces a eugenically driven visual narrative that reinforces the idea that racial mixing would eventually "whiten" Brazil. In imagery evoking the Madonna holding baby Jesus, a mixed-race mother holds a milky-white baby, while a white-skinned European father sits to their right. The black grandmother throws her hands in the air in an expression of gratitude at the blessing that whitening has become possible through multiple generations of miscegenation with European races. Her lineage has acquired the racial identity of the aristocratic class.

The need for new immigrant labor was paired with the predominant fin-de-siècle belief in *branqueamento,* which intertwined eugenic and racial whitening ideology with an emerging national consciousness. Eugenic-driven ideas, Jeffrey Lesser observes, entered into policies aimed at constructing a national race invested in producing a "healthy mixed population growing steadily whiter, both culturally and physically."[67] Newly arrived immigrants from Europe, Asia, and the Middle East were incorporated into the national project of whitening.[68] Immigrants were assimilated or discriminated against according to how they fit into a set of racial and moral values that defined whiteness as a symbol of progress, modernization, and liberty, implicitly creating derogatory notions of blackness and indigeneity—as synonymous with enslavement, colonialism, and backwardness.[69] Racist social evolutionary theory thus played a foundational role in defining national identity in a way that continues to determine a person's access into the functional, juridical, and ethical framework of the nation-state and racialized nationalism.[70]

Branqueamento, a white supremacist belief that advanced the project of whiteness through racial mixing rather than racial purity, was a critical discourse on Brazil's road to becoming a republican state.[71] Racial and eugenic theories about generative and degenerative miscegenation played a crucial role in determining who warranted national inclusion and who prefigured as an ever-threatening other. The boundaries for inclusion in the Brazilian state—as citizens or alien citizens—still operated according to slavery's racial regimes that deemed certain races more intellectually and morally capable of fulfilling the promise of liberty and self-governance. Less superior races were considered better suited to be ruled and to perform exploitative, subhuman labor. The fictions

FIGURE 1.3. *A redenção de Cam* (Ham's Redemption), by Modesto Brocos e Gomes, 1895. Source: Permanent Collection of the Museu Nacional de Belas Artes, Rio de Janeiro/Ibram/MinC.

that certain racial identities belonged to an imagined community while others did not became far more powerful than the political science of who was actually deemed a citizen.[72] Thus, we arrive at the cultural expressions that depicted Chinese laborers as simian primates—chimpanzees—a topic addressed in later chapters of this book.

This book may concentrate on Brazil; however, I am interested in fostering a revised notion of Latin American cultural studies, one that considers Chinese racialization as a circumoceanic discourse that is critical for understanding hemispheric American histories of racial difference. I begin my inquiries in the mid-nineteenth century, when racial representations were instrumentalized in political struggles having to do with national independence and abolishing slavery. I compile an archive of Chinese racialization across narratives and repertoires invested in shaping the national and racial identity of Brazil, drawing on abolitionist journals and diplomatic correspondences from Brazilian, Portuguese, and late Qing officials. Next, I show that vaudeville and yellowface performances were primary sites on which to rehearse new scenarios about race and national inclusion, which actors and playwrights negotiated on the stage by "performing" Chinese sexuality and gender. In the mid-twentieth century, with Brazil's entrance into World War II, I turn to musical forms like samba and marcha to hear what musicians and singers had to say about Chinese sexuality in relation to existing notions about the mulata. I conclude by taking another look at Brazil's image as a racial democracy, as discussed in the works by sociologist Gilberto Freyre.

The battle for how circumoceanic memories of race are remembered is also about the contest for jurisdiction over "the maintenance of any system of racial domination" and their organizing principles of governmentality.[73] To exercise power, racial regimes depend on discursive and embodied acts to engender ways of seeing and reacting to certain bodies. This book gathers an archive that brings together fragmentary appearances of Chineseness in textual encounters, embodied acts, songs, and visual representations that became socially bound to circumoceanic memory in the making of the modern world dependent on racialized, disposable workers. As a whole, this book brings together an archive of the migrant stories of people who were scripted into race. Like Coolie Street in Macau, this past is not forgotten; it remains in the material and symbolic ruins of memory and survives in unpredictable cultural expressions.

ONE

Brazil's Oriental Past and Future

In 2009, China surpassed the United States in becoming Brazil's largest trade partner; today, the largest Chinese population in Latin America lives in Brazil, totaling approximately 250,000 to 300,000 people. What may appear to be a new economic and political relationship, however, has a history that dates back nearly five hundred years.

Within the first decades of the sixteenth century, European voyages opened new trade routes that connected vastly distant parts of the world through establishing new links among Asia, Europe, Africa, and the Americas. While extensive trade networks had already been in place for centuries along the silk and spice routes, sixteenth-century globalization, migration, settlement, and cultural exchange reshaped trade on a global level, and marked a world historical transformation.[1] Geopolitics and global trade established the beginning of international law, and state power was extended to the seas.[2] World trade relations produced new collisions of local and diasporic knowledge, and it created new ways of knowing and representing places, people, and objects from distant lands.

Following Christopher Columbus's discovery of the New World, King Manuel I of Portugal commissioned Portuguese explorers Pedro Álvares Cabral and Vasco da Gama to lead their fleets to find swifter trade routes to the Indies, a name that stuck even after Europeans quickly realized that the Americas were not India. Indeed, the earliest map to depict the Western Hemisphere, made by German geographer Martin Waldseemüller (1470–1519) in 1507, shows that the Americas are located on a separate continent from Asia, Africa, and Europe (Figure 1.1). Regardless, European explorers and cartographers continued to refer to Asia and the Americas as the Indies. The malleability of the word *Indies*—it could refer to Asia or the Americas—indicates that the notion of continents as a fixed and evident aspect of the Earth's surface is itself a myth whose borders, place names, and regions like Orient and Occident tell us more about the spatial divisions through which people organized knowledge about themselves and the world than the earth's geographical terrains.[3] Multiple and at times conflicting names for people and places indicate the emergence of a new, modern world order where imperialist projects were emerging and had not yet defined and claimed geopolitical borders. For example, the word *Indies* could refer to people or objects from Mexico or India. Its variable definitions never referred to culturally and historically significant Indigenous Mexicans or Indians, but the word racialized Mexicans and Indians together. Processes of overlapping racialization give insight into how notions about nearness and farness became bound to emotions, bodies, and collective imaginaries.[4] This economy of racialization reveals geopolitical and economic interests that shaped the imaginative geography of a place and ideas about people in that place.

Race to the Indies

The race to find the quickest route to the Indies—which instead led to the discovery of the Americas—was also about the founding of the modern/colonial order.[5] The *Carreira da Índia*, a transoceanic trade circuit led by the Portuguese, established a global trade route that linked distant and not-so-distant economies. In 1500, when Pedro Álvares Cabral first reached the land that would come to be called Brazil, he was in search of the natural and cultural materials of China and India. Portugal's efforts to reach Asia were closely linked to the desire for the colonial riches that the Americas would come to symbolize and fulfill. Vasco da Gama became the first person to make the ocean voyage from Europe to Asia, when in 1497 he set sail from Lisbon and led his navy down the West African coast, around the Cape of Good Hope, and upward along the East African coast to India. Then he continued on to Southeast Asia and China. In 1511, Gama arrived in Macau. Mercantilism drove the voyages to the Americas, Africa, and Asia,

FIGURE 1.1. First known map to name America, by Martin Waldseemüller. *Universalis cosmographia secundum Ptholomaei traditionem et Americi Vespucii alioru[m]que lustrationes.* (Strasbourg, France?: s.n., 1507) Source: Library of Congress, Geography and Map Division. https://www.loc.gov/resource/g3200.ct000725C/.

and Portuguese trade interests were often unilateral. Portuguese mariners, who had quickly gained a reputation for violence, attempted to establish trade in the South China Sea, but due to mismanagement and the Ming dynasty's reluctance to deal with the "barbarian intruders from the Great Western Ocean," initial attempts were met with hostility.[6] According to a letter written by Father Gregorio González in 1557, the Portuguese were at first allowed to stay only through winters, at the end of which they had to tear down their temporary homes made of wood and straw and leave.[7] Nevertheless, a combination of persistence and clandestine trading eventually led to the first Portuguese colonial settlement in Macau in 1557.[8] Although the Portuguese settlers created a local government and paid an annual fee of 500 to 550 taels per year to the magistrate of the Heungshan district, Chinese authorities in Macau asserted that ultimate sovereignty belonged to the Ming and thereby overruled Portuguese claims to authority.[9]

The Ming forbade all maritime voyages and prohibited direct trade and migration between China and Japan.[10] Portuguese mariners swiftly capitalized on these bans, serving as intermediaries between Chinese and Japanese merchants. A single voyage consisting of loads of Chinese raw silks and textiles to Nagasaki would yield returns of 18 to 20 tons of silver. Profits earned from a single voyage provided a license holder of a carrack (Portuguese trading ships with three or more masts) enough financial security to last a lifetime.[11] By the end of the sixteenth century, Macau and Nagasaki became flourishing seaports, a result of mutually profitable and clandestine trade facilitated by Portuguese carrack circuits.[12]

The Delicate Art of Trade

The history of Sino-Portuguese trade might be better thought of in terms of transactions of inconsistencies, accidents, competition, and mutual acts of appropriation and exploitation that were propelled by new trade relations and the establishment of interdependent markets. Polycentric economic and political interests, as well as mutual acts of cultural appropriation such as those that occurred in the trade in porcelain, export porcelain, and chinoiserie (imitation porcelain), allow us to examine how visual and material objects circulated images and motifs of Asia and Europe to Asian and European consumers alike. These objects played a critical role in shaping new geographical imaginaries about Europe and Asia, filling many minds and rooms with otherworldly representations. The world trade in these highly coveted foreign goods also expanded the slave trade. Ships that carried porcelain teacups destined for the royal palace in Lisbon also trafficked slaves who would disembark in Brazil. The beginning of free trade went hand in hand with the worldwide expansion of the African slave trade.

Global economic ventures and competition-led production significantly affected geopolitical relations and cultural production about the so-called Orient and Occident. Portuguese mariners and merchants working with their counterparts in China jointly supplied the idea of the Orient in the form of hybrid material culture; for example, Chinese porcelain was inscribed with European-commissioned motifs and transported alongside other items that Europeans could sell, trade, or keep as souvenirs. Porcelain objects made in China were so popular that the word *china* became metonymic for porcelain. Shards of china found in archaeological sites around the world serve as evidence of the crucial role the porcelain trade played in establishing the interconnected global economy.[13] These shards also attest to the critical part that material and visual culture played in creating, displaying, and circulating ideas about China and Chineseness. Portuguese traders were particularly interested in porcelain, an item of high-art material culture that emperors throughout Chinese history prized. Each dynasty had characteristic patterns, forms, and motifs on its porcelain.[14] The lightness, durability, and impermeability of porcelain made it superior to clay ceramics. Its characteristics were unprecedented in Europe, and it was prized for both beauty and utility. For example, the bottom and top rims of a porcelain bowl enable its user to hold hot liquids without risk of burning.[15] Such innovations made these objects particularly attractive to elite European consumers who began to adapt Chinese customs such as drinking tea from porcelain cups. Along with shipments of porcelain, the Portuguese also brought back exotic teas from the Orient, and tea became a popular drink among the Portuguese court and elite society. The Portuguese word for tea, *chá*, is a transliteration of the Mandarin word for tea. Porcelain's exorbitant prices made it exclusively available to the wealthiest, and customs such as tea drinking that accompanied the use of porcelain quickly became a symbol of refinement and high culture.

Blue-and-white porcelain was a particular favorite of the Portuguese and later influenced the now famous blue-and-white tiles of Portuguese archi-

FIGURE 1.2. Mandarin in blue and white on tile, Portugal, c. mid-nineteenth century. Source: Aaron David Smith Private Collection.

tecture (Figure 1.2). The Sino-Portuguese porcelain trade represents the earliest example of porcelain objects with Chinese motifs sold to a European empire. The armillary sphere motif was invented in China in the second century (Figure 1.3). In the sixteenth century, it acquired new meaning when Kings Manuel I (1495–1521) and João III (1502–1557) used it to symbolize Portuguese maritime discoveries.[16] Along with the armillary sphere, it became a common practice for Portuguese royalty and aristocrats to commission familial coat-of-arms designs on Chinese porcelain objects.

FIGURE 1.3.   Porcelain bowl with armillary sphere motif, Lisbon, Portugal, sixteenth century. Source: Nuno de Castro, *A porcelana chinesa ao tempo do Império* (Portugal and Brazil: ACD Editores 1987): 68.

The royal Portuguese commissions of motifs on porcelain emblematized the Portuguese standard of the cultured and military man. The armillary sphere continues to hold significant political symbolism for modern-day Portugal. The sphere forms part of the Portuguese national flag, a reminder of its great seaborne imperial history, and testimony to a nostalgic part of Portuguese national identity that remembers its empire with longing.

The global trade in porcelain, export porcelain, and chinoiserie objects attests to how the production, circulation, and consumption of material and visual culture, including representations and motifs about both the East and West, made Asia and Europe into exotic products and status symbols for consumers in China, Japan, France, Portugal, England, the Netherlands and other places around the world. To understand the complexity of these relationships, we must analyze the way that both the East and West profited from and exploited images of each other to expand and reach larger markets. In some instances, trade produced enterprising alliances as well as competitive markets in Asia and Europe, and in others, market demand induced new genres of porcelain production. It is not enough to examine this history as an example of Orientalism or Eurocentric cultural hegemony in which Europeans produced an imaginary of the Other, thereby facilitating colonial domination.[17] The porcelain, export porcelain, and chinoiserie trade produced and circulated images of Asia and Europe that were seen as foreign by Asian and European perspectives alike and thus appeared exotic to all who looked at the objects depicting images from these differing cultures.

A number of significant moments in the global porcelain trade reveal the impact that the trade had in conditioning ways of seeing and knowing the East and West. During the transitional period between the Ming (1368–1644) and Qing dynasties (1644–1911), political turmoil in China led to a halt in porcelain production, which caused a supply shortage in the highly profitable European market in Oriental luxury goods. In the period that coincides with suspended porcelain production in China, a new genre of imitation porcelain and motifs known as chinoiserie developed in Europe. European emperors were eager to capitalize on the lucrative china trade and invested heavily in discovering the secrets to porcelain production.[18] However, because a key ingredient of the hard-paste clay that composes porcelain is the kaolin mineral that is richly abundant in places like Jingdezhen, China, but unavailable in Europe, a type of crude, soft-paste imitation called porcelainacau (or faience) developed. In the Netherlands, the Dutch could neither completely replicate the material properties of Chinese porcelain nor the techniques of Chinese art, so they developed a cheaper version of porcelain made from clay that was fired and then coated with a tin glaze. This imitation china—chinoiserie—developed into a unique style known as Hollandware. Dutch potters produced chinoiserie objects and decorations that circulated imprinted images of not only an imagined Asia but also an invented Europe. Eventually Dutch scenes of seascapes and windmills replaced Chinese motifs of pagodas, lotus flowers, and philosophers.[19] Although Dutch manufacturers developed their own motifs, they retained the popular blue-and-white color scheme. In turn, Japanese artisans embraced the exotic imaginary of Europe painted onto Hollandware (*Orandaware*), and imitated the chinoiserie in return.[20] When the Qing dynasty reestablished the main center of porcelain production in Jingdezhen, a new genre of cheaper export porcelain developed to satisfy the market. This variety of export porcelain was called *kraak,* likely derived from *carraca,* the Portuguese word for carrack, the merchant cargo ships that transported porcelain and other trade goods, along the routes of the Carreira da Índia. While *kraak porselein*, underglaze blue-and-white porcelain, became all the rage in Europe, in China, it was made only for export: it was of no interest to Chinese consumers, who considered its quality to be "low-grade" and its aesthetic to be "barbaric."[21]

Material and visual cultural evidence of a longstanding Sino-Portuguese cultural history exists throughout Brazil, serving as symbolic and physical reminders of the once vast Portuguese global empire and Portuguese colonization. Portuguese carracks circulated Asian material culture to all socioeconomic levels of Brazilian society, including enslaved people. Sociologist Gilberto Freyre, in his seminal 1936 study, *Sobrados e mucambos* (*Mansions and Shanties*), observes that Brazil received from Asia "large supplies of cheap fabrics for the use of slaves and the poor, and not merely high-grade materials for the wealthy."[22] The driving force behind Portuguese imperialism and its role in expanding the African slave trade depended on the global expansion of mercantilism, which led to the ceaseless search for trade goods, raw and natural material, and labor.

The traffic in people accompanied the trade in luxury objects like porcelain, export porcelain, and chinoiserie objects and decor. Since contraband formed a significant part of Portuguese trade, it follows that beginning in the fifteenth century, Portuguese explorers participated in covert and explicit slave trading negotiations.[23] The Portuguese, along with other European slave traders and African counterparts, established the African slave trade through linking the largest slave markets and port cities in present-day Angola, Cabo Verde, Guinea-Bissau, Mozambique, São Tomé and Príncipe, Brazil, the United States, Cuba, and Portugal, among other places. The ruins of the oldest known slave market in Europe built in 1444 still stand in the sleepy port town of Lagos in southern Portugal, once the epicenter of the European slave trade. In Rio de Janeiro and Salvador da Bahia, Portugal ran the largest slave markets in the world. Portuguese carracks also contributed to the Cuban slave trade, and thus linked Brazilian ports to Havana to the Caribbean to the southern United States. The trade in luxury goods and slaves moved along a vast transoceanic network that connected once-distant societies, cultures, and ideas to a circumoceanic memory of race, where the trade in racialized human labor moved alongside the trade in otherworldly objects—foreign luxury goods. Brazil was a major player in this global history of the slave trade where slavery lasted until nearly the twentieth century, May 13, 1888, making it the last place in the Americas to abolish inherited slavery.

The Brazilian Gilded Age

The Brazilian Golden Age was a story that literally began and ended with gold. Extravagant gilded church altars built during the late seventeenth and eighteenth centuries are remnants of this history, as is the architecture in cities located along the *Estrada Real* (Royal Road), a 1,013 mile colonial highway sanctioned by the Portuguese government during the mid-seventeenth century as the only legitimate road for travel and commerce.[24] At the height of the gold rush in the eighteenth century, the road connected Brazil's colonial cities, many of them named after the precious stones, metals, and minerals abundant in the area. The cities' names cast a shiny thin veneer over the social and physical destruction that had occurred in those lands due to gold and diamond mining; for example, "Diamantina" refers to the area's once plentiful diamond mines. The former capital city of Minas Gerais, Ouro Preto (meaning black gold), alluded to the area's bountiful amount of gold covered with iron ore. Gold was first discovered at the end of the seventeenth century; in response, the Portuguese brought over half a million Indigenous and African slaves to the region to mine the precious minerals. With the aid of horses, carriages, and gunfire, the gold, iron, diamonds, and other precious materials were funneled through Minas Gerais, São Paulo, and Rio de Janeiro. The Estrada Real ended in Paraty, where ships transported the valuable goods back to Portugal.[25] By the conclusion of the eighteenth century, most of the gold had made its way to Europe, but the devastation caused from mining and slavery remained.

The Portuguese government used the Catholic religion to create allegiance to the Portuguese flag across vastly diverse places held under colonial administration.[26] Church architecture, especially altars, produced a didactic experience for the faithful. When the faithful entered the sacred place of worship, they also entered a *Theatrum sacrum* (sacred theater), where reality was suspended for the full theatricalization of church and state power. The ritual of worship was also a process of becoming educated and disciplined by the Portuguese visual-spatial apparatus that taught attendees about their relationship to God and the state.[27] Each level of the church altar conveys an ornament of discourse wherein a material object serves a figurative function such that *b* represents *a*.[28] Baroque altars abided by a strict representational system that visually conveyed the juridical-theological power of the Portuguese empire within Aristotle's theory of mimesis, dependent on rhetorical forms of *memoria* (memory), *inventio* (invention), *dispositio* (disposition), *elocutio* (elocution), *actio* (action), *delectare* (delight), *movere* (persuasion), and *docere* (education).[29] The church altar had an allegorical function: it showed faithful worshippers their rightful place in the theological political hierarchy, which was at the bottom of the altar, just below the archangels. The saints would be above the angels, and above them, the Virgin Mary and baby Jesus. At the top of the altar would be symbols of God and Jesus, commonly shown as golden star-shaped rays to represent Jesus as light of the world.

It is common to find chinoiserie imagery that imitates Chinese porcelain design motifs like pagodas, fishermen, and famille rose (rose-colored enamel), among others, on baroque church altars throughout the Brazilian cities that once constituted the Estrada Real. On transoceanic trade routes, these motifs turned into "free-floating" symbols that lost their original meaning.[30] As they circulated, docked, and anchored, they gained new meaning with new contexts, as occurred within religious matrices. Located atop the highest peak of Ouro Preto is Nossa Senhora do Rósario do Alto da Cruz do Padre Faria, also known as the Church of Santa Efigênia. During Ouro Preto's Golden Age, the church congregation members consisted mainly of enslaved and freed people of color who were trafficked to the Espinhaço Mountains to work in its plentiful gold mines. The church is still in use today, and the majority of the church's members are personally connected to that history. In the sanctuary, two paintings on either side of the main altar depict men wearing knot button shirts and women with hair buns (Figure 1.4). They are holding parasols or using walking sticks and standing beside palm trees and elephants. The Portuguese word for walking stick is *bengala*, a derivation of *Bengal*. Bengala developed from the trade history between Portugal and Bengal. Bengala, like chinoiserie imagery, are exotic free-floating markers that fill the mind's eye with otherworldly representations and appear foreign to all who look at them. Whereas these South Asian canes may have once been a popular commercial item, African diasporic religious elements mixed with the Portuguese juridical-theological order on this church altar and produced a uniquely syncretic religion that is particular to the collisions and encounters that occurred in this space.[31] When I visited the church in June 2011, I asked the sexton about the visuals. He replied that they were likely created by artisans who had lived in Macau, Goa, or other parts of the Portuguese empire in Asia and migrated to Brazil along the circuits of the Carreira da Índia. The circuits of world trade that moved items like the bengala also moved the people who founded the church of St. Efigênia and produced new ways of seeing both local and distant places. These images serve as an ongoing reminder of the myriad forms of resistance and creativity that occurred in face of a slave-holding society that thrived on eradicating personhood.

The transoceanic movement of goods and human labor among Africa, Asia, Europe, and the Americas also produced overlapping processes of racialization. For example, *chino* or *china,* the female equivalent, was an ambiguous category, and as historian María Elena Martínez notes, it usually designated "the child of a black and native woman, but colonial officials often used it as a generic name for Asians, particularly from the Philippines."[32] The malleability of the word *chino/a* functioned like the evasive designation *Indies.* Under one ambiguous descriptor, *chino* referred to a wide range of racialized exploited laborers branded together in a circumoceanic memory where the China trade could refer ambiguously to both the trade in people and porcelain. Chinos could refer to people from either China or India, or Chinese Indians who had set sail aboard galleons (three- to four-masted oceangoing Spanish war vessels that were turned into trading ships) as "sailors, slaves, or servants."[33] In Acapulco, migrants took on jobs as laborers and craftsmen, as well as slaves and servants.[34] Portuguese traders working in the *Estado da Índia* (a reference to the more than fifty Portuguese colonial holdings and outposts in Asia) aided in supplying the Manila slave market and Manila galleon trade with enslaved people from Goa, Macau, and other parts of Asia.[35] Accounts of Chinese slaves appear in various writings that reveal different perspectives on Chinese slavery. Jesuit priest Matteo Ricci, who favored the commerce, noted he had seen Chinese slaves in Lisbon in 1578.[36] By the seventeenth century, Chinese slavery had reached such levels that to appease Chinese authorities, King Felipe IV declared on February 19, 1624, that Chinese men and women could not and should not be slaves, and he ordered the liberty of all enslaved Chinese men and women.[37] Regardless, the illegal sale of Chinese slaves, including young boys and girls, continued. In 1715, a Portuguese diplomatic cor-

FIGURE 1.4. Men wearing knot button shirts, holding walking stick and parasol, on lateral sides of main church altar, Church of Santa Efigênia, Ouro Preto, Brazil, c. mid-eighteenth century. Source: Photograph by the author.

respondence from Miguel de Amaral, who was stationed in Japan, to the governor of Macau, D. Francisco de Alarcão Soto Maior, stated the need to prohibit the trafficking of Chinese girls to Goa, Manila, and other areas outside China. The Qing court punished slave traffickers with execution or exile, and he feared that the Chinese slave trade put the entire Portuguese mission in Macau at risk of banishment.[38] Two years later, the Portuguese king, João V, ordered the viceroy of India to forbid the trafficking of *mui tsai* (bondmaids or handmaidens) from Macau.[39] Yet neither Portuguese nor Qing officials had control over the illegal selling and trafficking of Chinese slaves. In 1744, Emperor Qianlong forbade all the Chinese and Portuguese in Macau from selling children.[40] Nevertheless, the sale continued. Chinese men, women, and children were sent aboard vessels that stopped in Lisbon, along other entrepôts on Spanish and Portuguese world trade circuits, including Mexico and Brazil.

Racial Transits and Transformations

Portuguese imperial expansion was not concerned with maintaining racial purity. Portuguese colonial settlements around the world produced a mythology around miscegenation that had a significant impact on shaping later discourses in Brazil about mixed-race national identity. Heavy investment in imperial expansion produced dire economic conditions in Portugal, driving people to migrate and settle in other places, either long term or temporarily. The population in Portugal during the sixteenth century was about 1.25 million, with a further estimated 10,000 Portuguese males in Asia.[41] Portuguese playwright Gil Vicente wrote about these conditions in the Portuguese discovery play, *Auto da Índia* (1507), a remarkably insightful piece that uses adultery as a metaphor to criticize expansionism and the efforts at global commerce that were depleting the local economy and destroying domestic relations by driving men to emigrate to Africa and Asia to chase after the insatiable desire for adventure and colonial riches. By the end of the sixteenth century, as the Portuguese settled around the world, *Portuguese* increasingly referred to people of mixed European and Asian, Indian, or Indonesian descent.[42]

In theory, "native" miscegenation with Portuguese blood and cultural heritage produced an imperial discourse of multiculturalism wherein Portuguese language, religion, foods, and customs not only unified societies but also integrated cultural differences across the reaches of the Portuguese seaborne empire. In practice, a different story becomes evident when we look at records of interracial marriages. Maria Eugénia Mata observes that registered marriages included records of the participants' different skin tones, attesting to social and race-based prejudice.[43] In Spanish America, Martínez observes that marriage and baptismal records often qualified grooms or fathers with terms like *español* and *índio*, but the bride's identity was not listed. A patrilineal logic dominated the processes of establishing *vecindad* (citizenship) in local communities and *naturaleza* (nativity) membership in the kingdom.[44] Categories like *mestizo* and *mulato* that developed in the Americas did not originally have the racial connotations that those terms hold today. Rather, these terms conveyed legal rights over claims to land and citizenship.[45]

The Spanish and Portuguese American colonies gave rise to a set of unique and complex social, political, and religious developments, adding layers of racial categorizations to existing Iberian classifications that were based on religious lineage and purity. On the Iberian Peninsula, the Spanish and Portuguese Inquisitions forced society to undergo brutal genealogical investigations to determine the degrees to which people had Christian, Jewish, and Muslim blood.[46] The colonial caste system (sistema de casta) developed during the formal establishment of the Inquisition, which began in the fifteenth century and lasted four centuries. The sistema de casta was a genealogical fiction and a complex system of social hierarchy that developed in the Americas as a means of securing Iberian territorial control by classifying power through bloodline.[47] The sistema de casta was a response to the threat that the elite mestizo class posed to the Iberian crown's claim to territory and power.[48] More than 110 racial identity categories developed, providing a visual and linguistic rubric that determined one's social and economic ranking. This rubric indicated degrees of mixed-race ancestry, as well as taxonomy; for example, categories included "Spanish, Indian, black, mestizo, castizo, morisco, zambahigo (or zambaigo), and in the eighteenth century, also *lobo* [wolf], *coyote* [coyote], *pardo, moreno* and occasionally *chino.*"[49]

The sistema de casta also defined bloodline within a colonial division of labor. Slave regimes in Latin America and the Caribbean were in line with the Aristotelian tradition of the natural slave that held to the idea of inherent attributes determining a person's relationship to labor. Plato's myth of metals provides an early example of eugenicist thinking that imbued the division of labor in society with ideas about the inherent attributes of people. In the myth, Plato divided social hierarchy into four categories symbolized by the metals gold, silver, iron, and bronze. Each metal corresponds to one's ranking in society. Since gold is rare and the most precious of the four metals, the gold people were the philosopher-kings, born with the natural ability to rule, whereas silver people were the auxiliaries, and those classified as iron and bronze were born to labor with their hands as farmers or craftsmen.[50] Aristotle, Plato's most famous student, developed Plato's teachings in his philosophy of the natural slave. In *Politics* (c. 350 BC), Aristotle advanced the idea that citizenship and its virtues did not extend to certain people who were born suited to be slaves.[51] For Aristotle, to be born a natural slave was an inherent condition, which by logical reasoning related an ontological relation to natural freedom. Whereas some echelons of society were suited to rule and thus inherently granted freedom, others were better off being ruled. Following this logic, Aristotle proclaimed that citizenship and the virtue of deliberation necessary for exercising political rule was not attainable by certain segments of society, including slaves and foreigners.[52] This exclusionary principle of citizenship developed new horns in the context of hemispheric American colonialism and the African slave trade.

During the conquest of the Americas, theologians and conquistadors referenced Aristotle's philosophy of the natural slave to argue over whether Indigenous people of the Americas were indeed naturally suited to be slaves.[53] In the well-known Valladolid debate (1550–1551), Dominican friar Bartolomé de Las Casas and lawyer Juan Ginés de Sepulveda debated each other about the treatment of Indigenous people of the Americas. To argue for or against their freedom, Casas and Sepulveda had to first establish whether the nature of Native Americans made them capable of self-governance or if they were too childlike and thus better off under Spanish rule. These debates were also directly linked to land claims. Sepulveda argued against Casas on behalf of the colonists' property rights. He rationalized the way the Spanish colonists treated Native Americans by arguing that so-called Indians were natural slaves and that Spanish rule in the New World would benefit them.[54] Casas, however, denounced the atrocious acts of the conquistadors and condemned them as anti-Christian.[55] While both men fiercely debated the matter on opposing sides, both placed Aristotle's natural slave argument at the center of a moral interpretation of Christian law to then decide the status and rights of Indigenous people of the Americas. The category of natural slave, which logically extended to a person's qualifications for citizenship, thus accrued a spectrum of racialization alongside imperialist efforts to expropriate Indigenous lands and expand the African slave trade.

A set of thirteenth-century codes known as the *Siete Partidas* declared slavery to be an institution "against natural reason."[56] However, the Iberian empires treated slaves as both subjects and property, a necessary part of the body politic, constituting the lowest and natural rank of order. Since slaves were subjects, Klein and Luna explain, laws regarding liberty and slavery did not fully foreclose enslaved people from the rights to property, security, and the religious ceremonies of Christianity, even though personal liberty was voided.[57] We can observe the persistent logic of the natural slave in the way the institution of slavery operated in dictating the unions with women of African ancestry. To protect the financial interests of slaveholders, children born to enslaved mothers were attributed to the maternal bloodline. This explains the legal underpinning of the Free Womb Law, which protected the property rights of slave owners.[58] In Brazil, slavery continued as an inherited condition, passed through the bloodline of enslaved women, until the Free Womb Law passed in 1871. The law granted freedom to newborns, thus breaking off the slaveholder's inheritance of property via matriarchal lineage.[59] That sexual reproduction defined lawful freedom from enslaved labor provides one legal example of how the violence of the Middle Passage and chattel slavery had dehumanized and "ungendered" the body.[60] In the struggle for abolition, the ruling over black female sexual reproduction also signified the juridical possibility for societal emancipation.[61]

Slavery was finally abolished on May 13, 1888, almost sixty years after the Brazilian regency passed a law on November 7, 1831 that prohibited slave trafficking due to pressure from England. On paper, the prohibition on slave trafficking was made to appease the English, but in practice, laws were futile and defiantly broken. Coined during this time was the popular expression *para inglês ver* (for the English to see), meaning to do something for appearances only and without any practical intention.[62] The British prohibition on slave trafficking had not only backfired in Brazil; it also opened the floodgates to illegal trafficking, as well as hike in the price of slaves. Regardless of the official end to the slave trade, illegal enslavement continued, and the aristocratic ruling class turned a blind eye because it had rapidly become a major source of revenue and labor.[63] Between 1830 and 1850, traffickers brought approximately 700,000 Africans to work on Brazilian sugar plantations.[64] The constant threat of illegal enslavement made liberty a volatile state. It produced a condition of unfreeness in which the liberty of freeborn or freed people of color was precarious and had to be proved and litigated.[65] Court records, police correspondence, and prison books indicate numerous examples of illegally enslaved people who took their cases to court to create "a paper trail to safeguard the right to freedom."[66] This environment in which slavery was the default upheld the power and wealth of the aristocracy and agriculturalist oligarchy who fought fiercely to maintain their elite status. The struggle for power occurred predominantly between the government and the seigniorial class. The seigniorial class was often at odds with government attempts to limit their full control over slaves since whoever controlled the institution of slavery controlled the wealth and power of Brazil. The precarious condition of freedom for nonlanded laborers developed into a precarious labor system defined by personal as well as economic dependence on wealthy patrons and their paternalistic treatment of workers, slave and free.[67]

Duplicitous and elusive acts for the purpose of prolonging slavery in clandestine forms developed alongside—often in convergence with—the road to gradual emancipation and liberty. Because the English prohibition of slave trafficking created a scarcity model, it brought extravagant wealth to its traffickers. Along with the aristocracy, they decadently spent their fortunes as if each day were their last.[68] Rio de Janeiro transformed into a city of soirees, in which the wealthiest passed their time in dance, music, debauchery, and gambling. Socialites occupied their time in the activity of seeing and being seen, which required dedicated hours in beauty salons and promenading on the Rua do Ouvidor, the place to be for cafés, literary activity, and European fashion.[69] Specialty shops showcased the latest in wool hats and suits. Irrespective of Rio's year-round tropical temperatures that rarely dropped below 70 degrees, cariocas sported Parisian winter styles to signal the haut monde taste of a privileged noble class. If storefronts displayed the high culture of the elite slaveholding class, the streets were paved in *pé de moleque,* a type of cobblestone laid down by enslaved men.[70]

Slavery—a system that was both a backward means of production and a necessity—now shows its legacy in the practical, social, and emotional structure of the independent nation.[71] The scarcity model of equality—that is, the idea that equality is limited and thus has the potential to cause intense expansion or contraction of liberty—is observable in Brazil's exclusive mode of liberalism that upholds access to the full rights of citizenship for some and its wholesale denial to others, regardless of citizenship status.[72] This phenomenon is observable in Brazil's racial whitening project that followed abolition. The First Brazilian Republic, established in 1889, turned to immigrant labor to replace the labor once done by enslaved people. Newly arriving immigrants entered into a spectrum of racialized hierarchies within this Brazilian political complex. The ideas that had deeply shaped the institution of inherited slavery that governed and disciplined enslaved female sexual reproduction continued to operate within national frameworks. In the context of Chinese labor migration and eugenics-based ideas about labor, miscegenation, and national identity, the predominant rhetoric in debates over Chinese labor productivity centered on Chinese sexual reproduction as a threat or potential for abolition and republicanism.

The continuing charge for racial and social equality, and the opposition to those demands, exposes the processual nature of racial regimes that function as a continuum. The Brazilian nation-building project of whitening via immigrant labor produced a racialized national identity that arose contingently out of colonial racial hierarchies. With the formation of the modern Brazilian nation-state, we can observe how national sovereignty has defined itself through a racialized national consciousness that functions as a governing principle to determine the degrees of one's access to citizenship and inalienable rights to liberty in the state. As of 2010, the Brazilian census accounted for five racial identities: white, black, mixed race, yellow, and Indigenous. These stratifications attest to the way that the colonial caste system's racial logic continues to inform racialized national categories. Yet these classifications also expose the instability of racial identities, since all of these terms are relational and depend on self-identification and reasoning that is as personal as persons themselves. While race is discursive and performative, the vastly diverse experiences of racialization exceed representation.

Emancipation to Immigration

Branqueamento (racial whitening ideology) played a critical role in fin-de-siècle debates over Brazilian nation building when politicians and agriculturalists looked to immigration from Europe, Asia, and the Middle East as a means to modernize the economy from slave labor to free labor. Liberal reform intertwined with racial whitening and eugenic ideology wherein ideas about free labor became coterminous in discussions over whiteness and national identity. In the public at large, concerns about economic necessity during the shift from slave labor to free labor were intertwined with those about the nation's racial demographics. Defining whiteness meant defining how the nation would modify its population from blacker to whiter and assimilate immigrants who were neither white nor black.[1] While whiteness was highly regarded, it was a relational and dynamic construct that did not simply refer to skin color.[2] In some cases, the belief in whitening the population expressed abolitionists' desire for free labor via European immigration.[3] In other cases, whiteness expressed the desire to align with imperialist states, namely Euro-America and Meiji Japan. Leading abolitionists believed the Chinese were a "yellow race" who presented a threat to the whitening project, and thus could only serve as a temporary solution to the labor crisis.[4] Representations of Chineseness circulating in Brazilian mass media allow us to examine how yellowness played a role in defining whiteness and blackness. Print media circulated caricatures and parodic commentaries about the Chinese that related economic and political anxieties regarding assimilation with the so-called yellow race.[5] Racial representations of Chineseness were not limited to defining Brazilian national identity, but they show the emergence of a global racialized national consciousness.

For their part, the late Qing and Meiji governments had their own expansionist ambitions, which took shape in labor migration schemes that established national symbolic and structural ties between overseas settlers and the homeland. Late Qing intellectuals and diplomats were interested in creating their own versions of China in Brazil, via *yizhi* (a word that means both immigration and colonization). Late Qing intellectuals feared that the end of China was near, and they looked to Brazil as a possibility for building a new China through economic and political expansion via overseas Chinese labor settlements. Their visits sparked much debate among abolitionists and proslavery advocates alike. Late Qing diplomatic visits to assess these possibilities entered into the imaginations of abolitionists in Brazil who were struggling for emancipation and republicanism. Bringing together Brazilian and late Qing views about the figure of the migrant Chinese laborer reveals an emerging global consciousness about racialized national imaginings that expanded beyond individual state territories. Examining late Qing dynasty diplomatic missives about the role that overseas Chinese could play in opening immigration and trade routes between China and Brazil—bearing in mind the context of Brazilian abolitionists' preoccupations over emancipation and national independence—shows how racial representations of Chineseness contained these geopolitical layers of significance. These were the transitional years leading up to economic liberalization, which must also be understood within the global transition from slave labor to new systems of migrant labor. Brazilian cultural production as well as Qing diplomatic writings contradictorily produced ideas about Chinese laborers as both the colonizing settler and the newly enslaved population; the figure of the Chinese migrant laborer would both fulfill the dreams of expansionism via immigration/colonization and serve as the necessarily disposable collateral for nation building.

In Brazil, antislavery advocates created emancipation narratives that made Chinese immigration or so-called yellow labor into a trope for the precarious condition of freedom following the end of slavery. Depictions of Chinese laborers vacillate as both the hope for and threat to the nation: they may provide a solution to the labor crisis, but their deemed unfreeness made them unsuitable for Brazil's whitening liberalism. Whereas Chinese laborers were undesirable, Japanese migrants were welcomed, for the time being. Shifting ideas regarding Chinese and Japanese immigrants were tied to Chinese and Japanese state goals, which figured into Brazil's whitening project and transition towards republicanism.

In Brazil, fin-de-siècle views regarding labor, race, and liberty were largely focused on social Darwinist and eugenic ideas about miscegenation. Debates over Chinese labor productivity intertwined with discussions over miscegenation, Brazilian national identity, and republicanism. We can readily observe the interrelated rhetoric of sexual reproduction, mixed-race identity, and democracy in early nineteenth-century political theorist Alexis de Tocqueville's study of US democracy (1835; 1840), which he deemed the exemplary model for all nations. The Brazilian Constitution of 1891, Brazil's first republican constitution, was modeled after the US Constitution. For Tocqueville, there were two plausible solutions for forging unity and democracy: miscegenation or complete segregation. Integral to Tocqueville's discussion of racial democracy was sexual reproduction, in which "inter-breeding" could allow a "third race" to arise.[6] He told his readers about a hybrid race that had developed in the Spanish and Portuguese Americas and described the mixed-raced children of European men and Indigenous women, "half-castes," who were the "natural link between civilization and barbarity."[7] Black and Indigenous female sexual reproduction were to serve as a bridge between exclusion and inclusion into civil society. Tocqueville's vision of a democratic nation thus promulgated a racial discourse wherein he posited a naturalized relationship of racial identity, liberty, and democracy that depended on governing sexuality. Following this logic, Alberto Torres (1865–1917), jurist and president of Rio de Janeiro from 1896 to 1900, expressed the view that mulatos occupied an intermediary social position, hierarchically ranked above the black population but never fully accepted by the white nobility.[8] The mulato emblematized the intermediary position for negotiating the nation's racial identity, which gained positive or negative value according to a hierarchical relationship between blackness and whiteness.

Competing narratives about miscegenation with Chinese laborers figured into these existing ideas that entangled mixed-race identity and national identity. Some believed that miscegenation could redeem their undesirability such that they could be assimilated to the point of eradication.[9] Other perspectives presented the viewpoint that miscegenation with the Chinese would pose a virile threat wherein yellowness would not only eliminate blackness but also take over the possibility of whiteness. Chinese gender and sexuality gained a functional meaning in how it was used to negotiate the state's economic institutions. The Chinese became a figuration of a two-way bridge that could take Brazil from either a backward colonial economy based on slave labor toward a progressive state based on civilized free labor or keep it in a rearward direction.

Social Darwinist ideas about generative or degenerative miscegenation with the Chinese were in fact circulating around the globe, including US political cartoons that depicted Chinese laborers in a spectrum of dehumanizing stereotypes. Recurring depictions of the Chinese visually marked them with slanted eyes, knot button shirts, pointed-toe shoes, and, most prominent, the Qing dynasty queue, a men's thin ponytail hairstyle that symbolized loyalty to the Qing. In one image, titled "Darwin's Theory Illustration—The Creation of Chinaman and Pig," that appeared in a San Francisco–based publication, *The Wasp*, the Chinese were caricaturized in an evolutionary stage between rat and pig. The illustration shows physical features like a queue that resembles a hybrid rat and pigtail.[10]

These depictions were not merely products of the imagination: in the United States, cultural constructions of Chinese laborers as a yellow race prepared the cultural environment for unprecedented race- and class-based restrictions. The so-called Chinese question circulated on a worldwide scale the doubt over whether the Chinese were suitable for national integration. It created a homogeneous category, a "coolie race" that posed a threat to white free labor, and paved the way for anti-Chinese exclusion policies in the United States and around the rest of the world. The global Chinese or coolie question, as Ngai observes, lumped all Chinese laborers regardless of their status into one orientalist representation that flattened empirical differences among the various kinds of Chinese labor systems. It also obscured transnational dynamics, including racial politics.[11] The racialized nationalisms that emerged alongside the formation of a global system of nation-states did not arise from a single political system, but they possessed many centers of power.[12] The worldwide spread of anti-Chinese sentiment during the second half of the nineteenth century demands that we understand the polycentric and global dimensions of racialized nationalisms.

The US Chinese Exclusion Act of 1882, signed by President Chester Arthur, was the first federal law to ban immigration on the basis of race and class. The act restricted US borders from economic competition through claiming to defend the racial integrity of the nation.[13] The exclusion act caused a ripple effect in other countries, demonstrating the global dimensions of racial nationalism: US immigration restrictions and attempts to secure its racial and national borders produced a southward shift in migration patterns. These patterns also carried with them the racialized categories that US white liberal democracy wished to exclude. From 1890 to 1892, Africans and Asians were prohibited from entering Brazil.[14] Anti-Chinese sentiment that homogenized Chinese laborers as a coolie race conveyed the perception that they were unassimilable. The Chinese were racially and ethnically coded as uncivilized, subhuman, and filthy—as markers of the "exotic alien."[15] They were undemocratic, unfree, and thus un-American bodies.[16] Therefore, they were unfit political subjects and excludable from entering into US citizenry. In the United States, racialized nationalism and economic competition between white and Chinese laborers fueled anti-Chinese sentiment that circulated on a global scale and entered into the completely new context of Brazil's whitening project and national independence movement.

In the years immediately following Chinese exclusion in the United States, late Qing officials looked to places in the Americas like Brazil as a favorable option for Chinese political and economic expansion via the overseas Chinese. During the second half of the nineteenth century, the Qing steadily lifted bans on Chinese emigration. In addition to signing the 1860 Peking Treaty and the 1868 Burlingame Treaty that both lifted bans and legalized Chinese emigration, the Qing governmental attitude about overseas Chinese people also shifted, no longer perceiving them as traitors to the motherland who deserved a punishment worthy of death but as victims of "greedy foreigners" and "Chinese smugglers."[17] This shift helped further the view among Chinese people that the restriction of overseas Chinese people from the United States by means of the Chinese Exclusion Act was "particularly unjust and despicable."[18] Qing diplomats grappled with the negative perception of the Chinese that led to Chinese exclusion. Xue Fucheng claimed that the US public at large deemed Chinese people unsightly, with animal-like eating styles and appearances. Likewise, Cui Guoyin, Chinese minister to the United States, Spain, and Peru, noted that the illegal actions of overseas Chinese, including opium smuggling and tong wars, had been the grounds for exclusion. These critiques obscured a larger problem: the lack of overseas Chinese voting power in the US democratic system.[19]

In the face of global anti-Chinese sentiment and the decline of Manchu rule, late Qing leaders and diplomats took great interest in Meiji Japan's treatment of Japanese migration and overseas settlement as a model that Chinese migration could adopt to further Chinese state goals. The Meiji attached a nationalist meaning to migration and treated it as an extension of the state's economic and political objectives.[20] With the decline of the Qing empire and Japan's rise as a superpower following the successes in the Sino-Japanese War (1894–1895) and Russo-Japanese War (1904–1905), many Chinese intellectuals and statesmen looked to Meiji Japan as a model of governance and modernity.[21] The Meiji Restoration ushered in a new period of modernization and national development, and it also transformed Japan into an imperial power, with the goal of expanding throughout Asia and to other parts of the world, including Brazil. Meiji leaders believed that in order for Japan to be considered a "civilized" nation, it would have to follow the European practice of colonization.[22] Japanese standards for modernization may be viewed as having been "subject to the approval or legitimacy granted by the West or the White."[23] However, Japan's emergence as an Asian superpower, and its expansion into former European colonial outposts in Asia, challenged Western dominance and the "mystique of white supremacy" on which European and American expansion depended.[24] The Meiji empire was heavily invested in establishing the racial and cultural uniqueness of the Yamato race as having a divine lineage with morally superior virtues.[25] A secret study conducted in 1942 and 1943 and prepared in the civilian bureaucracy, titled "Global Policy with the Yamato Race as Nucleus," contended that it was the destiny of the Japanese empire—the Yamato race—to become the "leading race" in Asia and the rest of the world.[26] Meiji expansionist ideas consolidated around the notion of a superior Yamato race and culture to drive Japanese militarism and occupation throughout Asia; its colonial takeover of former Western colonies, and the Greater East Asian Co-Prosperity project was not to "invade" but to liberate Asia from Western domination.[27] However, Japanese military leaders made expansion itself into an act of racial and cultural purification in the form of annexation, colonial rule, and mass extermination.[28]

The "Yellow Peril" discourse emerged in 1895 when Kaiser Wilhelm II of Germany coined the expression in reference to Japan's victory over China in the First Sino-Japanese War (1894–1895), also known as the Yellow War. However, as Tchen notes, the tropology of the Yellow Peril formed part of a larger social malaise, so it would be incorrect to attribute an entire discourse to any one person.[29] The Yellow Peril expressed the threat of Asian domination over the West and homogenized ideas about the Japanese and the Chinese. It became a metonymy for Japanese imperialism as well as anti-Chinese labor. The Yellow Peril produced one-dimensional Asian political subjects who posed a threat to Western military power and economic domination. The Yellow Peril discourse provides an example of a racial regime that deployed racial difference for geopolitical and economic objectives. Visual and print cultures played a critical role in disseminating depictions of Asians as a threatening yellow race. Such constructions of racial difference were powerful political weapons that enabled the "psychological distancing" that facilitated ethnic cleansing, genocide, and killing during military confrontation.[30]

Fin-de-siècle and early twentieth-century anti-Japanese images circulating in Brazilian print culture mirrored prevalent anti-Chinese discourse, which depicted Chinese people as racially inferior, unhygienic, and backward.[31] Anti-Chinese attitudes influenced general perceptions about the Japanese, and the Japanese government worked concertedly to change those negative views through diplomacy and by providing economic and political support to Japanese immigrants. Japanese diplomats and immigrants also changed perceptions through appropriating and performing whiteness in order to further Japanese state goals. In 1894, Japanese diplomat Sho Nemoto arrived in Brazil and touted Japanese subjects as the solution to Brazil's labor shortage and path to national progress; contrary to Europeans, Japanese settlers would be hard working, quiet, and eager to become Brazilian.[32] The year 1908 marked the official start of Japanese immigration to Brazil. The first vessel to travel between Japan and Brazil, *Kasato-Maru*, provided transport for 781 passengers. The fifty-one-day voyage prepared them for life in Brazil through screening short instructional films to prepare them for arrival and by offering Portuguese lessons.[33] The passengers' journey marked the official and bilaterally sanctioned start of Japanese immigration to Brazil.[34] Upon arrival, Brazilians were impressed to see them wearing European clothes that the Japanese had purchased in Japanese factories in Japan.[35] These efforts pointed to a larger campaign among Japanese elites to portray Japan as a "white" country.[36] In all these ways and more, Japanese immigration was different from the experience of immigrants from China who confronted similarly harsh conditions and treatment but lacked government protection. The Japanese settlers had the powerful Meiji government supporting them, and the empire was quite present in their daily lives on the other side of the world. In 1908, a Japanese diplomat mediated a labor dispute between laborers and a plantation owner, and within a year, Japanese public-private firms created Japanese-only colonies in São Paulo State.[37] The Japanese colonies had school systems that followed the Japanese school year, and the government sent them textbooks and other supplies.[38] The Japanese state had close watch and control over the Japanese colonies since their productivity was a great source of revenue for the growing military empire, and the government played a critical role in transforming negative images of the Japanese to facilitate Japanese state goals in Brazil.[39]

China in Brazil

The Qing government addressed its weakened political and economic state by ordering a series of information-gathering missions to Japan, the United States, Europe, and the Americas. Its leaders were hoping to gain intelligence about the condition of overseas Chinese workers and assess modernization possibilities in agriculture, industry, and commerce. In 1876, the Qing government officially began to send regular missions abroad, ordering envoys to periodically send diary entries and reports that addressed such topics as canalization, military development, industry, literature and culture, and geopolitical relations.[40] The missions were divided into Eastern and Western *youli* (investigative) groups, whose findings would bring a global perspective to the insular Qing view. These missions opened paths for sending new waves of overseas Chinese populations abroad to mobilize an emerging Chinese national consciousness in the political realm and through economic entrepreneurialism abroad.[41]

Fu Yunlong, senior secretary in the Ministry of War, led the Dongyang (or Eastern ocean) group, responsible for investigating six countries: Japan, the United States, Canada, Peru, Brazil, and Cuba.[42] One of Fu Yunlong's main concerns was to make haste on lenient immigration policies in the face of the global effects of US Chinese exclusion policies.[43] Latin America symbolized a new start for the expansion of China via the export of labor, which could greatly benefit China. Totaling sixty-eight volumes and illustrated maps, the diary entries of Fu Yunlong provide a wealth of materials that outstrips the contributions of his peers (Figure 2.1).[44] Except for a few preexisting notions about Brazil as a savage country, until the turn of the twentieth century, the Qing knew almost nothing about Brazil.[45] Fu Yunlong's travel writings and maps played a pivotal role in transforming insular Qing views and attitudes regarding Chinese emigration.[46] Fu Yunlong debunked existing ideas about Brazil and instead attributed them to the *Zhi fang waiji* (*Chronicle of Foreign Lands*), a text created in 1623 during the end of the Ming dynasty, in which Indigenous Brazilians were depicted with the negative rhetoric of the European conquest tropes, as uncivilized and unlearned barbarians. They were portrayed as naked hunters and cannibals, innocent and illiterate.[47] Although Fu Yunlong rejected those negative images as falsities, he emphasized favorable aspects about the Brazilian landscape and Indigenous people that created a positive image of Brazil—the Brazilians' love of leisure, eating, spending time with family, and their great affinity for swimming in the rivers. He was clear to emphasize that they did not labor; rather, black people performed all labor.[48]

Because Brazil was a young nation and in the initial stages of immigration, he estimated that it could accommodate 200,000 to 300,000 Chinese workers, immigration on a scale without parallel anywhere else.[49] Countering well-known accounts of the exploitative treatment of overseas Chinese workers in places like Cuba and the United States, he instead portrayed labor conditions favorably by painting a one-dimensional, romanticized portrait of the conditions of enslaved people, stating that Brazilians rarely treated slaves cruelly and social mobility existed. They were given room and board; they could plant and sell crops, the proceeds from which many people used to purchase manumissions; and once they attained liberty, they became citizens. These views sold a vision of Brazil as a vast land of opportunity, ripe to take in China's peasant agriculturalist population. By romanticizing slavery and projecting the view of Indigenous people as a leisurely class, Fu Yunlong created a portrait of Brazil and its inhabitants that depicted the land's agricultural possibilities, extractive industries, and its potential to reward hardworking immigrants. His written and illustrated portrayals of the Brazilian landscape and people drove forward the idea that it was a hospitable place for Chinese settlement. Emphasizing available lands and favorable labor conditions, he divided Brazil's population into *minzu* (ethnos): (1) Chinese, (2) Portuguese, (3) British, French, Italian, and Swiss, (4) emancipated black slaves who became citizens, (5) Indig-

FIGURE 2.1. Fu Yunlong's travel map of Brazil. 1901. Double-leaved
book in case with folded map (26 cm). Source: Fu Yunlong. Youli baxi
guo tu jing, 10 volumes. China.

enous, and (6) miscellaneous groups without clear lineage.[50] Fu Yunlong's
classifications of minzu suggest that ethnic and racial identities were not
coterminous with nationalism and statism for him but in flux.[51] As he tried
to make meaning out of Brazil's diverse population, he did not use language
bound to a collective memory about Brazil's racial and eugenic ideologies
to describe Brazilian racial identities such as mulato, a commonly used but

derogatory word that described people of mixed-race parentage. Instead, he created a miscellaneous category for people "without clear lineage." He included emancipated black slaves, whose liberty transformed them into minzu, citizens, and thus members of the national body. He did not give meaning to Chinese ethnicity in terms of Brazil's existing racial caste hierarchy; rather, he created a separate minzu category for the Chinese in the Brazilian landscape. He was producing a new understanding of an emerging Chinese national consciousness that intertwined his understanding of minzu with circumoceanic memories of racial formation, including the processual transference of colonial racial ideologies into notions of racialized nationalisms.

In a mission to Brazil in 1889, he learned that overseas Chinese people were quite mobile; they moved along a vast Chinese migrant network in search of better economic opportunities.[52] For example, his writings about encounters with the Chinese who settled in Rio reveal that at one point, there had been more than a thousand settlers in Rio, but that number had fallen to approximately two hundred by 1889.[53] The decrease in the Chinese population conveys a larger picture about Brazil as a temporary stopover along a larger route that connected Cuba, Peru, San Francisco, and other places, attesting to serial migration patterns that occurred once local economic opportunities dried up or were usurped.[54] Among the Chinese who remained in Rio, some had opened businesses such as groceries or restaurants.[55]

For Fu Yunlong, developing a strong sense of Chinese nationalism would also unify the Chinese who were living away from China. Maintaining patriotic ties to China also meant securing economic contributions to China from workers aboard. Diplomat Xue Fucheng noted that the Chinese who were living in San Francisco were already sending millions of dollars to China each year. If they continued sending remittances in that quantity, the overseas population would equalize China's trade deficit.[56] While China benefited from receiving the earnings of the overseas Chinese, these plans proved unfavorable to host countries and served as tinder for fueling anti-Chinese sentiment.

Fu Yunlong's plan to expand Chinese political and economic objectives to Brazil was not unique among his ilk. The prominent Chinese scholar and political thinker Kang Youwei, for example, shared similar visions for Brazil. By 1895, China, weakened by many things including wars, had begun ceding territories to foreign powers. Kang Youwei, a leading Chinese scholar and major figure in the development of the modern Chinese state, was pre-occupied that the Chinese civilization might soon be extinguished. For him, Brazil offered a possible solution for preserving China, wherein overseas Chinese could build a new China in Brazil.[57] Colonial ideas about racial whitening influenced Kang Youwei's racialized notions of national identity and created a paradox. As Liang Zhan notes, on the one hand, Kang Youwei believed that Chinese emigrants could create a new China in Brazil. On the other hand, the project of whitening threatened to assimilate the Chinese to the point of extinction.[58] While racial whitening ideology was a main factor, Brazilian abolitionists feared that the Chinese would enter into the hands of voracious proslavery advocates who would consume them without ac-countability. The late Qing was too weak to extend political protection over the Chinese in Brazil. Japanese immigrants thus became a favorable option since the Meiji government was powerful and could invest in Brazil by way of investing in permanent settlements for overseas Japanese subjects.[59]

The dream of building a new China in Brazil was also apparent in the writings of Chinese diplomat Liu Shixun. He visited Brazil in 1909, one year after the official start of Japanese immigration to Brazil in 1908, at-testing to ongoing Chinese interest in investigating Japanese economic and political expansion via migration schemes. He called it a "pity" that China should sit back and watch Japan seize land in Brazil where the Japanese were successfully cultivating rice, beans, coffee, and other crops.[60] Liu traveled to Brazil on a special mission to establish diplomatic relations between Bra-zil and China, which actually implied mutual interest in establishing com-mercial treaties that included redirecting Chinese migration from North America to South America.[61] Liu, along with a delegation of Chinese diplo-mats, visited Rio de Janeiro, Petrópolis, São Paulo, and Santos to assess the prospects of Chinese settlement.

In 1914, Liu established the first Chinese legation in Rio de Janeiro. Shortly after, diplomat Wu Guangzhuo, in support of Liu's aims for Chi-nese immigration to Brazil, sent a report to the Chinese Ministry of the Interior. Wu's missives echoed the Meiji government's views regarding mi-gration as a mode of economic and political expansion. In a correspondence dated January 29, 1918, Wu advocated sending Chinese laborers to Brazil.[62] He argued that the outbreak of World War I had caused many European immigrants to return to their countries to fulfill military duties and that at the end of the war, these European nations would have a shortage of labor and require the returned migrants to remain, exacerbating the labor shortage in Brazil. Praising the success of Japanese immigration and settlement in São Paulo, Wu noted that there was room for China to replicate those efforts, since the labor shortage in Europe would inadvertently provide the means for Chinese laborers to settle in Brazil, thus achieving the goal of economic expansion. Since Japanese immigrants were limited to settling in São Paulo State, Wu used this point to emphasize the possibilities of directing Chinese *yizhi* (immigration/colonization) to other states like Bahia, Minas Gerais, Rio de Janeiro, Paraná, and Rio Grande do Sul.[63]

Diplomatic attempts at promoting Chinese labor were successful to a small extent. Small waves of Chinese immigration to Brazil happened throughout the twentieth century. Immigrants settled in places like Rio de Janeiro and São Paulo, as evidenced by the establishment of various social aid and cultural centers. For example, in 1919, about one hundred merchants and businessmen, including restaurant and laundry owners, established the Centro Social Chinês do Rio de Janeiro (Chinese Social Center of Rio de Janeiro) located near the city center (Figure 2.2). Today its members maintain strong ties with the Taiwanese government.[64] Ultimately, however, the Chinese statesmen's interests in replicating the scale of Japan's migration and settlement model in Brazil were not realized.

Regardless, these ideas regarding Chinese migrant labor reveal the emergence of a global hierarchy of race in which colonial racial hierarchies transferred to new racialized national categories. These identities informed an emerging Chinese national consciousness as well, which prevailed among leaders of Chinese Nationalist and Communist Party circles alike when deliberating the future of China. The movement toward Chinese nationalist unification signified a rejection of imperialism from foreign nations, as well as from the Manchurian Qing empire that had colonized the Han Chinese people.[65] In 1924, Sun Yat-sen delivered *Sanmin zhuyi* (Three Principles of the People), in which he questioned how it could be that China, with its great population and oldest civilization, its "single, pure race," could have become victim to such indignity: "The rest of the world is the carving knife and the serving dish, while we are the fish and the meat. Our position now is extremely perilous . . . we face a tragedy the loss of our country and the destruction of our race."[66] In the same year, Li Dazhao, cofounder of the Chinese Communist Party, condemned white supremacy and Western cul-

FIGURE 2.2. Street placard of the Chinese Social Center of Rio de Janeiro. June 15, 2017. Source: Photograph by the author.

tural hegemony, repudiating "the white peoples as the pioneers of culture in the world; they place themselves in a superior position and look down on other races as inferior."[67]

Abolition and Sinophobia

In Brazil, mixed views toward the Chinese existed, and terms such as *yellow race, yellow labor,* and *coolie race* were used interchangeably in discussions over Chinese labor. Opponents echoed the rhetoric circulating in the United States that the Chinese would bring new forms of unfree labor. While proponents like the Baron of Cotegipe, a proslavery advocate, favored Chinese labor for precisely the same reasons. Brazilian political leaders, intellectuals, writers, and artists created a discourse about Chineseness to participate in political and economic debates over Chinese labor. Late nineteenth-century Brazilian abolitionist cultural production is replete with depictions of Qing officials (*mandarim* in Portuguese) and Chinese laborers who figured into emancipation narratives as liberty's antithetical Other.

Interestingly, anticoolie sentiment did not always mean anti-Chinese sentiment, but it conveyed the precarious labor conditions that would confront the Chinese due to proslavery advocates who viewed unfree Chinese labor as a solution to the labor crisis anticipated by abolition. For example, Henrique Carlos Ribeiro Lisboa, diplomat and former secretary of the Brazilian special mission to China of 1880 and adversary of the coolie trade, wrote a detailed account of his mission in a book published in 1888, *A China e os chins: Recordações de viagem* (*China and the Chinese: Travel Memoirs*). Lisboa wrote the Chinese into a relational and global history of slavery's racial regimes. The book's text and images present a deceptively realistic account about the land and people of China. Lisboa's observations were part of an information-gathering mission to China. Even though he attempted to debunk stereotypes about the Chinese, including the widespread idea that all the Chinese belonged to the Mongol race, he meticulously names, classifies, and categorizes the Chinese as racialized, ethnicized subaltern others. During the time of Lisboa's publication, expressions like "Mongol race" fueled Yellow Peril fears. Words like *Mongolian* conjured up powerful and undefeatable figures like Genghis Khan, but *Mongolism* was used to signal congenital disease.[68] Such misconceptions or, in Lisboa's words, "vulgarized opinions" and "crass errors" might have originated as early as the thirteenth century in Venetian merchant Marco Polo's accounts of his visits to China while it was under the rule of the Mongol empire.[69] Nevertheless, Lisboa could not imagine the Chinese as equals. He positioned them within the field of what Mary Louise Pratt calls the imperial eye.[70] His accounts were characteristic of the ethnographic projects of the nineteenth century that decidedly contributed to the archives of the colonial imagination, which Appadurai observes, were undeniably "classificatory, taxonomic, penal, and somatic."[71] Within the shifting global order of abolition and the turn to a new international division of labor, he was also negotiating their place in Brazil within globally constituted racialized national categories. Lisboa's contradictory treatment of the Chinese as either assimilable immigrants or excludable others was symptomatic of existing views concerning whether they would unravel or consolidate a national symbolic order itself an aspect of a shifting geopolitical order.

Lisboa sided with abolitionists, and thus opposed coolie labor, which was incompatible with the belief in whitening. The chapters "Chinese Emigration" and "China and the Chinamen" provide a detailed analysis of migration within China and abroad. He defined the latter as having two natures: contract labor and free labor. He explained that contract labor or "yellow traffic" produced the same deplorable conditions that had occurred with African slavery and then denounced the slave trade's atrocities as "crimes of Western civilization" and European colonization.[72] The chapter includes an illustrated scene, titled "The Bleeding Coolies in America" (Figure 2.3). The words beneath the title indicate that it is a Chinese drawing. The scene depicts dozens of victims of yellow trafficking in front of a plantation house. Two plump men wearing European-style clothing sit on the elevated porch, and below them on the ground sit groups of coolies whose arms and legs are tied and impossibly contorted. In the right-hand corner of the image stands an overseer dressed in a Western-style coat, pants, and hat. He is holding a knife and looks as if he is about to cut off the hand of a coolie depicted with the archetypical characteristics of a hair bun and a loose flowing knot button shirt that differentiate his race and class from the overseer. Through this report and illustration, Lisboa attempted to offer fellow abolitionists another perspective on the global Chinese question. For him, the issue of Brazil's future as a nation was not only about whether the so-called yellow race would be suitable for a whitening national identity. He urged his readers to find concern in the plantation economies that formed the basis of the economic and social structure of Brazilian society, and warned about the unsustainability of continued dependence on enslaved and slave-like labor whose ends would lead to economic crisis.[73] It is not a coincidence that he published his book in 1888, the same year that Brazil declared the emancipation of all slaves. Ultimately, for Lisboa, liberty and free labor were not possibilities if the first republic's wealth depended on the economic demands of the plantation and ongoing forms of slavery in disguised form.

Blurring the line between art and politics, contributors to the Rio de Janeiro–based abolitionist journal *Revista Illustrada* (*Revista Ilustrada* in modern Portuguese) responded to Chinese immigration in ways that shed light on the emergence of a new political consciousness regarding race, liberty, and national citizenry. Founded in 1876, the widely read journal had a twenty-one-year run, issuing its final publication in 1897.[74] The *Revista Illustrada* deployed humor to put forward and comment on the most pressing events of the day. Angelo Agostini, an Italian immigrant from Piedmont, was the founder of the journal and the artist responsible for most of its illustrations. The journal's collaborators included immortalized names of the Brazilian literary tradition, among them Machado de Assis and Arthur Azevedo. They were acclaimed and well regarded in their day, bolstering the journal's reputation and popularity. Political satire, cartoons, and writings enable us to see how artists and writers deployed a discourse of Chineseness to oppose the proslavery sentiments of the seigniorial colonial elite class whose agendas often did not coincide with the general public's welfare.

Scattered throughout different issues of the *Revista Illustrada* are caricatures of Chinese laborers as well as Qing officials. They appear among illustrations of the Indian and the Slave. Allegorically, indigeneity stands in for colonial territory, which must be liberated and emptied in order for newly arriving immigrants to settle and constitute an independent state. Blackness personifies slavery, and Chineseness embodies unfree labor. Such were the antithetical Others that represented the barriers to liberty and nationhood. Racial representations are a critical site for examining modern liberalism's emancipation narratives, wherein the superior political soul is conceptually possible only within a dialectical relationship to its antithesis, the hypothetical slave or coolie.[75] Recognizing how constructions of Chineseness have been deployed across heterogeneous states of liberalism that unfolded in synchronic orders of modernity/coloniality requires reckoning with the polycentric statist and economic liberalization projects that discourses of Chinese racialization have served.

The illustration, "Chinaman as a Transition," advanced the idea that, rather than helping to whiten Brazil, the Chinese would transform the country into a

FIGURE 2.3. "The Bleeding Coolies in America." Source: Henrique Carlos Ribeiro Lisboa, *A China e os chins: Recordações de viagem* (Montevideo: Typographia a vapor de A. Godel, 1888): 345.

predominantly yellow race. Four caricatures—a black slave, a Chinese laborer, a white agriculturalist, and a mulato—convey the idea that the Chinese would act as an economic and racial bridge between blackness and whiteness (Figure 2.4). The *Revista Illustrada's* image suggests that the Chinese might take the place of the mulato in serving as an intermediary between blacks and whites. The Chinese could "dilute" the "negative interferences" of the black slave, thereby facilitating the process of creating a lighter, freer Brazil. The captions state: "In regard to the idea of bringing the Chinaman here as a transition . . . will it be the transition of color between black and white toward a yellow hue? In this case, the mulatos have the right to protest . . . and with reason." Off to the side is the drawing of an outraged mulato—for what will happen to him? Chinese miscegenation is depicted as a threat to the mulato figure, the ideological bridge between blackness and whiteness. As the caption implies, Chinese labor brings

*Acerca da idéa de mandar vir chins como transição...
Será transição de cór entre a preta e a branca
que querem attenuar pela amarella?*

*Neste caso os mula-
tos estão no direito de
protestar... e com ra-
zão.*

FIGURE 2.4. "Chinaman as a Transition," *Revista Illustrada*, no. 120 (1878).
Source: Rare Book Collection, Latin American Library, Tulane University. Reprinted
with permission.

with it the virile threat of Chinese sexuality that could biologically transform
everyone into an unfree yellow race.

The turn from emancipation to immigration aided in enforcing the eradication of black and Indigenous people. The drawing sarcastically titled "September 7—Brazil Celebrating Its Independence" declares that under the Brazilian
empire, the church and state hold "Native" Brazil captive (Figure 2.5). The
drawing allegorizes Brazil as a "Native" male whose right leg is chained to the
state and his left leg to the church. To achieve independence, indigeneity—
symbolic of a colonial captive state—would have to be eradicated and replaced
with new life. The figuration of the Indigenous man portrays anti-Brazilian imperial sentiment as well as the struggle for land and liberation, and it also shows
that it is inconceivable to imagine a place for indigeneity within ideas of Brazilian national independence.[76]

The illustration depicts Brazilian independence by presenting a turn in racial

FIGURE 2.5. "September 7—Brazil Celebrating Its Independence," *Revista Illustrada*, no. 34 (1876). Source: Rare Book Collection, Latin American Library, Tulane University. Reprinted with permission.

ideas, showing what Doris Sommer describes as Brazil's "two-faced indigenism," in which cultural elements of indigeneity were absorbed into national narratives, while Indigenous people were facing eradication and land dispossession.[77] This two-faced treatment of the Indigenous population in Brazil might also be understood as forming part of the "settler-colonial tendency," in which contests for land are also a contest for life.[78] Brazil's perfidious treatment of the Indigenous population is apparent in Brazilian literary romanticism. For example, José Alencar, a fervent advocate of slavery, wrote *Iracema* (1865), whose title is an anagram for America.[79] In this origin story about the founding of Ceará, in Northeastern Brazil, Iracema dies and leaves behind a son, who becomes the first Cearense. Before Iracema dies, she gives her son to his father, Martim, a white European Christian warrior. Her body, sickly and weak, cannot survive the road to the nation's future. This allegory of her death transforms indigeneity, and Indigenous struggles for land and the actual enslavement and elimination of Indigenous people, into an affective bond, a "bitter *saudade*" (nostalgia) that forges a national imaginary on the disappeared site of the Indigenous body.[80]

In the story sketch titled, "*Colonisação*" ("Colonization"), indigeneity stands in for the disease-infested Brazilian empire (Figure 2.6). The images introduce the idea that Brazil, represented as an Indigenous woman's body, is unfit for European immigrants. The diseased Brazil warns European settlers to keep at bay. The illustration narrates the story of a European family that immigrates to Brazil. The narrative begins in Europe, where an elderly man is blessing the father of two young children. Standing beside them, among a few bundles that are their worldly possessions, is their mother, who is crying into the shoulder of another woman. Their dog is equally sorrowful in this scene of departure with no return—a tender farewell to the emigrants whose lives in one land would end to find sustenance in another. Upon arriving at Guanabara Bay, the family is hopeful. The father's hand motions upward to all the possibilities for the future. Their bundles are replaced with farming tools. These European settlers represent Brazil's future, a new working class that will build and whiten the country. However, these utopian ideas are not so easily fulfilled, as the frames indicate. Soon the city of Rio de Janeiro, depicted as an Indigenous woman, will transmit to them the miasma of yellow fever, represented as a snake coiled around a tree that bears the Brazilian empire's rotten fruits. The settlers' fate is grim. The last two scenes show that this diseased Brazil has orphaned the children, who are left alone kneeling before their parents' graves. Meanwhile, relatives in Europe receive the announcement of death that concretizes the finality of their departure. The longed-for immigrants who could whiten Brazil's colonial and enslaved past, and thus propel it into nationhood, could not survive Brazil's backward conditions, defined in terms of its failure to accommodate the ideal European nuclear family.

The drawing titled "A colonização chinesa" ("Chinese Colonization") advises against racial and cultural miscegenation with the Chinese, warning that Chinese labor would only contribute to already existing problems in Brazil (Figure 2.7). While the images give caution regarding Chinese labor's negative effects, they also turn a critical gaze to Brazil's colonial history. The Indigenous figures portray a cannibalistic, diseased Brazil that literally eats the Chinese. Chinese labor is shown as precarious, untrustworthy, and unfree. One frame shows that Chinese laborers have committed suicide. Another depicts them stealing farm animals, portraying the fear that they will take away local wealth. Yet the cartoons are also critical of the agriculturalists, rendered as slave drivers; one stands high above a circle of Chinese men whose queues have been tied to a pole. They are chained while they are forced to perform field labor. Collectively, these images configured Asian, African, and Indigenous bodies as the antithesis of lib-

FIGURE 2.6. "Colonization," *Revista Illustrada*, no. 12 (1876). Source: Rare Book Collection, Latin American Library, Tulane University. Reprinted with permission.

erty: the currency for the transactions of dispossession and exclusion structured in liberalism's dialectic of freedom.[81]

Published six months after the *Lei Áurea* abolished slavery, the illustration titled "Brazil-chim" ("Brazil-Chinaman"; *chim* is a derogatory word in Portuguese that referred to Chinese immigrants; its closest English equivalent is Chinaman) addresses the ongoing issue of unfree Chinese labor and conveys the viewpoint that the Chinese will transform Brazil into a degenerate, hybrid Brazil-Chinaman (Figure 2.8). The first frame in the third row shows that the Chinese would not whiten the country. Instead, they will assimilate with the black population. The images show Chinese men who have become wild from dancing samba. Their uncontrollable, erect queues emit a political and sexual message while they recklessly dance with Bahian women. The caption reads: "This samba is half Bahiano, half-Chinese, what a fun and splendid thing. Well, it is decided. The Chinaman will come."[82] At this time, samba was discriminatorily viewed—as were other forms of African diasporic cultural production—and restricted in public spaces; thus, the scene of Chinese men *sambando*, dancing samba, is meant as a sarcastic portrayal of a morally suspect activity. The next frame provides another example of the contradiction between what is written

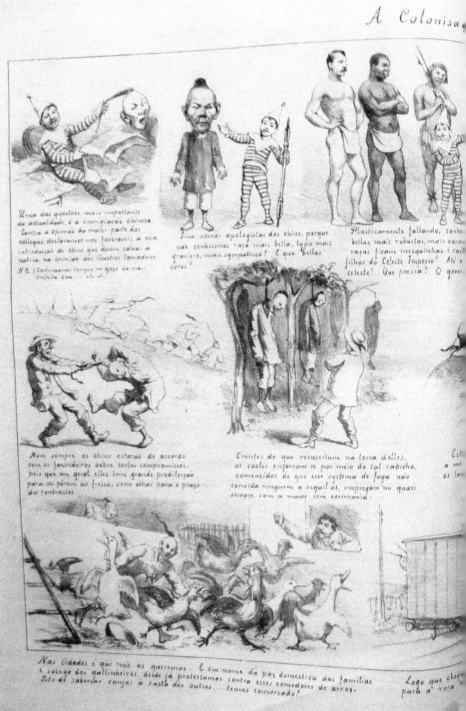

FIGURE 2.7. "Chinese Colonization," *Revista Illustrada*, no. 558 (1883). Rare Book Collection, Latin American Library, Tulane University. Reprinted with permission.

a.

O chim é um pouco descançado é verdade, mas incontestavelmente, ninguem trabalha melhor do que elle... em abanar-se

melhores colonos!

Porem confiamos muito na intelligente vigilancia dos nossos lavradores. Varios systemas se inventarão para impedir os chins de se deitarem por occasião do trabalho. Os Srs Jannay, Telles e outros que inventaram tantas machinas para beneficiar o café, inventarão tambem outras applicadas aos cultivadores deste abençoado grão.

de que
ará entre
colonos.

E ja que os fazendeiros querem chins: pois teremos chins.

O que é que nos queremos afinal?
E que os lavradores fiquem satisfeitos!

E como em negocio de lavoura, elles entendem mais do que nos, é possivel que o café se dê bem com os seus novos cultivadores.

incontinenti

Um excellente lugar é o sertão das provincias do Matto-Grosso ou Alto-Amazonas. Excellente lugar para cultivar a terra e o espirito dos habitantes da mesma, que se acha muito inculto.

Estamos certos, que estes dariam provas do maior reconhecimento.

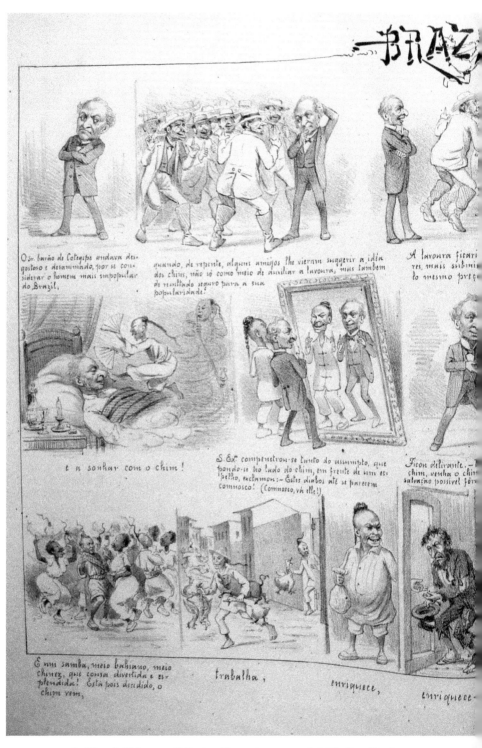

FIGURE 2.8. "Brazil-Chinaman," *Revista Illustrada*, no. 523 (1888). Rare Book Collection, Latin American Library, Tulane University. Reprinted with permission.

CHIM...

..., tendo trabalhado antigos e quasi pezaria queitão da côr...

E o Sr. de Cotegipe começou a pensar no chim,

a estudar o chim,

a calcular o chim,

E demais, varietio delectat! Como deve ser agradavel mudar de habitos e de costumes,

Comendo arroz com dois pausinhos

e apreciando um fricandó de lagartixas com minhocas recheiadas em torno!

é uma felicidade geral!

Vencidos pelo numero, resolvemos todos mudar-nos para a outra vida...

Ficam só no Brazil o Sr. Cotegipe e os chins. Estes, no delirio do enthusiasmo proclamam-n'o mandarim Tchim-Tcham-Fó 1º imperador d'esta colegibica china.... Um pagode!

FIGURE 2.9. "Liberty," *Revista Illustrada*, no. 522 (1888). Source: Rare Book Collection, Latin American Library, Tulane University. Reprinted with permission.

and what is happening. A Chinese man is shown stealing farm animals, but the caption says "he works." Following that scene is a picture of an impoverished white Brazilian man begging a heavyset Chinese man for money. Underneath the caption it says, "The Chinese will enrich us."

The last frame of the series depicts a Chinese version of the Baron of Cotegipe, a zealous antiabolitionist and the head of the Council of Ministers during the last years of the Brazilian empire (1885–1888). His support for unfree Chinese labor was also aimed at maintaining the aristocratic order and preserving the power of the empire. For all his advocacy for Chinese immigration that the images invoke, he has gotten his wish of bringing China to Brazil. Even he does not escape the fate of degenerative miscegenation, shown as having acquired Chinese biological and cultural traits. Finally, the caption warns that Brazil will become Chinese if the Baron succeeds in establishing a Chinese labor migration scheme with types like the fictionalized mandarin Tchim-Tcham Fó. The Baron of Cotegipe, it warns, will turn Brazil into his version of an enslaved China— "this Cotegipe-ified China." If this venture is successful, Brazil would degenerate into a hybrid Brazil-Chinaman, thereby directly hindering the formation of a white liberal republic. The figure titled "Liberdade," published on November 11, 1888, literally and figuratively conveys the notion that Chinese laborers would serve as a substitute for black slavery. Liberated black slaves cheer while the Baron of Cotegipe cuffs the wrists of the newly enslaved coolies (Figure 2.9).

On November 4, 1909, a photograph with the title, "The Chinese in Rio," and the caption, "Are we in Peking or Rio?" appeared in Rio de Janeiro's *Gazeta de Notícias* (Figure 2.10). The reporter claims to have found Chinese settlers living and cultivating tea in Rio's Botanical Garden, nearly one hundred years after João VI brought the first group of Chinese agriculturalists to Rio and confined them to the Botanical Garden to plant tea. The unfocused photograph features three people wearing Western-style clothing and implies that the Chinese diplomatic mission to Rio brought the idea of Chinese labor into fashion. The caption continues: "Not all Chinese smoke opium and sell fish. Here in the Botanical Garden, they cultivate tea just as they do in the provinces of the Celestial Kingdom." These constructions of racial difference signal the production of new forms of exclusion. The Chinese in Rio are in Brazil, but they are confined to the grounds of the Botanical Garden. Like the construction of the coolie race, these settlers are shown as the unfit figure of emancipation. Although they wear Western clothing and do not indulge in the racialized vices of Chinese settlers, their indistinct appearance within the restricted borders of racialized agricultural

FIGURE 2.10. "The Chinese in Rio," *Gazeta de Notícias*, November 4, 1909.
Source: Newspaper Archives of the Biblioteca Nacional, Rio de Janeiro, Brazil.

labor—tea cultivation—became a necessary and disposable structural element in the making of the modern world.

The *Gazeta de Notícias*'s Chinese settlers shared more in common with the *Revista Illustrada*'s fictional portrayals of mandarins and coolies than with actual people who settled in Rio de Janeiro. These widely circulating images, words, and concepts about liberty and nation constituted part of a language that was bound to a circumoceanic memory of racialized labor. Beyond print culture, popular theater was a main stage where performances of racial impersonation like yellowface recast debates about citizenry.

THREE

Performing Yellowface and Chinese Labor

As the nineteenth century ended and the twentieth century began, Qing diplomatic officials and businessmen went to Brazil to examine the prospects there for Chinese settlement. In Brazil, political debates over Chinese immigration, and accompanying fears about miscegenation between Chinese and Brazilians, arose in response to the visits, which were sponsored by both Chinese and Brazilian state and private entities. Political and economic issues associated with Chinese labor were reflected in popular entertainment at the time. Fin-de-siècle *teatro de revista* (revue) performances and their carnivalesque constructions of Chineseness intersected the issue of Chinese labor with miscegenation and the racial makeup of an independent Brazil. Performances of racial impersonation—that is, yellowface—during which actors performed caricatures of Chineseness, staged encounters not only between Brazilian aristocrats and Qing officials but also Chinese immigrants and Rio de Janeiro's downtrodden economic classes. These performances show how theater was not purely about entertainment; it was a critical site to deliberate citizenry and Brazil's future. Toward the end of his life, Arthur Azevedo, arguably the most renowned Brazilian playwright for the genre of teatro de revista, drew a parallel between the work of theater and nation building: "The theater of each country should not be public entertainment, but rather a national institution."[1] Playwrights used the genre of teatro de revista to turn Rio de Janeiro into a topsy-turvy world in which race and gender were in flux. They used the spectacle of racial impersonation to reimagine circumoceanic memories of race and colonial narratives about racialized labor. The stage became the site for new performances about liberty wherein Chinese labor was debated in terms of the positive or negative potential of Chinese sexual reproduction. Performances of Chinese sexuality and gender asserted their unsuitability for the national body politic in ways that intertwined liberal ideas with racial ideologies to structure an emerging Brazilian national imaginary.

Yellowface Rio de Janeiro

The relatively few yet significant yellowface performances in Rio de Janeiro's teatro de revista scene used the stage to explore debates about Chinese laborers, miscegenation, and nation building. Yellowface, like blackface, performances are acts of racial impersonation in which an actor or playwright uses performances of race to reflect the social structures and power dynamics that have been integral to national self-imagining.[2] Interpreting the appearance of yellowface on the stage as an expression of anxiety about Chinese sexuality suggests that these performances were based on a set of codes similar to those used in blackface performances. These performances of race depend on theatrical conventions that treat the racialized, commodified body as an empty vessel to project others' feelings, desires, and values.[3] In the United States, for example, white American fantasies, desires for racial hierarchy, and rules of domination were played out through blackface performance.[4] Along this line, performances of racial impersonation shed understanding on the interconnected workings of race, gender, and nation.

Arthur Azevedo played a critical role in establishing teatro de revista as a national institution. It provided an alternative to the imperial theater's state-sponsored narratives that served the didactic purpose of "civilizing" the tastes, morals, and character of the population.[5] Imperial theater was a form of "cultural colonialism" in which European models of urbanization and modernity were displayed on the stage—an efficient mode of cultural domination that was a cost-effective alternative to war.[6] In his work, by contrast, Azevedo paired humor with current events to make theater a place to engage public debate and cultural phenomena.[7]

Although Azevedo and his contemporaries were consciously inaugurating a national institution, they did so under the censoring eyes of the Conservatório Dramático Brasileiro (Brazilian Drama Conservatory), which represented Brazil's imperial court's political and economic interests. The conservatory censored works that criticized the institution of slavery or the monarchy, which may explain the frequent use of satire as a strategy that gave audiences a dose of laughter with each bitter commentary on political and economic crisis. Satire enabled playwrights to textually convey scenarios that would be pleasing to censoring eyes, but the performances that occurred on stage often contrasted with what was written in the script. The playwrights created laughter in the disjuncture between what was written and what was performed—what Taylor calls the performatic space.[8] The performatic disjuncture induced satire and laughter, and it also served to help their writers evade censorship and accusations of transgression.

The theater was not limited to the Rio de Janeiro elite, but rather aimed at reaching a broad audience that included both erudite and the illiterate masses. Because it offered the occasion to see and be seen, going to the theater was as much a social occasion as it was a national institution. Popular theater allowed diverse audiences to participate in public discourse about contemporary political events. Brazilian theater historian Antonio Herculano Lopes remarks that theatergoers' demographic profile is difficult to define since we have only approximate sources such as newspaper commentaries—many written by Arthur Azevedo—and information about the value of the tickets compared to the purchasing power of the various groups in society. Records show that the usual theatergoers were small-trade employees such as clerks. Portuguese immigrants accounted for a high percentage of attendees. Several wealthy families attended and were fond of the genre. It is important to note that the term *popular theater* refers here to mass audiences rather than class, since *popular* in Portuguese also means working class or poor.[9] While the curtain call may have signaled the end of the performance, the shows imparted new notions of nation, citizenship, and liberty and had a lasting impact on their mass and diverse audiences.

A characterizing aspect of teatro de revista is a chase through various spaces—a constant pursuit from which a character escapes only by the skin of his teeth.[10] Teatro de revista was a unique genre for the way that the chase sequence took audiences directly into Brazilian society's current issues. It provided a logic that did not need to follow narrative coherence or linear time; characters could run through different public and private spaces, as well as in and out of conversations, with no direct relation to the main plot. Multiple escape-chase action sequences enabled playwrights to thread the year's unrelated events into one coherent theatrical piece, a device that enabled social critique that might not otherwise have been openly discussed. Following this same logic, we can map appearances of Chineseness across seemingly disparate works to piece together a larger story about the issues concerning Rio de Janeiro society at this time.

Performing the Mandarin

Performances of Chineseness were more than figments of the imagination; they also harbored the cultural memory of race. During Brazil's transition to a modern nation-state, we can observe how representations of Qing dynasty officials and Chinese laborers gained additional layers of meaning in deliberations over the new nation's imagined community. Spectacles, images, and literary depictions of mandarins (Qing dynasty officials) circulated in the works of various playwrights, journalists, diplomats, authors, artists, and musicians. In these works, depictions of mandarins are connected with the business of the trade in Chinese labor as the negotiator or protector. If we are to trace the recurring appearance of mandarins across these different artistic and political spheres as a common narrative thread, we may map a larger story about the symbolic function of the "hypothetical mandarin" in Brazilian narratives about political emancipation and abolition.[11]

While the idea of the mandarin gained new meaning in Brazil during the nineteenth century within debates over the suitability of Chinese labor and the so-called yellow race for Brazil's nation-building project of racial whitening, etymologically the word *mandarin* contains the long history of Sino-Portuguese trade dating back to the sixteenth century. In Portuguese, the word *mandarin* exists as a Lusophone invention in the sense that the word originates in the sixteenth century from the Portuguese *mandarim*.[12] The word might have derived from the Portuguese *mandar*, meaning to command or to order. However, the addition of the *im* to the verb stem *mandar* transforms the verb into a noun meaning "a person who commands," and even suggests a sense of bossiness. One could playfully imagine that this derivation might have been created by Portuguese voyagers who interacted with Ming and Qing governors who were particularly commanding during exchanges that officially began in 1557, the year when Macau was leased to Portugal. On the flip side, the Chinese (Mandarin) word for *Portugal* is literally translated to English as "Grape Tooth." "Portuguese people" in Mandarin translates to "Grape Tooth People." The word sounds like *Putaoya,* the Mandarin transliteration of the word *Portugal,* but one could also just as playfully imagine how the Chinese imagined the lot of Portuguese mariners in southern China with grape teeth, that is, teeth stained by cheap wine.

Today *mandarin* carries a range of different and even contradictory meanings. It could be used to refer to a Qing governor or senior official, to porcelain decorated with Chinese motifs, a type of clothing worn by Chinese officials, a dialect of Chinese, a variety of citrus fruit, a Marvel Comic supervillain, or an adjective that conveys refinement and class.[13] In the Chinese language, the word *mandarin* does not exist. Qing governors have different names that correspond to their ranking, as determined by the imperial government civil service examination. The Chinese dialect of Mandarin is known as *Guanhua* (official speak) or *Guoyu* (language of the nation), as well as *Putonghua* (the common language). There are no citrus fruits in the Chinese language that are called mandarins. However, in Portuguese, the fruit *mandarina* was likely named after the citrus colors of Qing (mandarin) robes.[14] Arguably, the friction in linguistic definitions nods toward the shared economic, political, and social histories of China, Portugal, and Brazil, which were linked at the cusp of the sixteenth century when Portuguese fleets connected trade ports in Europe, Asia, Africa, and the Americas.

In October 1883, one year after the United States passed the Chinese Exclusion Act of 1882, Tong Jing Xing (1832–1892), known as the *Mandarim Tong King Sing* in Portuguese accounts, late Qing official, Cantonese comprador, and managing director of the China Merchant's Steam Navigation Company, visited Rio de Janeiro to assess Brazil's willingness to accept Chinese immigration labor.[15] Tong's visit is one example of how US immigration exclusion acts redirected Chinese immigration to places like Brazil. His trip produced a series of literary and fictional incarnations of the real man as a fictional mandarin—a figuration of Brazil's volatile road to emancipation (Figure 3.1). Tong was portrayed to personify the idea that an economic alliance between Qing-ruled China and Brazil, a composite Mandarin-Brazil, would impede white free labor and emancipation. When Tong visited Brazil to assess its conditions for Chinese laborers in October 1883, he probably never guessed that his business trip would transform him into a series of caricatures or that events from his life would end up memorialized in institutional archives as cartoons. While Tong quickly left Brazil after learning that Chinese laborers there would meet a fate similar to slavery, his departure did not stop Brazilian writers and artists from using literary and visual cultural production to deliberate the significance of Tong and other Qing officials' visits. Even after Tong denounced Brazil's labor conditions, Qing officials and Chinese migrants continued to arrive in Brazil, and fictional appearances of mandarins proliferated across many works. By paying close attention to how writers and artists deployed the symbol of mandarins to circulate and debate abolitionist concerns, we can examine how ideas about race shifted during slavery's gradual emancipation and the transition to wage labor via immigrant labor.

Tong Jing Xing, who had learned English at the missionary Morrison Education Society School in Hong Kong, had invested in steamships and mining, earning his title as "China's first modern entrepreneur."[16] He visited Rio in response to the Brazilian government's formation of the Companhia de Comércio e Imigração Chinesa, a shipping company intended to bring twenty-one thousand Chinese workers from China at the cost of 35 milréis per laborer, the equivalent of nearly $US100.[17] If successful, the venture would have established direct maritime routes between Brazil and China, thus circumventing Portugal and loosening its economic hold over Brazilian trade. G. A. Butley ("Butler" in some reports), an educated African American man described as having "refined Parisian elegance," accompanied Tong on the visit, serving as his assistant.[18]

Newspaper accounts of Tong and Butler were skeptical and curious: Butler's dress was too bright and excessive, while Tong still used what was described as his "national" clothing, a likely reference to a formal court robe granted to men who passed the civil service examination, indicative of status among the ranks of Qing government officials. Their formal dress and educated aura were unfamiliar to Brazilian society. The sight of two well-dressed Asian and African American men traveling together was indeed a rare, if not unique, occurrence and thus caused quite a sensation. While Tong's presence inspired many fictional accounts, Butler disappears. Textual, visual, and staged racial impersonations of mandarins were numerous, but Butler's erasure suggests that the integration of an educated and refined black man was impossible in the Brazilian imagination at the time.

Tong and Butler's visit to Rio de Janeiro was for the purpose of assessing the suitability of Brazil's natural and raw materials for a Chinese market.

O Mandarim Tong-King-Sing.

FIGURE 3.1. "The Mandarin Tong King Sing," *Revista Illustrada*, no. 8 (1883). Rare Book Collection, Latin American Library, Tulane University. Reprinted with permission.

Brazilian rubber, tobacco, wood, and its potential cotton industry could find a large market in China. Brazilian coffee was under consideration as a substitute for opium, but this substitution was deemed unlikely since the Chinese would not "adopt" a taste for coffee despite having had "contact with Europeans."[19] However, if the exploratory visit were successful, the shipping company would open a direct trade route between China and Brazil, thus reducing the costs for transporting passengers, Brazilian raw and natural materials, and Chinese merchandise. Fully aware that Chinese laborers had endured indentured labor and slave-like conditions in places like Peru, Cuba, and British Guiana, where the governor had recently proposed the introduction of Chinese laborers as a substitute for black slavery, Tong went to Brazil to inspect labor conditions to prevent a similar outcome.

During his business trip, Tong negotiated with Brazilian coffee industrialists for pay rates and living conditions for Chinese laborers. He requested the pay rate of 20 to 25 milréis per month per Chinese, on top of room and board, to be paid to each laborer.[20] However, since the latifundium structure that depended on slave labor formed the basis of the Brazilian economy, fulfilling Tong's requests were unfavorable for coffee industrialists' profit margins. In addition, Tong had also requested a yearly Brazilian governmental subsidy of $100,000.[21] However, the government, perhaps under pressure owing to anti-Chinese sentiment, planned to pass the bills to agriculturalists. They in turn planned to take their losses out of the wages of the Chinese laborers, essentially creating a slave labor condition. Upon discovering this, Tong called off negotiations and left for England. Shortly after, he wrote a letter proclaiming that he would play no part in putting the overseas Chinese into positions of forced labor.[22]

Journalists covering Tong and Butler's visit depicted their "fascinating" and "startling" presence in newspaper accounts, and this preoccupation entered into the work of fin-de-siècle writers, artists, and playwrights. In a drawing of Tong that appeared in the *Revista Illustrada* shortly after his arrival in Rio de Janeiro in October 1883, his figure is placed next to caricatures of men who are meant to represent Chinese laborers—so-called coolies. The image depicts the apprehensive local reaction to Tong's visit to Brazil and his intention to open direct trade routes with China. The placement of Tong among ghastly masses of Chinese laborers, Brazil's newest wretched victims of slavery, reflected the larger social milieu regarding Sinophobic anxieties about the formation of a Chinese colony in Brazil.

This particular image conveyed a common awareness among abolitionists that slavery was taking on a new racial identity, which they expressed with recurring terms like *yellow labor* and *yellow trafficking*.[23]

At the time of Tong's visit, advocates for whitening Brazil via European immigration were also contributing to heightening the Sinophobic climate. The Sociedad Central de Imigração (Central Society of Immigration), founded by three highly influential German immigrants, Karl Von Koseritz, Hermann Blumenau, and Hugo Gruber, worked to advance initiatives that favored European immigration, liberalism, and latifundium reform.[24] The longstanding society operated for eight years from 1883 to 1891 and also published a newspaper, *A Imigração* (*Immigration*). In 1883 and 1884, the newspaper positioned the Chinese as an "inferior race" with an "innate hatred toward the white race," and therefore a potential threat to the racial whitening project.[25] This supposed hatred of the white race was portrayed as the Chinese immigrants being unwilling to intermix sexually and thus racially. The writer's views give an indication of how the global Chinese question was shaping diverse debates in Brazilian media regarding Chineseness and whiteness.[26] The Chinese question circulated on a worldwide scale an orientalist discourse that homogenized all Chinese laborers as an unfree "coolie race" who stood in the way of white liberal democracies.[27] The journalist writes disparagingly about the US practice of using Chinese labor as a substitute for enslaved labor, citing contemporary events in California as evidence of the unproductive experiment with the "coolies" in California, warning that an influx of Chinese immigrants to Brazil would "repel" and "completely destroy" the possibility of European immigration.[28]

Teatro de revista playwrights engaged in these conversations through staging yellowface performances to enact new modes of thinking about national independence and economic self-interest, harnessing debates over racial divisions of colonial labor, the project of whitening, and nation building. Tong Jing Xing's visit to Rio de Janeiro directly inspired the acclaimed fin-de-siècle teatro de revista *O Mandarim* (*The Mandarin*). In 1883, Arthur Azevedo partnered with Sampaio Moreira to cowrite *O Mandarim*. First presented on January 9, 1884, in Rio de Janeiro at the Teatro Príncipe Imperial, the well-known playwrights drew an audience of upwards of 650 attendees.[29] In writing *O Mandarim,* Azevedo and Moreira were engaging in a larger dialogue with their contemporaries about major topics like slavery of the time. Consisting of a prologue with three acts and original musical scores, *O Mandarim* brought to the stage the major events of 1883, which included Tong Jing Xing's visit to Rio de Janeiro. It deliberated the opinions about the mandarin that were shared by some elites, politicians, and working-class sectors of society.[30]

O Mandarim represented a range of hopes and fears about Chinese labor. Its depictions of Chinese gender and sexuality as androgynous and strange became a mode to negotiate the introduction of Chinese labor and accompanying discussions over their suitability for Brazil's racial whitening project. The perceived negative biological traits and immoral character of the Chinese made them wonky candidates for assimilation. Yellowface depictions of the mandarin index the idea that miscegenation with the Chinese was also perceived as the threat of the potential domination of yellowness over whiteness. There was no desire to assimilate with the mandarin, who was metonymic for accepting Chinese labor. In light of Brazil's whitening project, the teatro de revista performances of yellowface that we will explore put a fine point on the idea that the Chinese would only ever be candidates for exclusion.

The wildly successful *O Mandarim* served to cement Azevedo and Sampaio's reputations as playwrights and also established the genre of teatro de revista.[31] The duo created interlaced plot lines with parodic allegories of actual events, people, or things. Anyone, anything, and any issue could be caricaturized on stage. For example, *O Mandarim*'s cast included characters like Abolition, Gambling, Streetcar, and Yellow Fever. These parodic performances allegorized larger societal issues. Streetcar served as an allegory for new transportation systems and rapid modernization in Rio de Janeiro. The character Yellow Fever personified the uncontrollable epidemic that plagued Brazil at the time. The introduction of these kinds of characters was a new development in the history of Brazilian theater and performance, and it created much public excitement that garnered the attention of the police, which generated free publicity and even more feverishness for the show.[32]

O Mandarim's main storyline centers on the Baron of Caiapó, symbolic of the proslavery and pro-Chinese labor statesmen, who attempts to convince the Mandarin, Tchin-tchan-Fó, to invest in Brazil, which would bring China to Brazil. In the staging of *O Mandarim*, Tchin-tchan-Fó, guided into the scene by the Baron of Caiapó, introduces himself to Brazilian society as the "First-Class Mandarin."[33] He has arrived on business, seeking to inspect Brazil's labor and resource prospects for China. Brazilian society gathers to meet him, including Olímpia (a courtesan and the leading lady), along with the whole gamut of Rio de Janeiro—including microorganisms and other nonhuman things that compose the diverse lot of Rio de Janeiro's problems. Collectively referred to as "bad and evil," the motley crew open the show by establishing a larger social critique about the current state of Rio, where every element, from people to bacterium to institutions, is cast into a negative light. The Mandarin enters the story as the solution to their problems. But he is set up to fail since a single solution to a society's complex array of challenges is impossible.

It is notable that the Mandarin makes his appearance on stage among the most marginalized figures of society and is thus aligned with the evils of society. Upon his entrance, the chorus proclaims:

Oh what strange faces!
What odd visitors!
What good types both are,
The Chinaman as much as the Baron![34]

In Portuguese, the plural tense of strange faces, *caras esquisitas* is made to rhyme with odd visitors/odd visits (*esquipáticas visitas*) to refer to both the Mandarin and Baron as "good types." However, the audience would have understood the scene's sarcastic tone. First, the actors portrayed the Mandarin and the Baron as caricatures; second, the audience would have the context from various newspapers and journals to understand that the Mandarin and the Baron were potential business partners due to their shared interest in both bringing Chinese laborers to Brazil and establishing a Brazilian-Chinese trade alliance. In this scene, it is clear that for Brazil, nothing good could arise from their intentions. The satire in this teatro de revista derives from what is written in the script about the Mandarin and what he actually performs during the unfolding of the plot—the perceived threat that unfree yellow labor would pose in Brazil's transition to an independent republic.

The Baron and the Mandarin's joint desire to open trade between China and Brazil is conveyed in a way that ties debates over Chinese labor production with Chinese sexual reproduction, thereby tacitly acknowledging the social discourse about labor crisis that was coupled with the preoccupation over miscegenation and Brazil's racial makeup. *O Mandarim* rendered Chinese gender and sexuality as ambiguous, bizarre, and comedic. The Baron's primary aim is to convince the Mandarin to bring Chinese laborers to Brazil, yet the Mandarin is sidetracked from his business dealings. He falls for the money-hungry Olímpia; however, to be with her, he must hide from his wife, Peky (a name derived from "Peking"), whose masculine features cause the play's characters to repeatedly mistake her for a man. Whereas the script depicts Peky as a hypermasculine woman, the Mandarin is portrayed as a hyperfeminine man, thus demanding that actors perform yellowface by reversing and mixing the gender codes of Brazilian society at a time when slavery's paternalism and patriarchal agrarian infrastructure governed the social milieu. To portray the Chinese body as sexually deviant and ambiguously gendered hinders the Chinese body from entering into the heterosexual reproductive sphere, thus symbolically barring the Chinese from Brazil's eugenic project of whitening and domestic spheres. These racial impersonations relate a spectrum of danger at the myriad contagions that Chinese labor would bring to the Brazilian body politic.

Soon enough, Peky discovers that her husband has run off with Olímpia, beginning a chase sequence between Peky and the Mandarin. Peky's pursuit of the Mandarin and Olímpia acts as the narrative thread that links otherwise disconnected current events. On the heels of the Mandarin, the audience follows the plot line as it traverses Rio de Janeiro's current events. In one scene, he literally enters the debate over abolition and Chinese labor when he encounters characters representing Rio's major periodicals who are on different sides of the abolitionist struggle. Among those is the abolitionist journal *Revista Illustrada,* in which Angelo Agostini, an Italian immigrant, drew numerous sketches of Tong King Sing, and the *Gazeta de Notícias*, where Machado de Assis published chronicles of the Mandarin's visit to Rio de Janeiro and his views on Chinese labor immigration.[35]

However, *O Mandarim* warns its public, Chinese labor would bring with it reproductive labor in the form of Chinese offspring capable of supplying an unending labor force. Chinese sexuality would produce *too many* exploitable laborers, who would turn Brazil's racial and ethnic makeup into a dystopian Brazil-China. For example, the chorus exclaims, "He's from China," and the Baron adds, "He has come to visit this country. He wants to bring China here!"[36] The Mandarin confirms the Baron's statement, explaining his rationale to the audience: "There are so many people in China that they no longer fit there, and they do not know where to go. All are impelled to enter Brazil, but the Chinaman is insightful; I have come to verify that this land dignifies him."[37] Invoking Chinese overpopulation as a motive for assessing whether Brazil is a good fit for the population of Chinese laborers whom the Mandarin represents—depicting the substantial geopolitical landmass of China as so overcrowded to the point that people can no longer fit into it—implies an uncontrollable Chinese sexuality. However, the implication is that surplus laborers would perform the opposite effect of providing a solution to the labor shortage; instead, they would threaten both Brazil's economic growth and territorial resources. Accordingly, the stage encodes the Mandarin's intentions in terms that render Chinese sexuality as overly productive, and it echoed contemporaneous debates that deemed the Chinese a so-called yellow race unsuitable to the project of racial whitening.[38]

O Mandarim stages Chinese sexual voraciousness in the form of multiple love triangles. Each triangle includes both the Mandarin and Olímpia, with the third party as either Peky or Lírio (Lily), a shrimp peddler from China. In one triangulated affair, the Mandarin attempts to have an affair with Olímpia. When he approaches her on the street, however, she coyly resists his kisses. He responds that Brazil's customs are unfamiliar to him, saying, "Love in China is more ardent."[39] We take from this that Brazilian prostitution's lewdness thus pales in comparison to Chinese sexuality. In another love triangle, Chinese female sexuality is rendered unappealing by depicting Peky as hypermasculinized. The play also emasculates Chinese male laborers. For example, Lírio, named after a flower (the lily), is a poor Chinese shrimp peddler who loves Olímpia but has no financial power in this society to purchase her favors. Thus, he cannot afford to buy Olímpia's commoditized love, available only for the right price.

O Mandarim brings up several potential paths to assimilation for the Chinese, only to foreclose them. *O Mandarim* illuminates three ways in which the Mandarin will be unable to achieve assimilation. The first is by biological means. During the production of *O Mandarim*, yellow fever had become an epidemic in Brazil. In the play, the Mandarin may be a naturalized Brazilian only if he catches the disease or receives an inoculation against it. In the following scene, Yellow Fever is a character in the play. The Mandarin learns from Olímpia that "[Yellow Fever] preferentially attacks foreigners, but it spares nationals" to which he replies, "Oh! Really? In that case, I naturalize myself!"[40] The Mandarin wishes to vaccinate himself against foreignness. To assimilate into Brazilian society, a transformation must occur at the microscopic level, permeating every aspect of the Mandarin, down to his biological and genetic coding.

In another irreconcilable contradiction, the Mandarin is depicted as androgynous and unfaithful. His affair with the courtesan Olímpia means that he is committing adultery against his wife, but the play depicts Chinese gender and sexuality as unfit for Brazilian gender norms that regulated a heterosexual binary. Peky's masculine femininity is made freaky and grotesque precisely to provoke doubts about Chinese female sexuality, harnessing the discourse of sexual anxiety and competition. The Mandarin describes his wife as "a man who looks like a woman! A woman who looks like a man!" Yet he shrugs off this observation, saying, "It's all the same."[41] With this assertion, he suggests that his own Chinese masculinity is questionable, since it does not matter if he is with a "man who looks like or woman" or a "woman who looks like a man," projecting the unsuitability of Chinese sexuality of any kind for the larger Brazilian project of miscegenation.

The Mandarin is shown to be culturally and patriotically untrustworthy, leading to the third impossibility for assimilation. Peky discovers his infidelity to her and, by extension, China. She looks for him at Olímpia's house. Before she can find him, the Mandarin makes a deal with a group of magicians to hide him. In doing so, he sheds his Qing clothing and offers them the pledge of his *rabicho* (queue), symbolic of his patriotic ties to the Qing. However, due to the ambiguity of the Portuguese word *rabicho*, the Mandarin's promise to give up his queue conveys a number of mixed meanings. The line "I will pawn my rabicho to pay such a debt" presents the possibility of a number of translations. *Rabicho* can mean a hairstyle or the tail of an animal (ponytail or pigtail). It also implies "to tag along," which can be used affectionately or in annoyance, like a child who is always a rabicho following his or her mother. It can also be used to indicate a loved person or someone with whom one might be having a flirtation. In popular language or slang, it also connotes sodomy. Cutting his queue would convey an expression of unfaithful patriotic ties to the Qing, an act worthy of death, as well as a severing of his masculinity.

The following scene presents all three impossibilities for assimilation that serve to justify why the Mandarin and Chinese laborers should be excluded from Brazilian society. At the end of the scene, the Mandarin mysteriously disappears, indicating assimilation's final impossibility, and the Baron assumes the Mandarin's dress, which acts as a signifier for his national and cultural ties to China.[42] Dressing in the Mandarin's clothing transfers Chineseness to the Baron, a gesture suggesting to the audience that Chineseness is transmittable, contagious, and performed. The Baron's gesture of wearing the Mandarin's look reiterates lines from the play's beginning, when both he and the Mandarin are satirically referred to as the same "good types." This joining of the Baron and the Mandarin in shared attire highlights the creation of a relationship between them, which in the current events context referred to the Qing and Brazilian states' potential joint effort of initiating Chinese labor immigration:

> Servant: Here comes another man who looks like a woman.
> Olímpia: (Standing up) Who is it?
> Mandarin: A man who looks like a woman? For Fó's sake, I know who it is.
> Servant: He is furious.
> Mandarin: It's my wife!
> Olímpia: Your wife! A man who looks like a woman?
> Mandarin: She is a woman who looks like a man! But it's all the same. Buddha, save me! She is the most jealous spouse in Peking. She has discovered I am here and wants to catch me red-handed. Hide me!
> Olímpia: A scandal in my house!
> Servant: (In the background): She is coming!
> Hermann: (To the magicians) My gentlemen, let us show them we are great illusionists. We will conceal the Mandarin.
> Mandarin: (With volubility.): My friends, if you are successful, I will pawn my queue to pay back such a debt. / My friends, if you are successful, I will pawn my ass to pay such a debt.
> The Magicians: All hands on-deck! (They encircle the Mandarin, who mysteriously disappears, leaving his clothes in their hands).
> Olímpia: And these clothes?
> Hermann: Sir, you wear them. (They dress the Baron in the Mandarin's clothing. Peky enters furiously and the servant exits).[43]

The Baron's relationship with the Mandarin might be seen as symbiotic wherein the Mandarin symbolizes prosperity for the Baron, and an elite few, because he introduces new forms of slavery and colonialism. However, *O Mandarim*'s other significant Chinese character, Lírio, earns a modest living by peddling shrimp. He falls for Olímpia but lacks the means to purchase her love. Olímpia tells Lírio that she has her eyes set on the First-Class Mandarin, thereby proclaiming that her attraction to the Mandarin is bound to her desire for the money she believes he bountifully possesses. When, in the following scene Lírio professes his love for Olímpia, she replies that she is waiting for the Mandarin. She is not romantically interested in the Mandarin; her desire for him is always expressed through her desire for what he brings to her in financial terms. She does not want to be with him sexually per se. Rather, her desire is bound to an economic transaction.

Immediately after Olímpia expresses her true objective in pursuing the Mandarin is his money and conveys to Lírio that the Chinese are pleasing to her for this reason, Lírio confesses that he is also Chinese. Until this point, Olímpia thinks Lírio is Parisian. Through Lírio's declaration of his Chinese identity, the playwrights portray the idea that becoming Chinese is not so much bound to biological features but rather to the declarative gesture. Lírio must declare he is Chinese in order for Olímpia to read him as such.

In this confessional scene between the two characters, Azevedo and Moreira expose the ties that bind the biological body to the commoditized body. Olímpia's desire for the Mandarin is tied to the business deal, not his Chineseness. Lírio's declaration of his Chinese ancestry is therefore not enough, and Olímpia ushers him to the door. This scene explicitly signals that her affinity for the Mandarin and disinclination toward Lírio are purely transactional. It depicts Chineseness as dynamically and relationally constituted rather than fixed to biological or cultural traits:

Lírio and Olímpia (at the same time)
Lírio: Love I implore you Olímpia: Love you implore me.
Olímpia: Do you want me to tell you everything frankly?
Lírio: Tell me!
Olímpia: Well fine, I am waiting for someone.
Lírio: Who?
Olímpia: The Mandarin!
Lírio: The Mandarin?!
Olímpia: The First-Class Mandarin!
Lírio: An authentic mandarin?
Olímpia: Doubtful?
Lírio: Are you going to enter negotiations with China?
Olímpia: It seems so!
Lírio: Are the Chinese pleasing to you?
Olímpia: Very.
Lírio: In that case then I will confess a secret . . .
Olímpia: Now, no; later!
Lírio: It has to be now: I am also Chinese.
Olímpia: You? A Parisian?
Lírio: That is what you assume . . . In 1863 . . .
Olímpia: No! For the love of God! Later . . . later. (Pushes him to the door).

Lírio: Decidedly you send me away?
Olímpia: Yes! Yes! Leave me! (Takes him to the door).
Lírio (He disappears, returns and makes an ironic greeting): Salam Alec!
Olímpia: There goes my commerce. (Lírio disappears).
Lírio: Shrimp! (Exits lively).[44]

While Lírio, a shrimp seller, is a major character, there are other Chinese shrimp seller characters in the revue referred to homogeneously as "*o Chim*" (the Portuguese equivalent of *Chinaman*) in the play. They serve to portray part of Rio de Janeiro's quotidian society. The Chinese shrimp seller appears among newsboys and a street peddler who sells a hodgepodge of eggs, mint, pepper, Bahian coconut sweets, and matchboxes. Selling sardines and fish, Chim holds up his goods and calls out in a loud, heavily accented voice: "Slimp! Saldines! Fish!"[45] Although the Chinese shrimp seller enters the scene as a quotidian part of Rio de Janeiro society, he is depicted as an outsider who does not belong in the scene. The script indicates that the actor who plays this role should mock the Chinese accent in Portuguese. The script's description of the Chinese shrimp seller's foreign accent produces a form of yellowness that is mappable across a number of works from this period.

The recurring yet minor roles of the "Chim" in Azevedo and Moreira's *O Mandarim*, as well as in other works of this period, provides a glimpse into the kinds of precarious conditions that Chinese immigrants, and others in a similar situation, faced during Rio's urban development. Upon observing the multiple appearances of the Chinese shrimp peddler in creative works, I looked into newspapers during this time period and discovered reports about the wretched lives of Chinese fish sellers. On July 22, 1900, one reporter wrote that Chinese fish sellers had all but disappeared from the streets of Rio de Janeiro due to "yellow fever," "opium," and "nostalgia."[46] The reporter mentions the absence of Chinese fish sellers to convey relief that there are no more Chinese in Rio: "The Chinaman is already so yellow when he is calm, now imagine how the Chinaman becomes when he's yellow with rage."[47] The reporter then proceeds to portray yellow rage by describing the Boxer Rebellion, a peasant uprising in China that was largely targeting foreigners and Christian missionaries, as an "innumerable multitude of tails [*rabichos*]" who are "furiously" "assassinating," "torturing," and "burning" "the immense extension of the Celestial Empire."[48]

In similar rhetoric as these descriptions, a Chinese shrimp seller appears in a short scene from Aluísio Azevedo's *O Cortiço* (*The Slum*) (1890), a novel that gave a fierce critique of Brazil's postslavery republic. *Cortiço* was a colloquial name given to the tenement-like, overcrowded housing developments that had formed in Rio de Janeiro's center during the latter half of the nineteenth century.[49] The houses were often made of low-cost, light materials—such as sheet metal, wood, bricks, and concrete—that people could carry and construct without the use of expensive tools or machinery. Due to economic restrictions, homes were usually built in components or stages and constructed on rented lots.

Aluísio Azevedo and Arthur Azevedo were brothers—they also influenced each other's literary works as well as cowrote pieces. Aluísio's *The Slum* provides a complex portrayal of ideas regarding mixed-race identity, whiteness, blackness, gender, sexuality, and class during a period of rapid urbanization, internal and international migration, and the development of overcrowded and substandard housing settlements in Rio de Janeiro. The explicitly raunchy novel was a sensational success, becoming an instant classic, and it provides an indication of the rising moralistic bourgeoisie's earthy reading tastes. *The Slum* emblematized the height of Brazilian literary naturalism. The novel personifies the slum as a living creature, an organism that grew out of Brazil's "brutal and exuberant world," growing in strength by day, an "implacable jungle" that mercilessly "devours newcomers."[50] In the novel, the Chinese shrimp seller enters the slum, but he is quickly kicked out. Its dire economic state cannot handle any more newcomers like him. This Brazilian entity will not ingest the Chinese migrant, who has no place in this body politic, however miserable.

The novel presents the Chinese shrimp seller as an innocent bystander, pulled into Brazil's domestic problems. Caught in the wrong place at the wrong time, the Chinese man unknowingly walks into a heated argument between the couple Bruno and Leocádia. In an attempt to escape from her abusive relationship with Bruno, Leocádia has made a deal with Henrique, a student, to exchange sex for a rabbit he acquired at an auction. The deal would not only provide her with the rabbit, but possibly a source of wealth—a baby—which would then enable her to work as a wet nurse, another example of how women's reproductive abilities translated into economic terms. The narrator emphasizes the student's grip around the rabbit, the symbolic object that transforms their sexual act into a financial exchange. However, Leocádia's plans are spoiled when her husband, Bruno, catches them. In a public rage that all the neighbors gather to witness, Bruno throws out all of her belongings. Amid this squabble, a jug hits an innocent bystander, a Chinese shrimp peddler, on the head. A fierce Portuguese woman named Machona (the nickname means "masculine woman") yells at him, "Salamaleque." Azevedo and Moreira's Lírio made a similar remark, "Salam Alec," when he bid farewell to Olímpia before returning to vend his shrimp. Colloquially the phrase is a negative one, indicating a pompous or exaggerated greeting from a courtesan.[51] Machona's scornful use of the Arabic expression *salamaleque* cites the long-fraught history of Christian and Islamic tensions on the Iberian Peninsula. The expression maps this historical division onto the body of the Chinese migrant whose yellowness overlaps with other racialized bodies who were historically excluded from the Iberian Catholic order. The pessimistic tone of the novel heightens with the Chinese shrimp peddler, who is not only the figuration of the unassimilable alien or Oriental Other, but his presence becomes a mirror that reflects Rio's urbanization problems, including new forms of housing inequality that continued the master/slave plantation structure in the urban setting in the divide between mansion and slum.

The Chinese shrimp peddler crosses into the social borders of Rio's inner city, where sex and reproductive labor are commodities, but his body has no place in this disturbed Brazilian organism:

> A shrimp-peddling Chinaman had entered the cortiço. He had absentmindedly stopped beneath the Bahian woman's window, got hit on the head with a jug, and screamed like a child who had just received a beating. Machona, who couldn't bear anyone shouting louder than her, fell upon him with her fists and, insulting him, dragged him to the gate and threw him out. "The last thing we needed was the arrival of some *salamaleque* from hell to disturb a creature more than it was already.[52]

Aluísio Azevedo's portrayal of the Chinese shrimp peddler intertextually referenced similar preoccupations as those expressed in *O Mandarim* that Chinese immigration would not solve Brazil's existing problems, but only add onto them.

In a teatro de revista performance titled *Fritzmac* (1888), cowritten by the playwriting brother duo Arthur Azevedo and Aluísio Azevedo, the Chinese are depicted as an unfit labor force, either too lazy to work or too unscrupulous to be trusted, because they would turn Brazil into a hybrid Brazilian-Chinese mass who would spend their days in an opium stupor. Adhering to the genre norms of the teatro de revista by addressing current events, *Fritzmac* tackled quite a wide range of issues that occurred in 1888, including the abolition of slavery; increased Chinese and Italian immigration; women's entrance into professional fields such as medicine, pharmacy, and even bullfighting; and the beverage scandal involving the industries of two men, Fritz and Mack, who were fined and imprisoned for falsifying beverage ingredients.[53] The highly successful show sold out a record-breaking forty-nine performances.[54] The box office numbers created quite the sensation, since most theater revues did not last more than one week.[55] *Fritzmac* filled to capacity the "hygienic and tastefully" reconstructed Teatro Variedades Dramáticas of Rio de Janeiro. Its capacity was similar to that of the Teatro Príncipe Imperial, which could seat upwards of 650 people.[56]

In particular, *Fritzmac* presented a vision of Brazil's future if the Chinese were to assimilate, allowing us to examine how global debates about the Chinese question gained new meaning in Brazil. In *Fritzmac*, the character Amorosa attempts to convince the Baron (likely a reference to the proslavery advocate Baron of Cotegipe) of the negative effects of Brazilian miscegenation with Chinese. Referring to the Chinese Exclusion Act in the United States, Amorosa uses the example of how Chinese immigrants were "repelled" in North America due to their "misery and corruption."[57]

Through an act of sorcery, Amorosa takes the Baron to Brazil one century into the future to show him what Brazil would look like if his desire for Chinese immigration were fulfilled. They enter into a hybrid and dystopic Brazilian-Chinese future, recalling both the *Revista Illustrada*'s drawing of the "Brazil-Chinaman" that was also published in 1888 and the scene in Azevedo and Moreira's *O Mandarim,* in which the Baron puts on the Mandarin's clothing.[58] The *Fritzmac* characters have hybrid Portuguese-Chinese names, such as Fonseca-Tching and Tzéng-Tzéng-Sodré. The curtain opens to a room in "Chinese decor"; the script clearly indicates that this room resembles the interior of actual Brazilian homes of the future. Fonseca-Tching is seated in a chair, smoking opium and fanning himself. Fonseca proclaims that he is content to live a life of leisure, where work is out of the question. Tzéng-Tzéng-Sodré is eating rats, a depiction of how his ability to sustain life on sewer rats, which he considers an "economic morsel," threatens a decent way of life. If Chinese immigration succeeds, *Fritzmac* warns, Brazil would transform into a mixed-race, degenerate population and obstruct the project of whitening. Enhancing social deterioration, the Chinese would bring an opium market and other illicit activities to Brazil.

The Azevedos also bring back the character of Peky, the Mandarin's ambiguously gendered wife from 1883's *O Mandarim.* In this version, Peky is no longer the wealthy wife of the Mandarin; instead, she is addicted to opium and depicted cleaning the animal trough. All of the hybrid Chinese-Brazilian characters are unhygienic and immoral: they eat rats and spend their time smoking opium in this future dystopia. Peky lives with Fonseca, and the two are tied by relations of dependency and protection. This state of hierarchical codependency constituted a typical relationship that occurred during colonialism in Brazil's patronage system (*sistema de favores*) that was based on exchanging favors and obligations and was guided by social hierarchy. Looking for a suitable fiancé for Peky, Fonseca subtly conveys that Peky is not a virgin. In fact, she is three months' pregnant, but it is not clear who the father is. Fonseca in fact speaks of Peky's offspring in terms of providing a transaction that will secure them both a good financial future—her womb has a commodity value. Fonseca and Peky are looking for the suitor who will pay the highest price for the developing child. Furthermore, she is addicted to opium. The scene ends with her dozing into a narcotic-induced slumber. Her virtues are questionable; she, like the others in this dystopic world, is intoxicated and useless. This scene makes the case to the pro-Chinese immigration advocates to turn against Chinese labor. *Fritzmac* in this way juxtaposes the possibility of liberty from slavery and colonialism with an anti-Chinese stance:

> Fonseca: I am happy because in essence there is no better job in the world than to be idle and not do anything. A knock at the door. Who is it?
>
> Sodré's Voice: It's your infamous servant! . . .
>
> Fonseca: Enter at your will. (Sodré enters.) Oh! God be praised! It is Sir Tzeng-Tzeng-Sodré! Welcome to this poor and filthy house. This rubicund face is all health and life! (He rises and both greet each other in Chinese style.)
>
> Sodré: So how have you eaten?
>
> Fonseca: Perfectly. Thank you.
>
> Sodré: Getting fatter each day!
>
> Fonseca: I take after how Buddha is served.
>
> Sodré: My immoral family asks that I give my compliments to your excellent wife. Where is she?
>
> Fonseca: Working. My wretched little woman reciprocates your compliments. She is meddling in the kitchen, washing knives and dishes; she cannot appear. And you, sir? Are you really eating more than enough?
>
> Sodré: Even just today I ate two rats that I found in the trash barrel.
>
> Fonseca: Did it give you gas? You did not have heartburn? (Sodré gives affirmative and negative signals.) It might be a thrifty dish, but it is a very good snack. (Feeling the effects of opium.) I have smoked too much! Go ahead and have a smoke from my pipe. See how good the opium is from Minas

Gerais! (Passes the pipe to Sodré, who smokes it.)

Sodré: (Seeing Peky enter.) Wow! Beautiful Peky!

Peky: Was washin' the trough; I heard your voice . . .

Sodré: Isn't she beautiful!

Peky: And quickly ran here.

Sodré: (Taking Peky's hand, to Fonseca.) I have had the honor of twice asking for this hand.

Peky: It's time to decide: I've been expectin' for three months . . .

Fonseca: This interesting possibility is still not visible, and finding a more important fiancé to present himself is still possible! Even the knowledge of this state can be pleasing to many fiancés, and even more, one finds a woman, the work has already begun, because in the end, dear Sodré, ambition is resourceful; if a woman dies childless, the husband does not inherit anything! (With resolution, hugging them both.) Now goodbye! I do not wish to be deceived; Get married! Be Happy!

Sodré: Oh! What happiness! A kiss! (Kisses Peky. Fonseca falls on the floor completely intoxicated.) The old man is drunk, and I too already feel . . . (Falls down.)—Come to my arms, oh come! Give me ardent kisses . . . (Falls asleep.)

Peky: Both asleep . . . Well now, from this golden pipe I'll smoke my bit, and fall into slumber like these two . . . (Takes the pipe from Sodré's hands and starts smoking. Curtain goes down. Music stops).[59]

Recurring characters such as the Mandarin, Peky, and the Chinese shrimp seller made it clear that the page/stage, to reinstate the words of Azevedo, was not pure entertainment. Rather, like the teatro de revista chase scenes that threaded seemingly disjointed narratives into a single but highly complex story, following figurations of Chineseness as they traversed Brazil's emerging national literary and theatrical spaces makes it possible to see how stories about Chinesenesses related a larger narrative about the attitudes that were shaping labor, race, gender, sexuality, and citizenship. Mandarins and Chinamen became tropes of emancipation, projecting both proslavery advocates' hopes and abolitionists' fears about new modes of racialized labor, which these works portrayed with scathing satire.

FOUR

The Chinese Question in Brazil

This chapter builds on the analysis of overlapping racialization examined throughout this book, focusing in particular on the constructions of the Chinese as a yellow race in the works of Machado de Assis and Eça de Queiroz, arguably the founding fathers of modern Luso-Brazilian literatures. They were influential authors because they crafted new genres of literary expression, and they were also prominent public officials. The topic of the Chinese question entered into their work as writers and as public servants. Studying their literary production provides us with insight into Brazil's decision to ultimately reject large-scale Chinese immigration in favor of laborers from Europe, the Middle East, and Japan.

Machado de Assis and Eça de Queiroz were both vehemently against Chinese labor. Throughout the last decades of the nineteenth century, they wrote a number of pieces that associated the construction of citizenship with racial identity and labor.[1] Examining the way the Chinese question is addressed in the work of these two prominent authors and public servants allows us to probe the transnational dimensions of what representations of Chineseness meant to the Brazilian nation as it struggled to craft its image on the world stage and within new geopolitical and trade alliances. While the discourse of Chineseness in their works was directly related to debates about wage labor, liberty, and Brazilian national independence, similar polemics about Chinese laborers were circulating around the world in what became known as the Chinese, or coolie, question, which disseminated assimilationist debates over the suitability of Chinese laborers for white liberal democracies.[2]

North American perceptions of Chinese laborers influenced debates about the Chinese question between Brazilian abolitionists and proslavery advocates. In the United States, the idea that the Chinese were a "coolie race" was used to bolster US nativism and Anglo-American hegemony.[3] The Chinese question often transpired as cultural constructions that shaped ideas about the Chinese as Orientals, or a yellow race, such as in nineteenth-century US music and performances of yellowface that spread stereotypes like *Heathen Chinee*, *John Chinaman*, *Ah Sing*, and *Yellow Jack*.[4] These expressions of racial difference give an indication of how economic competition and political threat took shape as a form of anti-Asian cultural expression referred to as the Yellow Peril.[5] US popular culture disseminated the belief that the "heathen and alien ways" of the Chinese threatened the moral fabric of free labor and US republicanism.[6] Negative images dehumanized the Chinese with facial features and body shapes that made them into creatures. These depictions circulated in the Caribbean as much as in the United States, Canada, and Mexico, attesting to their potential for global transit.[7] Although it is difficult to pinpoint the exact origins of these negative portrayals, these ideas circulating in the northern part of the American hemisphere eventually made their way south to affect Brazilian views about the Chinese.

On February 18, 1871, the New York City–based *Harper's Weekly* published the political cartoon "The Chinese Question" (Figure 4.1). Geared toward middle- and upper-middle-class audiences, the publication played an important role in shaping public opinion dating from the Civil War era to the dawn of the twentieth century.[8] Circulation numbers ranged from 100,000 to 300,000, and its readership exceeded half a million people.[9] In the illustration, Columbia, the figure of a woman who resembles the Statue of Liberty, is depicted as protecting a Chinese laborer who is sitting on the floor beside her, curled inward with his head in his hand. On the wall behind them are words that convey extreme anti-Chinese sentiment. In large type, "Chinese Question" is prominently posted on a wall at the top center of the illustration. Crowding the wall are derogatory phrases stemming from Yellow Peril discourses, including "Coolie, Slave, Pauper, Rat-Eater," "Degraded Laborers," and "Importation of Chinese Barbarians." While Columbia stands over the caricature of the Chinese laborer who has a Qing queue and is wearing Qing-style garb, the caption reads: "Hands off, gentlemen! America means fair play for all men."[10] This *Harper's Weekly* illustra-

FIGURE 4.1. "The Chinese Question," by Thomas Nast. *Harper's Weekly*. February 18, 1871. Source: HarpWeek.com, electronic database of *Harper's Weekly*.

tion furthered the notion that the United States would defend the rights of all people, regardless of race. However, anti-Chinese sentiment persisted. Images of this sort give a glimpse of the cultural climate that made possible the US Chinese Exclusion Act of 1882, which prevented Chinese laborers from entering the United States and prohibited Chinese residents of the United States from becoming US citizens.

The Chinese question, along with ideas about the Chinese as a race, took on a different, yet connected, form in Brazil where these debates constructed a racial identity for the Chinese as the personification of unfree yellow labor. A site-specific analysis of how Sinophobic discourse took shape in an emerging Brazilian national imaginary provides a way to examine the emergence of racialized national categories that retained the race-based exclusionary, paternalistic logic of chattel bondage. In Brazil, debates about the Chinese question addressed whether Chinese laborers would enable proslavery Brazilian agriculturalists and government officials to create new forms of unfree labor. Because yellow labor was viewed as an extension of slavery or unfree labor, Chinese laborers were portrayed as an impediment to free white labor and republicanism—similar to the way they had been portrayed in North America. These views entered into Brazilian debates about the Chinese question, but they also intertwined with discussions about generative or degenerative miscegenation with the Chinese. Debates over miscegenation in favor of or against unskilled, unfree Chinese labor became a central element in discourse about the nation's future and concerns over the whitening project.

Gradual emancipation laws like the Free Womb Law of 1871 rendered clear the entanglement of agricultural and labor needs with sexual reproduction that would secure a workforce born into bondage. This view was developed within the ideological structure of Brazil's slave-holding, paternalistic, and scientific racism. The Free Womb Law simultaneously liberated children born to enslaved mothers and rendered clear the paternalistic ideology of slaveholders.[11] While the Free Womb Law severed the inheritance of slavery, it revealed an operational principle of slavery's racial regime that had constructed the enslaved black mother as the means of production for future laborers. Chinese labor and sexuality accrued their racialization within slavery's legal terms, which had stipulated that the children of enslaved women also inherited the condition of their mother's bondage. Since it had been through reproduction with enslaved, or semi-enslaved races that the future of Brazil's subjugated labor force and agriculturalist economy was secured, the question of whether to accept Chinese labor linked closely to the topic of sexual reproduction. Economic necessity intertwined with questions of eugenics and social evolution, and so it is not a surprise that legal cases regarding the condition of freedom, including those involving Chinese laborers, were often debated in Brazil's Ministry of Agriculture.

Machado de Assis headed the department of the Ministry of Agriculture that was in charge of enforcing the Free Womb Law. As director, he defended regulations that favored the freedom of slaves over the rights of slave owners and their claims of chattel bondage as private property.[12] Machado's duties at the Ministry of Agriculture, mainly his mandate to monitor the implementation of the Free Womb Law, allow us to connect his literary production from the 1870s to the 1880s to his duties as civil servant who worked to advance the abolitionist movement. In response to politicians', agriculturalists', and aristocrats' advocacy for Chinese labor, Machado wrote a number of pieces about China and Chinese immigration throughout the last three decades of the nineteenth century. In 1868, Quintino Bocayuva, who served as Brazil's minister of exterior relations (1889–1891) and as president of Rio de Janeiro (1900–1903), published a pamphlet about the agricultural crisis anticipated by abolition and advocated a short-term solution involving state-financed Chinese immigration.[13] Chinese labor would provide a temporary solution during the transitional moment from slavery to abolition, a period bookended by two significant dates, 1871 and 1888, due to two transformational laws. On one end is the Free Womb Law of 1871. On the other end, the year 1888 saw the passing of the *Lei Áurea* (Golden Law), which completely abolished slavery in Brazil. From 1887 to 1888, the great immigration of 150,000 salaried laborers from Europe arrived at Brazil's ports to perform the labor previously enforced by slavery.[14]

In July 1870, a year prior to the passing of the Free Womb Law in 1871, a ten-year plan to hire Chinese laborers had been implemented. Public discourse debated whether this plan was suitable for Brazil. At the Sociedade Auxiliadora da Indústria Nacional (Auxiliary Society of National Industry), arguments rehearsed anti-Chinese rhetoric that was contemporaneously circulating around the world. The Chinese were inferior; they could not improve society; they were dependent, docile, ambitionless, and worked for little pay.[15]

The question over miscegenation between Brazilians and the Chinese also entered into conversations. There were different sides to the miscegenation issue that related incompatible views for the nation's future. On the one hand, generative miscegenation focused on the whitening project and a desire to transform Brazil into a free white liberal society by means of European immigration, and on the other hand, degenerative miscegenation with those deemed enslaved or unfree threatened a new era of colonization and slavery. The widespread belief that Chinese laborers would eventually return to China and take Brazil's wealth with them provoked additional layers of racial anxiety toward the Chinese as a new colonialist labor force that had no intention of staying in and improving Brazil. Nicolão Moreira, of the Agricultural Sector of the National Industry, voiced his fears that the Chinese would not stay in the country and thus would not be good for miscegenation.[16]

While abolitionists and opponents of Chinese labor saw the turn to yellow, unfree labor as an impediment to national independence and liberation movements, the paternalistic social Darwinist evolutionary discourses that dominated Brazil's colonial liberalism continued to shape the development of racialized national categories that drove Brazil's entrance into a new era of racial nationalism via whitening.

In addition to his work as a public servant, Machado was a prolific writer. He developed and experimented with his craft across diverse literary genres. Machado's masterful skills in satire and irony were powerful tools in the abolitionist work he did while working for the Ministry of Agriculture, and his work provides a prismatic view on the Chinese question, which, for abolitionists, represented the opposite of social progress toward liberty for all. In some instances, Machado engaged anti-Chinese labor rhetoric from the perspective of British officials and Qing mandarins. In other instances, he subverted Yellow Peril tropes that deemed the Chinese a threat to the moral values of a republican state.[17]

Machado's literary production was political, in the vein of how Arthur Azevedo viewed the role of playwriting and the theater as not just purely entertainment but as a space to construct, debate, and even dismantle national institutions. Machado deployed Sinophobic views strategically, as a way to point an accusatory finger at the Brazilian, British, and Qing empires' respective self-interests in setting up Chinese labor settlements in Brazil. Machado's writings allow us to see how the racial regimes of slavery persisted in the postslavery nation. Moreover, the actual memory of slavery may have been obliterated, but it was replaced with new narratives involving immigration, a national myth sustained through national amnesia requiring the elision of genocidal histories of slavery and indigenous land expropriation.

The paternalistic scientific racist logic that provided the infrastructure for the institution of slavery in Brazil continued to determine how race was perceived during Brazil's transition to a republican state. Rhetoric about the new body politic intertwined moral values with racial discourse and class hierarchy. Nietzsche explains that those in positions of power have historically determined the meaning behind moral value judgments like good or evil. If we trace the genealogy of morals, he contends, we can observe how the aristocratic class, which holds the power and has access to self-representation, designates morally good attributes to itself such as noble, superior, and privileged soul: a development that always runs beside that hypothetical other in which peasant, commoner, or working class are transformed into concepts like immoral, low, and bad.[18] The aristocracy upholds its own superiority when it attributes the common class with ignoble characteristics as incapable of virtue, excellence, and the other qualities that are necessary for citizenship—that is, for achieving political independence, self-governance, and justice. Fin-de-siècle writers internalized this genealogy of morals and used race-based descriptors to make moral arguments about which kinds of racialized bodies were equal and good and which ones were inferior, commodifiable, and socially degenerate. Conflicting representations of Chinese migrants did not always follow dominant political and racial ideologies, and the contradictions in these representations give an indication of the complex moral debates over liberty and life occurring in Brazil during this time.

No silver lining can be found in Machado's writings about Chinese immigration, which would at best be an irrational, if not completely delusional, solution to the labor crisis. His concerns about miscegenation and labor were intertwined in his approach to the Chinese question. In 1878, under the pseudonym H. Pito, Machado de Assis wrote the poem "Chinoiserie" for the abolitionist journal *Revista Illustrada*. While the poem's title refers to objects or designs that imitate or are evocative of Chinese porcelain motifs and artistic techniques, the content actually referred to the misleading promise of Chinese labor as a form of free labor:

"Chinoiserie"
Gê-yué is in China—and here, José.
Says Amen,
But says this very well,
since he tells in his by which he means—sun and moon
Now this Chim-Zé [Jo Chinaman]
Or Chimpanzee
Your mentor is dear
the things from China
Gé Yué is a mine
worth an enormous lot
for whom is
the beautiful Amen
Recounts the quasi-assassination
The Emperor William
And Gè-Yuè
The Chim-Zé,—
drops the duck
picks up the fan,
Makes its salamalek,
Sits on his knees and says:
By the laws of my country
Made by Confucius and Mencius
Amended by Kincio and Sencio,
Punish any Chinaman—with treason—
Who punctures a citizen
As the Kaiser in Berlin
Agrees Amen
With Gè-Yuè
—the Chim-Zé—
Wonders if the *Ta-hio*
Without having—-gone beyond—
In the name of Fú or Fó
—is hanged
Laughs the Chinaman—and I as well,
I understand, here in my,
Only the plucked Chinaman in the kitchen/ A Chinaman only in the
    kitchen, what a pity
—is well

o mesre Amen
Kakòlé.
Like something from China or Amen.[19]

The poem is composed of a series of indeciphrable words and strange grammatical constructions. For example, *ge yue* does not refer to any actual place or thing in China, but the poem gives form to contemporary stereotypes about the Chinese as an inscrutable other that were circulating with the Chinese question.

The poem contains a number of syllepses, so that one word conveys a number of meanings in the same sentence. Machado used this stylistic technique to enter into the Chinese labor debate. Depictions of the trade in Chinese labor, as well as objects from China, specifically Macau, have the same symbolic function in the poem; they express the parallel trade in luxury goods and human labor. A multilingual reading of this poem reveals layers of nuance; for example, the word *amen* simultaneously hints at a religious utterance at the end of a prayer and the Cantonese word for Macau, or *aomen*. The last line of the poem makes this double meaning explicit: "like something from China or Amen" ("Como coisa da China ou do Amen"), since it makes sense that the object would come from China or the ports of Macau/Aomen. Referencing Macau in this way evoked the five-hundred-year history of Sino-Portuguese trade relations, which began in 1557 when Portugal leased Macau from the Ming dynasty. The reference to Macau was a contemporaneous reminder that just a few years prior to Machado's writing, Macau had functioned as a major port in the coolie trade until 1874, when international pressure forced the Portuguese to end the trade. As another example, the line, "Only the plucked Chinaman in the kitchen," which could also be translated as, "A Chinaman only in the kitchen, what a pity," plays with the Portuguese expressions [*cheio*] *de pena* and *depenar* (to pluck). In one definition, the phrase means "to pluck feathers," and in another sense, it means "to feel regret or pity." When read with the meaning "to pluck feathers," the Chinaman is dehumanized, becoming a fowl that has met its final end: flesh that a cook prepares to devour. At the same time, *pena* becomes an empathetic critique (pity, regret) of the political and economic situation that had begun to conflate slavery with the so-called Chinaman, the personification of racialized and exploitable immigrant labor.

Machado's use of *Chim-Zé* does not refer to any specific person. In English, the expression "John Chinaman" was a disparaging way of referring to Chinese immigrants and laborers in the gold mining and railroad towns in the United States during the nineteenth century. The moniker also personified the Chinese nation.[20] In this sense, *Chim-Zé* could be the Portuguese translation of Jo Chinaman since *Zé* is a common Brazilian nickname for *José*, the equivalent of *Joseph* in English and *chim* functions like Chinaman in how it homogenizes all the Chinese into one anonymous person. Monikers like *Chim-Zé* and Jo Chinaman communicated racial anxieties about the assimilation of the yellow race across national and linguistic spaces. The word *chim* homogenized all Chinese immigrants as a single yellow race. Its usage formed part of a multilingual vocabulary about the global Chinese question and the emergence of a globally racialized national consciousness that came directly out of colonial hierarchies of racial identity and labor. In writings concerning the construction of a free Brazilian republic, it could refer to skilled, voluntary Asian laborers or be used interchangeably with *coolie* to signify indentured, unfree, and unskilled labor. The line "Ora este Chim-Zé Ou Chimpanzé" (translatable as both "Now this Jo Chinaman or chimpanzee" or "Pray this Jo Chinaman or chimpanzee") plays on the double meaning of *ora*—it could be read as *to pray* (pray for the Jo Chinaman or Chimpanzee) or as an interjection. The word play between Chim-Zé and *chimpanzee* expresses a negative attitude about miscegenation between the Chinese and Brazilians and the resulting detriment to Brazilian society writ large. In this poem, miscegenation with Chinese immigrants would produce a Brazilian population of chimp-like people—a subhuman species.

The Chim is a recurring yet minor character in the fin-de-siècle Brazilian literary scene, constituting part of a linguistic economy of racialization that was bound to a collective memory about slavery's racial regimes. Often he is depicted as peddling his fish and shellfish, advertising what he has by shouting with a heavy Chinese accent. Machado de Assis also wrote a number of pieces about Chinese shrimp sellers with heavy Chinese accents in his depictions about the precarious conditions of the chim/Chinaman who migrated and settled in Rio's unforgiving climate. In a parodic letter addressed to the Emperor of China, "Carta do Dr. Semana ao Imperador da China" ("Dr. Week's Letter to the Emperor of China"), published on April 17, 1864, in the magazine *Semana Ilustrada,* Machado, under the pseudonym Dr. Semana, writes to the emperor, whom he addresses as "Your Obesity," to warn him of the fates of the Chinese who have immigrated to Brazil and have taken up selling "slimp and saldines."[21] That is, they had been reduced to hawking shrimp and sardines.[22]

Machado wrote other poetic expressions of Chineseness in addition to "Chinoiserie." In 1871, he translated into Portuguese eight poems from Judith Gautier's *Le Livre de Jade* (*The Book of Jade*) (1867). When Machado translated *Le Livre de Jade*, he inverted the trope of the exotic, escapist Orient that was common in French Orientalism and also influenced English literature. Judith Gautier was the daughter of celebrated writer Théophile Gautier (1811–1872), a prominent member of the literati often associated with the development of French Orientalism. She studied under the tutelage of Chinese scholar Ding Dunling (?1830–1886) and had supposedly learned enough classical Chinese to translate into French a collection of Tang and Song dynasty poetry and Ding Dunling's poems. When Chinese scholar Ding Dunling entered into Judith Gautier's life, he turned her eyes toward Asia, in particular China.[23] It is notable that the true story of Ding's arrival in nineteenth-century Paris wanders in and out of a larger narrative about the rise of French Orientalism and that accounts of his life in Paris are mainly told through the filters of the bright-eyed and infatuated perspective of Gautier. The original reference is lost to imagination, much like chinoiserie, but a process of fascination and imitation remains. While scholars have questioned the accuracy of Gautier's translations, her efforts nevertheless introduced Chinese poetry to the French literati, where the Chinese literary traditions she shared had lasting influence.[24] Yet the focus here is not on the Chinese literary influences via French Orientalism that might have influenced Machado as he undertook his translations of Gautier's work.[25] Machado transformed European Orientalist topoi into the beginnings of a discourse on economic crisis. Far from attempting to recreate Orientalist splendor, the poem realigns Orientalist symbols with a newly contested space in which the business of the coolie trade presents a direct obstacle to abolitionist struggles and the project of national independence.

Machado's translations of *Livre de Jade* can be found in a section titled "Lira Chinesa" ("Chinese Lyre"), in the collection of poems *Phalenas* (*Falenas* in modern Portuguese). When Machado chose to title his 1871 collection of poems *Falenas*, he was not merely crafting an analogy between metamorphosis and his own maturation as a poet, as some have argued: "It is obvious that by calling the volume *Falenas* Machado intended to emphasize his maturation as a poet, and indeed, in *Falenas* one can detect the further development of pre-Parnassian as well as Machadian elements." [26] Rather, I prefer to read Machado's *Falenas* as an example of how he harnessed literary expression as a means to enter the debate on Chinese labor. According to the *Michaelis Modern Dictionary of the Portuguese Language*, the word *falenas* is commonly used to describe "the geometrid family of butterflies whose larvae attack all sorts of trees and plants by eating their leaves."[27] Falenas are agricultural pests whose offspring ravage trees and plants. In another dictionary search, I found the adjective *nocivo* being used to describe the insect species.[28] *Nocivo* means harmful, noxious, and morally deleterious. The last definition coincides with the colloquial meaning of *falena*, which means a prostitute who wanders at night, attracted to the streetlights.[29] If we interpret Machado's writings as literary artillery, as he and his contemporaries envisioned, then we can observe the analogy between the etymological meanings of falenas and a wide range of commonly circulating ideas regarding Chinese laborers as invaders and insect-like.

His choice to use the title *Falenas* gains a political meaning when we situate his poems within the context of his social milieu where it was common for his contemporaries to refer to Chinese labor and sexual reproduction as a moral detriment. In a parliamentary address delivered in 1879, abolitionist and democrat Joaquim Nabuco claimed that Asiatic immigration to Brazil and new diplomatic relations with China would result in "mongolization," and he cited the popular belief that the Chinese belonged to the degenerative Mongol race.[30] He was against Chinese immigration, and he justified his reasoning by claiming that while China and Brazil were the two largest empires of the time, their societies were incompatible. China was trapped in antiquated traditions, but Brazil was headed toward a brilliant future.[31] Nabuco appealed to moral values to argue against the Chinese workers: "Morally . . . why introduce into our society this addictive leprosy that infests all cities where Chinese immigration is established?"[32]

If we read Machado's title "Lira chinesa" as constituting part of an abolitionist vocabulary that had developed among Machado and his contemporaries, we can also interpret the title as a shorthand reference to *de-lira chinesa*, or Chinese delirium. Distraction and delirium are recurring themes in fin-de-siècle writings about Chinese labor as a mad solution to the labor shortage. The word *lira* is the Latin root word of delirium. The verb *delirar* is the action state of delirium. Representing Chinese labor as a solution that would promote only delirium was a common literary trope in the works of abolitionists during this time. They deemed that there were no answers to the Chinese question; rather, they asserted that recruiting Chinese immigrant labor was a proposal so unviable as to be mad. For example, writers for the *Revista Illustrada* claimed that the Baron of Cotegipe was delirious with the idea of Chinese labor.[33] Furthermore, Lírio, an impoverished Chinese shrimp seller who makes a meager living as a street peddler, is a main character in Azevedo and Moreira's fin-de-siècle teatro de revista *O Mandarim*.[34] If we read his name within the abolitionist vocabulary that had developed in Brazil, it too signifies the truncated version of the word *delirium*: *de-lírio*. Lírio, the Chinese shrimp peddler, who has a star-crossed infatuation with the courtesan Olímpia, may very well reference a kind of unsound excitement and moral degradation that foreshadowed yellow labor.

Distraction is the dominant mood in Machado's translation of Gautier's poem "L'Empereur" ("The Emperor"). The poem is about an oblivious Qing emperor. The mandarin officials, who act as advisors to the throne, are deeply preoccupied with the failing Qing empire, which has been torn apart by civil war and multiple forces of colonization. However, the emperor is intoxicated with the scent of seduction, which draws him away from his duties and toward the concubines in his porcelain pavilion. While the mandarins pursue news about foreign affairs, the isolated Qing emperor continues with a myopic view. He chooses not to see the dangers creeping in and instead closes himself off inside a porcelain bubble. Machado's translation of the poem significantly transforms its opening. He begins with the imperative: "*Look*, the Son of Heaven, on a golden throne."[35] Gautier's version begins with a description: "On the golden throne/the son of heaven."[36] The emperor's story is an allegory for Brazil's aristocratic class, which lives inside a delirious elitist bubble, a hallucinatory state that is blind to the actual reality of Brazil. When the mandarins confront the emperor with the crisis facing the empire, the emperor frolics in his privileged spaces, deliriously unaware of the looming economic and political crises that are afoot.

A mandarin makes a brief appearance in Machado's canonized novel, *Memórias póstumas de Brás Cubas* (*Posthumous Memories of Bras Cubas*) (1881), in which a deceased but capricious narrator recalls the events of his life. *Memórias póstumas*'s narrator powerfully expresses the paternalistic slaveholder mind-set.[37] In a poignant scene about a black butterfly, Machado wrote about the absolute vulnerability of the black body in the

Brazilian state. One day a black butterfly flew into Brás Cubas's bedroom and landed on a portrait of his father, where it did not move for some time. Greatly bothered at the insect's "mocking way," Brás killed it. Afterward, he wondered if the insect would have met a similar fate had it been blue. Historian Sidney Chalhoub sharply interprets this scene as an analogy for slavery's paternalism.[38] In the seigneurial mind-set, slaves were completely subordinated to and dependent on the dominant class, carrying the full burden of physical and psychological labor. Brás projected his own psychological state onto the butterfly. The butterfly's life or death depended solely on the whims of Brás's own rather paranoid state. Because he believed the butterfly was mocking him, he killed it and analogically demonstrated his class's unaccountable power over the vulnerable black body.

The volatile personality of the narrator, Roberto Schwarz argues, is a critical element in Machado's novel. He contends, "Monotony, degradation, truncated arguments, wasted materials, dissonance, sterility, and so on are not accidental presences but important, basic effects of the movement of the prose."[39] Machado created a literary structure that gave form to the volatile personality of the Brazilian slave-holding elite, who turned a blind eye to their immediate social reality and passed their time in futile activities. They lived through the filters of "another system, precisely that of bourgeois, liberal Europe (principally Britain and France), whose lack of correspondence to local truths was perfectly plain to Machado," Gledson argues.[40]

The novel's themes of pessimism, boredom, and futility that repeatedly restart and delay the natural progression of a linear narrative present a temporal state of nonproduction and nonproductivity. Nothing accumulates and nothing progresses, since the narrator recounts his life's events posthumously, after all. The narrator expresses disaffection, alienation, distraction, and a whimsical regard for his readers. In the chapter titled "Delirium," abandoning the formal requirements of narrative, the narrator even takes a break from the labor of narrating. The narrator enters as a character in both the chapter and the state of delirium, transforming into a pot-bellied Chinese barber who attends to the caprices of a Mandarin: "At first I took the figure of a Chinese barber, potbellied, dexterous, giving a shave to a mandarin, who paid me for my work with pinches and sweets: the whims of a mandarin."[41] The passage makes a direct reference to the Mandarin's capriciousness. In other words, the Mandarin has absorbed the ideological structure of the slaveholder's paternalistic mind-set in his negligent attention to paying the actual debt he owes for the labor that has been performed for him. Machado's capricious Mandarin, like the novel's volatile narrator, give form to an ongoing pessimistic condition by ridiculing the falsity of emancipation, in which the Mandarin's payments in pinches and sweets make a mockery out of any transition toward free labor. That the peripheral literary appearances of a paunchy Chinese barber, and the recurring but always anonymous Chinese shrimp sellers, are located at the crevices of Brazilian society only bolster the fictions of who belongs at the center.

Memórias póstumas first appeared as serial episodes in the *Revista Brazileira (Brazilian Review)*, a journal dedicated to literary, theatrical, and economic concerns. [42] Its contributors and editors were among the founding members of the Academia Brasileira de Letras. Machado de Assis was one of the founders of the organization and served as its first president in 1897.[43] Along with Machado, Salvador de Mendonça Castro helped found the Academia Brasileira de Letras, and he wrote about the Chinese question in the *Revista Brazileira*. In 1876, Salvador was appointed Brazilian consul general in the "United States of North America," as he called it, and charged with reporting on the conditions of the Chinese in California, which resulted in a related mission to China.[44] In 1880, Salvador published his book review of *Trabalhadores asiático (Asiatic Labor)*, by Antonio Maria de Miranda e Castro. This same edition of *Revista Brazileira* also published chapters of *Memórias póstumas* that were sandwiched between two essays regarding liberated slaves and Asian labor—"A classificação dos escravos libertados" (A classification of liberated slaves) and Salvador's review of *Asiatic Laborers* in which he created a caste difference between two different types of Chinese labor. He referred to skilled laborers as "chim" and used the term *coolie* to describe unskilled workers who had arrived in the United States as a result of illegal or deceptive means and were forced into indentured labor.

Machado de Assis wrote about the Chinese question across many genres, including *crónicas*, a hybrid genre that sits between factual news reporting and fiction. Its key characteristics are the author's subjective and often parodic social commentaries. Machado had a keenly observant eye and could show his readers the most mundane occurrence as a microcosm of a dire social issue, and do so with an irresistibly sharp wit and biting humor. He had a wide readership and contributed crónicas for a number of Rio's popular and critical print publications, including *Balas de Estalo (Shooting Bullets)*, a section that ran from 1883 to 1887 in the *Gazeta de Notícias*.[45] The title indicates its mission to use journalism as metaphorical gunshots to shake up, or awaken, readers' attention.[46] The inauguration of the popular and affordable press in Brazil began with the *Gazeta de Notícias,* first published on August 2, 1875. Print media became critical platforms for deliberating questions of citizenship. They also exposed the corrupt interests of agriculturalists and the aristocracy. However, under Brazil's climate of heavy censorship and persecution, pseudonyms were a necessity—as were literary techniques such as irony and satire—because they allowed authors to make bold critiques, using humor to expose society's paradoxes and incongruities. In fact, the founder of *Balas de Estalo*, Ferreira de Araújo, declared that pseudonyms served as a "protective shield" against possible retaliation toward writers.[47]

From 1864 to 1895, Machado published approximately twenty crónicas that addressed the issue of Chinese immigration to Brazil, in such influential publications as *Gazeta de Notícias, Notas Semanais*; *Balas de Estalo*; *Bons Dias!*; *A Semana*; and the crónicas "História de quinze dias" published in the *Ilustração Brasileira*.[48] In a series of crónicas for the *Gazeta de Notícias,* Machado wrote about the Cantonese comprador Tong Jing Xing's visit (or the Mandarin Tong King Sing, as he was called in Portuguese) to assess Brazil's conditions for Chinese labor migration. Machado pointed out the multiple actors involved in administering the circuits of coerced Chinese labor, among which were British, Portuguese, and Qing governments and private enterprises. Writing under the pseudonym Lélio, Machado de Assis fired a number of proverbial bullets at Tong's visit, portraying Brazilian anxiety surrounding the visit. On October 16, 1883, Lélio published a letter that he jokingly claimed had been written by the greedy and corrupt First-Class Mandarin, the Qing government official and merchant Tong King Sing himself. The letter expresses nothing decent about him. Lélio contends that he has decided to publish the letter in its original language in an effort to uphold its value:

> Viliki xaxi xali xaliman. Acalag ting-ting valixu. Upa Costa Braga relá minag katu Integridade abaxung kapi a ver navios. Lamarika ana bapa bung? Gogô xupitô? Nepa in pavé. Brasil desfalques latecatu. Inglese poeta, Shakespeare, kará: make money; upa lamaré in língua Brasil:—*mete dinheiro no bolso*. Vaia, Vaia, gapaling capita passa a unha simá teka laparika. Eting põe-se a panos; etang merú xilin. Mandarim de 1ª classe. TONG KING SING.[49]

Some parts are so "crude," he warns the reader, that it is better to let only those who understand Chinese be privy to its contents. The Mandarin's satirical letter is composed of a series of nonsensical words, with a few lines that are written in Portuguese and English. He is depicted as a gibberish-speaking thief who forcefully demands money: "Put your money in the bag."[50] However, Machado critiques more than Tong King Sing; rather, Tong's nonsensical speech gains meaning when we focus on the three phrases that do make sense. Machado wrote two phrases in English and one in Portuguese: "Shakespeare," "more money," and "mete dinheiro no bolso" (put your money in the bag). Machado was not only crafting a negative view in regard to the Qing official; he also made a specific reference to an icon of British high culture, only to then align it with a money-making imperative. It is not a coincidence that the Mandarin's speech accrues meaning through employing the British and Portuguese words for money. Through loans to the Portuguese and Brazilian empires and import regulations that favored British goods, Britain was a hegemonic power in Brazil during most of the nineteenth century.[51] The Mandarin's speech references Portuguese and British economic interests—as Machado bluntly put it, "more money" and "mete dinheiro no bolso."

In another satirical letter written for the *Gazeta de Notícias*, published on October 23, 1884, under the pen name "Webster," Machado addressed a memorandum to Sir Conde George Granville, the British minister of foreign affairs from 1880 to 1885:

> The first advantage of the chimpanzee is that it is much more frugal than the common Chinaman. The chimpanzee does not use clothes, shoes, or hats. He does not live with his eyes fixed on the home country. On the contrary, Sir John Sterling and his relatives affirm that they have managed to make the chimpanzees eat their dead.[52]

Imitating the tone and language that a minister customarily uses in diplomatic correspondence, Machado made an acerbic jab at the British pro-slavery official, whom he portrayed as attempting to persuade his readers about the benefits of using Chinese laborers as a substitute for black slavery. Webster's correspondence referred to Chinese laborers as a "chim-panzé," again rehashing wordplay between *chim* (Chinaman) and *chimpanzee*, and the racist idea of the Chinese as primates, as a lower species. While the slur conveyed a racial stance that seemed fiercely anti-Chinese, by parodying the

British minister, Machado makes it explicit that the desire for Chinese labor was not solely about China or the Chinese; it was also representative of the desire to establish new forms of racialized, subjugated labor settlements in Brazil. In this way, Machado/Webster's critique morphed from representing anti-Chinese sentiment to a condemnation of British experiments with the "coolie trade." Machado's letter makes political satire out of "humanitarian" concerns about Chinese laborers' well-being. His critique exposes how so-called moral arguments were thinly veiled disguises that obscured the goal of finding the most cost-effective solutions to maximizing the profits from cheap and unfree labor. He conveyed the idea that the coolie trade produced a labor regime that dehumanized Chinese laborers, treating them like primates who did not need human things like clothing or shoes. Moreover, he warned, their continued dehumanization would cause them to lose patriotic ties and any desire to return to China. British experiments in labor migration were so successful, Machado sardonically attested, that they managed to beat all sense of humanity from the workers, even to the point where they would become cannibalistic.

The analogy between submissive Chinese laborers and the weak Chinese state runs throughout many of Machado's crónicas that address the Chinese question. In Machado's parodic epistolary exchanges between Webster and Sir Conde George Granville and several of his other crónicas, he consistently asserts that Chinese workers are obedient and cheap, an ideal combination for the seigneurial class since they would work hard and not rebel against unfair labor treatment. Moreover, China would not intervene in any mistreatment of them because it was too weak to protect its citizens overseas. Underlying the recurring representation of the victimized Chinese laborer was the message that the advantages of Chinese labor were indeed also disadvantages that would perpetuate Brazil's status as a peripheral economic state under the thumb of British hegemony. While Brazil's elite agriculturalist class would reap large financial benefits, society at large would suffer, existing only as a monoculture, a raw-product export market.

In a crónica published on September 18, 1892, Machado began from what he assumed was his readers' common understanding of China, aiming to educate them about their incorrect perceptions. He contends that the Orient is not an exotic land of porcelain, mandarins, teas, silks, and parasols—that Orient does not exist. In fact, that belief obscures the detrimental effect that actual Chinese immigration would have on Brazil:

"China is not just the land of porcelain, fans, tea, silk, mandarins, and para-sols made of paper. No, China demands that we plant coffee while it sits at home."[53] He asserted that as long as it relied on the import of Chinese labor, Brazil would not be able to transition out of its colonial state. In a harsh rebuff of Chinese settlement and assimilation, Machado asks his readers how they will be able to communicate with the chim, whose Chinese name sounded more like a sneeze than a pronoun. Indeed, he asks, "What other human *animal* is comparable to the Chinaman?"[54]

China is again a nonsolution in Machado's short theatrical piece *Don't Consult the Doctor* (1896). By using the theme of unrequited love, Machado presents his reservations about looking to China for any kind of answer to Brazil's domestic problems. In the work, D. Leocádia, a self-proclaimed doctor of moral illness, specializes in curing unrequited love.[55] To cure love-sick patients, she advises them to voyage to foreign places. In one extreme case, the character Cavalcante, whose love interest is the married daughter of a Peruvian diplomat, decides to become a friar and enter the cloisters be-cause he cannot be with his beloved. However, D. Leocádia convinces him that he would not forget his love object—he would instead obsess over her in his solitude; thus, the doctor prescribes that he become a missionary to China. D. Leocádia asserts that while China is a place full of infidels, it is still better than the confining walls of a convent, which are more "dangerous than the eyes of the Chinese."[56] The remedy is "bitter"; he must go to China for ten years, after which time he will be cured of the "devil." The characters in Machado's play discuss the amount of time it will take for Cavalcante to be cured—perhaps he will spend two, three, four, but no more than fifteen years in China. Finally, Calvancante finds another lovesick patient, D. Car-lota, who has also suffered unrequited love. Together, they decide the solu-tion to their problems is not in China but rather in Brazil.

Machado's writing about the Chinese question added layers of meaning to the Sinophobic rhetoric circulating around the world. His literary shots across the bow about the so-called chim belonged to the same economy of representation that formed part of Brazil's abolitionist vocabulary. Macha-do's references to China, Chinese culture, and Chinese laborers illuminate how he not only condemned slavery but also keenly and cynically showed that the culture of slavery, the ideological structure of paternalism, scientific racism, and Social Darwinism, would transfer successively and damagingly into Brazil's transition to a republican state. Moreover, for Machado, the potential for a substitution of yellow for black slavery warranted a pessimistic view on the human condition, whereby liberty signaled a passage to new forms of corruption and unfreedom.

Circumoceanic Cuba Brazil

Geographically distant yet connected by circumoceanic memory, Cuba and Brazil shared a common path forward with gradual emancipation laws before each achieved full abolition in 1886 and 1888, respectively. The Free Womb Law passed in Cuba in 1870, one year before a similar law passed in Brazil, prompting agriculturalists and elites to look to China for laborers to replace African slaves. Between 1847 and 1874, approximately 125,000 Chinese indentured or contract laborers were sent to Cuba.[57] Chinese contract laborers were not legally slaves due to the consensual nature of the contract agreements they had signed, which included a limitation period; nevertheless, when they arrived in Cuba, they were treated in the same manner as slaves.[58] Chinese men were sold on auction blocks that were former slave markets, their queues were cut, and their new owners renamed them—a symbolic act that further severed ties to ancestry and homeland.[59] The exploitative conditions that met Chinese laborers ushered in a new era of indentured, slavelike contract labor, and the ambiguous status of Chinese immigrants in Cuba brought forth new questions regarding the status of China's overseas citizens.

By 1856, after the British had banned the coolie trade from their ports in China, Chinese laborers began to depart in large number from Portuguese Macau. From 1872 to 1874, Ambassador Eça de Queiroz, on behalf of Portugal, went on a mission to Cuba to assess the conditions of Chinese laborers and rumors that the "yellow trade," as it had come to be known, was consigning to Chinese men a fate similar to that of enslaved Africans. In addition to having a long career as a celebrated author, Eça de Queiroz served as a diplomat for the Portuguese government for nearly twenty-eight years, traveling to Cuba, Egypt, France, England, and the United States, among other places. His diplomatic correspondences from Cuba shed a geopolitical perspective on his writings about Chinese labor as a bad solution for Brazil, which he wrote adamantly against and published in some of Rio de Janeiro's most widely read journals.

By the time Eça arrived in Cuba in December 1872, Chinese laborers numbered more than 100,000. His appointment to Cuba coincided with the visit of Chinese ambassador Chen Lanpin, for whom he served as an informant among the diplomatic corps in Havana.[60] However, he had his own motives for being there. Eça's humanitarian views about the exploitative labor conditions of the Chinese in Cuba, José Suarez argues, expressed a "*de facto* colonial" attitude that was rooted in the ideology of European superiority over subjugated colonized people.[61] Humanitarian claims implicitly allowed Eça to assert the narrative of the white man's burden: European liberation of subjugated people vis-à-vis new modes of imperialist domination.[62]

Eça's mission to Cuba was thus invested in asserting Portuguese claims over Chinese emigrants from Macau as Portuguese subjects, which would then enable Portugal to establish an economic stronghold in Cuba via the Chinese Portuguese laborers from Macau. Eça referred to the Chinese in a variety of ambiguous and contradicting ways. They were colonialists yet they were also coolies. He also used terms like *asiático, china, chim,* and *chinês* (respectively, Asiatic, China, Chinaman, Chinese). By consistently emphasizing the workers' ambiguous status, he argued for Portugal to assert a claim over the laborers and thus gain access to Cuba's sugar industry.

In a letter written to Andrade Corvo, minister of foreign affairs, on December 29, 1872, Eça made clear that the treatment of Chinese emigrants from Macau in Havana was in fact tied to colonial rivalries among such powers as England, France, the United States, Spain, and Portugal:

> Recent opposition taken against Chinese emigration has, undoubtedly, incited much interest. Philanthropy and charity are secondary influences. . . . England has been inciting opinion against Chinese emigration. This was inspired by the same colonial influences that caused it to take a decidedly hostile attitude against the traffic of Negros, which led it to oppose the whole operation that gives Cuba more numerous and cheap laborers than any of the other tropical colonies.[63]

Realizing Portuguese economic self-interest via Chinese laborers may explain why Eça repeatedly—and incorrectly—characterized Chinese emigrants from Macau as *undocumented* or *unclassifiable*, even while many were still under willingly signed labor contracts with planters. In his assessment over Chinese labor conditions, Eça contended that because many of the

Chinese entered into contractual agreements, the legal status of Chinese laborers was essentially bound to their relationship to a contract; a laborer without a contract therefore would be a laborer without political protection even though many had been lured. His discussion about the protection of the Chinese in Cuba was focused on which government could claim them as subjects. Those who had arrived prior to 1861, explained Eça, were allowed to request foreign identity cards.[64] When Eça arrived in Cuba in the 1870s, many Chinese laborers were still under eight-year or shorter contracts. Some had managed to acquire residency papers and identification cards, and a few were naturalized as Spanish citizens since Spain still administered Cuba as a colony at that time.[65]

However, the Central Commission for Colonization, made up of the island's richest landowners, interminably prolonged the process of granting foreign identity cards.[66] In essence, Eça explained, plantation owners profited greatly from denying civil and social rights to the Chinese.[67] Wealthy agriculturalists used the laborers' ambiguous legal status as a strategy to deny them access to full protection under the law, which therefore allowed the agriculturalists to exploit laborers and pay meager to no wages.

Eça recommended the Portuguese government grant Chinese laborers protection by giving them naturalization papers. If the Chinese gained "free agency" or naturalization, as was already happening with the Chinese who had become Spanish citizens, Eça asserted, the "subtle and skillful Chinese race" would "take large domain of the Island's industries."[68] Granting Portuguese citizenship to Chinese emigrants who passed through Macau would have enabled Portugal to secure a piece of Cuban industry and agriculture vis-à-vis the "Chinese race."[69]

He goes on to refer to the naturalized and documented Chinese as "colonialists" who would be well positioned to extract Cuban wealth. Thus, his proposal for naturalizing and claiming protection over the Chinese was also a proposal for measures that Portugal could take to gain a stronghold in Cuba:

> There are over a hundred thousand Asians that the Emigration Regulation of the port of Macau today explicitly places under the protection of the Portuguese Consulate. If Your Excellency takes into consideration that this high number of colonialists is one of the most vital forces of agriculture on this Island, and that this number will grow due to the conditions of this country that yield all of its labor to imported arms. Then the subtle and

skillful Chinese race may, in having free agency, take large domain of the Island's industries—Your Excellency will understand the importance of this consulate, as it can register Portuguese nationality to a hundred-thousand souls: it is therefore urgent that the Government of Your Majesty attend to the living conditions of this colonial population.[70]

Shortly after his arrival in Cuba, Eça discovered that Cuba and China refused to recognize Portugal's claims over the Chinese, thereby rendering his mission useless. Neither the Spanish administration in Cuba nor the Qing administration in Macau would recognize Portugal's declaration that naturalization papers would be awarded. This demonstrates a significant moment in international relations and international law, in which Spain and China, working for their own respective economic interests, were in alignment by denying Portuguese claims over the Chinese in Cuba. The Cuban administration, operating under the auspices of Madrid, did not recognize the Portuguese claims over Chinese emigrants via Macau; it only recognized Portugal's limited role in administering port police operations. The Qing officials who were sent to Cuba to compile the Cuban Commission Report for the purpose of gathering evidence about the mistreatment of Chinese laborers also challenged Portuguese sovereignty in Macau, claiming that Chinese emigrants from Macau were under Chinese, not Portuguese, protection.[71] Significantly, Portugal is left off the list of countries that participated in the Cuban Commission Report, a gesture that, arguably, may have been politically calibrated to negate Portuguese humanitarian and political claims over the Chinese in Cuba.

Since Eça's diplomatic role granted him international visibility, his views about Chinese labor reached a wide public in Brazil, Portugal, and other parts of the hemispheric Americas and Europe via print media, thus demonstrating how newspapers were shaping national imaginaries within a geopolitical context. Between 1880 and 1897, Eça wrote a number of crónicas for the Rio de Janeiro–based *Gazeta de Notícias*, including *Notas Contemporâneas, Colaboração Européia, Ecos de Paris, Cartas Familiares de Paris, Bilhetes d'aquém-mar,* and *Bilhetes de Paris*. In December 1894, Eça wrote "Chinezes e Japonezes" ("The Chinese and Japanese") for the *Gazeta de Notícias*. The piece begins by giving the reader a general history of China and Japan and the countries' respective relationships to Europe. Eça addresses popular Orientalist notions about China and Japan, and his tone is didactic and corrective. In his experience, his readers had a severely skewed idea of Asia because of European Orientalism. Their indulgence in stories about the exotic Orient as a distraction or a bourgeois pastime had created terrible misconceptions. For their part, Europeans regarded China and Japan as underdeveloped countries: China lacked railroads, gas, and electricity; Japan had only imitated European innovations. Eça urges his readers in Brazil not to follow Europe's mistaken underestimation of China and Japan. Rather, readers need to see the capabilities and savvy of two powerful Asian countries with expansion goals. Eça argued that the Chinese held on tightly to tradition, while in contrast, Japanese society transformed almost overnight into an imitation of Western civilization. Eça argued that Europeans had missed the point that these societies were highly civilized and powerful, which he evinced by discussing their long histories, literary traditions, and social institutions. At first, it seems as though Eça has used the rhetorical strategy of revealing stereotypes to dispel them; in actuality, his essay does the opposite: he debunks European Orientalism's tropes only to replace them with Yellow Peril ideas that painted the Chinese and Japanese as economic and military threats to the West.

Literary critique on Eça's essay about China and Japan has largely ignored his linguistic dehumanization tactics and use of violent metaphors in relation to Asians. To prepare the rhetorical logic for his argument, Eça made use of the globally circulating stereotypes that fabricated the Chinese as creatures that threatened to pollute the moral fabric of republicanism and free labor. He stated, "China has a population of four hundred million men (nearly one-third of humanity!); they are all extremely intelligent, an army of ants, with persistence and tenacity only comparable to bull-dogs."[72] They were "yellow rats" with "slanted eyes," "long tails," and "nails three inches long."[73] Eça contended that the Chinese believed themselves to be superior to Europeans, who, according to him, they held in bitter contempt for having violently forced China into trade agreements—first through opium and then the Opium Wars, when China refused to acknowledge the drug trafficking within its borders. Simply put, the Chinese considered Europeans inferior. He states, "The Chinese have a tremendous disdain for the European, and a conviction that he is in all points intellectually, morally, and socially superior, and should be his master."[74] For Eça, since the Chinese did not have a positive regard for European civilization, they would not be good candidates for Brazilian nation building because they posed a threat to whiteness. Chinese laborers were loyal to Chinese civilization; they would work for a few years in Brazil and then take the wealth back to China.

Because he is aware of Brazil's desire to turn to Chinese labor, Eça warns the Brazilian public of their ignorant view toward China and Japan. Chinese laborers pose political and social dangers, which, he claims, he has seen firsthand in Cuba. Eça asserts that Chinese labor would not only give China an economic foothold but also allow for China to build a new civilization in Brazil. Japanese immigration would be no better, since Japan poses a serious military and cultural threat to Western civilization. For Eça, Chinese and Japanese immigration would mean the extension of Chinese or Japanese political and economic power to wherever their overseas nationals settled.

Eça wrote that his readership's Orientalist imaginary of Japan could be broken down into one of two images: the samurai who represented the pre-Meiji past and the new Japanese soldier of the Meiji Restoration, depicted as wearing a pastiche of European military gear that is too big for him. The ridiculous image of the Japanese soldier, Eça emphasized, represented the readers' ignorant perceptions about expanding Japanese militarism. Japan was in fact militarizing, he asserted, and this needed to be treated seriously. Japan had acquired European military and scientific technology and established an alliance with Europe, which constituted part of a much larger military strategy to expand throughout Asia. By sharing its military intelligence, Europe had positioned Japan to become an Asian superpower:

> The cunning and forceful civilization of the "European devils" had converted a great Asian power, communicating to them its strategies, in order for the "Middle Kingdom" not to surpass the "Empire of the Rising Sun," once it was unfortunately proven that the Lebel rifle kills better than the elegant and venerable arrows of their grandfathers.[75]

Eça perpetuated Yellow Peril tropes in his writings about the Chinese and Japanese as a potential threat to Western civilization via militaristic, economic, and cultural mechanisms. In his view, these dangers manifested differently, however. Japan needed to be monitored due to its increasing military power, while China did not pose a military threat. The Chinese were dangerous because they could passively invade. Again likening Chinese laborers to an ant colony, Eça writes, "They will come, not to destroy, but to work. And this is the invasion that will endanger our old world— the Chinese laborer invades like a silent ant colony."[76] In conclusion, Eça proposes that Japan and China be contained in different ways due to the different kinds of threats each country and its citizens posed:

> For the European, the Chinese is still a yellow rat with slanted eyes, a long tail, three-inch nails—antiquated, childish, and full of outdated manias, exhaling sandalwood and opium, and eating large mountains of rice with two little sticks and spending their lives amid paper lanterns, bowing in reverence. And the Japanese are still for us skinny beings with shaved heads, two enormous swords secured at the waist. Jovial, frivolous, running and fanning themselves, whiling away empty hours by spending time at the tea gardens and clearing houses made of paper screens and chrysanthemum in order to sit cross-legged on a mat and perform ritual suicide. To both are attributed the inherited ability to make porcelain and silk.[77]

In a final irony-laden description, the author warned that Chinese immigrants would transform Brazil into China in a very short time. Chinese settlers would overpopulate Brazilian society, inevitably transforming it into an immense Chinatown, with markers of all the negative globally circulating "coolie race" stereotypes. Reiterating anti-Chinese rhetoric of hyper-Chinese virility and overpopulation, Eça contended that the large number of Chinese immigrants would impede the success of European immigration from countries such as Portugal, Italy, and Germany, and ultimately obstruct Brazil's project of whitening. Furthermore, in the shadows of Brazilian society, Chinese immigrants would organize crime and traffic drugs. Chinese traditions would overtake Brazilian ones, and Chinese-run businesses would crush all competition, devouring Brazil until everything and everyone became Chinese:

> But enough with the Chinese! You, friends, here in Brazil, it seems that you wish for them to plant and harvest coffee. You shall be inundated, submerged. One hundred will come, then a hundred thousand. In ten years, São Paulo and Rio will have large Chinatowns, with signboards mottled in red and black, strings of paper lanterns, infestations of opium dens, all sorts of secret associations, an immense force growing in the shadows, and Chinese dress and queues, incessantly seething. But you will have Chinese cooks, Chinese laundries . . . All the other colonies, Portuguese, Italian, German, will be subtly and sensibly pushed back to their land of origin— and all of Brazil, in twenty years, will be Chinese.[78]

The threat that Brazil would become Chinese recalls the circulation of the recurring characterization of the *Brazil-chim* (Brazil-Chinaman) mentioned in previous chapters. The Brazil-chim was regarded as the negative cultural mixing and degenerate offspring of Brazilians and the Chinese. The ideology of paternalism and scientific racism consumed Eça's writings. Eça, like his literati contemporaries, advanced the project of racial whitening at the crossroads of politicohistorical and aesthetic forms.

FIVE

Between Diplomacy and Fiction

Eça de Queiroz, Aluísio Azevedo, and Luis Guimarães Filho were celebrated authors and highly regarded diplomats during the late nineteenth and
early twentieth centuries. Each wrote fiction and nonfiction about China
and Japan during the rise of diplomatic relations among Brazil, China, and
Japan. All three served as diplomats in missions focused on immigration
and military interests at the center of the triangular relationship between
the three countries. Their diplomatic missions had a great impact on their
fictional writings wherein they used fiction to mediate larger debates about
how Sino-Japanese conflicts might affect the Brazilian nation, constituting
what literary scholar Timothy Hampton calls "diplomatic poetics," which
refers to diplomacy's authority as shaped by representation, whereby diplomatic authority is "mere representation and where representation must
claim whatever authority it can garner through negotiation instead of violence."[1] The aim of diplomatic poetics is to mediate, negotiate, and arbitrate
an alternative to the escalation of violence by prioritizing the function of
representation. This prioritization in turn creates a useful lens for examining
the intersection of diplomacy and fiction, politicohistorical text and aesthetic text. Diplomatic representations affect the form that new fictions take
on or experiment with, and poetic possibilities may enable new imaginaries
to emerge within the political.

The diplomat-authors delivered new depictions of Chinese and Japanese migrants to challenge existing preconceptions that governed ways of
seeing and reacting to Asians. Their literary production shows how novels,

as much as nonfiction essays, circulated political ideas and swayed public opinion about Asia and Asians. Racial representations of Chinese and Japanese people and culture gained new meaning through discussions about the morality of a burgeoning bourgeoisie, whose desire for luxurious status symbols drove ongoing colonialist endeavors. These diplomat-authors also mediated international relations through literature; in particular, they wrote about the effects that Sino-Japanese conflicts would have on Brazilian relations with China and Japan. They closely monitored proletarian uprisings in China, asking whether similar plebian rebellions would occur among Chinese migrants working under Brazil's unfree labor conditions.[2]

As a prominent author and public servant, Eça de Queiroz often entertained his highly influential friends in his home. During the receptions he held, Eça would recite familiar theatrical verses and dress in a *cabaia de mandarim* (a late Qing dynasty–era men's dress; see Figure 5.1).[3] In this figure, a black-and-white photograph taken circa 1893, Eça is simultaneously an emblematic Portuguese writer and diplomat, but his pose for the camera is that of a Qing dynasty official wearing a *changshan*, the dress of a mandarin. Eça's posing body symbolizes his roles as diplomat and fiction writer. His diplomatic posing body performs the convergence of nation and culture.[4] The effect of Eça's mandarin pose for the camera archives a representation of Chineseness that arrests a particular viewing subject and demands attention.[5] The photograph presents an "inevitable theatrical projection" wherein "posing is the representation of invisibility."[6] This pose references the idea of a mandarin, whose right-hand fingers flitter in the air while his left hand holds a book. Depending on the viewer's reception of the pose, the effeminate and pretentious hand gestures transmit the image of a cultured man of the Qing gentry, as well as a mockery of that same view.

Eça's pose, as well as his fictional writings on China and the Chinese, merges the fields of representation that exist between diplomacy and fiction; Chineseness is the spectacle that projects a political image and an imaginative fiction. His writings are a mediatory space in which he negotiates the place of China and Chinese immigrants within the Brazilian imaginary to achieve certain political and economic ends. China is not only the object of Orientalist representation, in which the West produces the idea of the East. Representations of China and the Chinese function as both sociohistorical and aesthetic texts that produce Chineseness with which to arbitrate geopolitical and economic situations.

FIGURE 5.1. Eça de Queiroz wearing a Qing dynasty–style changshan (c. 1893),
black and white photographic print. Source: Biblioteca Nacional, Lisbon, Portugal.

Eça's consul mission to Havana, Cuba, from 1872 to 1874 was directly concerned with investigating the situation of Chinese contract laborers there.[7] Eça's assignment to Havana had a great impact on the development of his literary realism. Indeed, he completed a short story, his first piece of realism, "Singularidades de uma rapariga loira" ("Peculiarities of a Blonde-Haired Girl"), during his diplomatic trip to Cuba, where he "exchanged mists, vultures and forests for harsh reality."[8] Eça first published the story in the *Diário de Notícias* on January 22, 1874.

"Singularidades" begins at a lodging house in the vinho verde–producing province of Minho in northern Portugal when the narrator meets Macário, a stranger with piercing black eyes and yellowish skin. The two strike up a friendship, and soon enough Macário confides in him a distasteful story about his romance with Luísa, "a light-skinned, blonde-haired girl, holding a Chinese fan."[9] The Chinese fan functions as a symbol of the desire for imperialist endeavors and colonial wealth. Eça uses symbols of the trade activity from European colonies, like ivory, feathers, and gold, to portray the decadent desire of Portugal's bourgeois class to accumulate property that may be acquired only through deception and thievery. These desires and interests, the novel moralistically teaches, are unsustainable and destructive to domestic Portuguese relationships and conditions. Luísa and Macário are both lured by fetish objects—material goods brought to Europe from colonies around the world via transoceanic voyages. Luísa will stop at nothing to obtain these fetish objects, going so far as to shoplift and destroy her engagement to Mácario. The short story asks us to reflect on Luísa's "peculiarities," which is not to say simply that her underhandedness is a quirky trait, but her actions direct us to reflect on the immoral character of colonial projects. At first, Macário overlooks her acts of thievery, and his infatuation with her prevents him from seeing the reality of her decadent behavior, which implicates him as an accomplice every time he neglects to speak out against her actions.

Eça's first piece of realism functions in a way that is comparable to Machado de Assis's formalistic exploration of monotony and pessimism, discussed earlier, in which tedium and distraction structure the plot. Macário's monotonous life leads him to find entertainment by watching his neighbors and imagining stories about them. The fictions he constructs become so real to him that they prevent him from realizing that those fabrications are taking advantage of him. One day, he notices a lovely young woman, Luísa, holding a Chinese fan made of a literal and figurative pastiche of exotic luxury items. Lace, ivory, and feathers initially attract Macário's attention. He conjures an elaborate daydream that Luísa, with her porcelain skin and blonde hair, is the daughter of an Englishman who had acquired the Chinese fan from his global travels:

> Only in the afternoons would the curtain wrinkle back, the window open, and she, placing a pillow on the windowsill, would lean there, delicate and fresh, fanning herself. The fan worried Macário: it was a round Chinese fan made from white silk, embroidered with scarlet dragons edged with blue feathers fine and tremulous as down; the handle was made of ivory inlaid with mother-of-pearl in the beautiful Persian style, and from which hung two golden tassels. It was a magnificent fan, and it was unexpected to see it in the hands of a plebeian girl dressed in muslin. But as she was blonde and her mother from southern Europe, Macário, with the intuitive interpretive skills of love, said to his curiosity: "She must be the daughter of an Englishman." The English go to China, Persia, Hormuz, Australia, and return loaded with jewels and exotic luxuries such as that; not even Macário knew why that mandarin fan worried him so, but as he told me—"it sparked his curiosity."[10]

While Macário is wary of the "mandarin's fan," which seems out of place in Luísa's humble hands, he decides that her blonde hair and light skin are enough to justify her possession of the luxury object. Macário attributes Luísa's wealth to her biological features and subtly echoes the predominant nineteenth-century racist eugenic discourse that linked intellectual, moral, and class differences to biological attributes such as skin color. This assumption gives rise to three moments of great self-deception, each unraveling Macário's delusion that whiteness is synonymous with the ideal bourgeois lifestyle. In each example, a theft occurs, but Macário is too distracted with the fantasy of Luísa to see the actuality of her actions.

In the first self-deception, Luísa enters the textile showroom where Macário works to shop for scarves from India. Infatuated and distracted by Luísa's visit, Macário does not notice the storehouse clerks declare that a box of Indian scarves has gone missing.[11] The second instance of theft occurs at the home of the rich bookkeeper who lives on Rua dos Calafates. There, Macário plays a game; however, in retelling the events of that evening to the stranger in the lodging house in Minho, he "could not remember what he played on that radiant night."[12] The mysterious game was likely a gambling game that Macário was not very good at, since after the game, he had to pay his debts to a gentleman from Malta. While he spins the coin that will pay for his losses, Luísa watches it intently:

> Luísa smiled as she watched it spin and spin, and it seemed to Macário that all of heaven, all purity, all the goodness of flowers and the chastity of stars were held in that bright, distracted, spiritual smile comparable to an archangel, which followed the spinning, spinning, spin of the new piece of gold. But, suddenly, the coin rolled to the edge of the table, fell to one side onto Luísa's lap, and disappeared without so much as making a metal clink onto the wooden floor.[13]

Luísa grabs a corner of her dress at the exact moment that the piece of gold falls from the table. Macário sees this but soon enough dismisses the incident when Luísa distracts him with a kiss, which seals a nuptial promise. He is too enamored of the idea of Luísa to accept that she palmed something that is not hers. Instead, he conjures up dreams of their bourgeois future together. To fulfill those fantasies, Macário must earn the money needed to purchase Luísa's dowry, filling her closet with a wardrobe of textiles and silks from China and India and giving her goods that symbolize the ideal European bourgeois lifestyle.

During the publication of the short story, Portugal was struggling with Britain to keep control of its colonies in Africa. Furthermore, the British held a trade monopoly in Brazil, exercising hegemony over monarchic Brazil's economy. Eça's first piece of realism merges the fields of representation between international relations and fiction. To obtain exquisite goods like the Chinese fan that he could never attain from working as a clerk in Lisbon, Macário travels to the Portuguese colony Cabo Verde, where he endures the brutality of plantation work. Off the West African coast, in the middle Atlantic volcanic archipelago, he suffers in a manner likened with enslavement:

> The next day Macário departed. He experienced the difficult voyages of hostile waters, the monotony of nausea in a suffocating cabin, the harsh colonial suns, the tyrannical brutality of rich plantation owners, the weight of humiliating burdens, the lacerations of absence, journeys into the dark backlands, and the melancholy of caravans that travel for days on end, alongside violent nights and tranquil rivers that exhale death. He returned.[14]

Mácario returns to Lisbon after his bitter sojourn in Cabo Verde, where his body and the grueling labor it could produce were demanded by the excesses of slave-driving, tyrannical agriculturalists. His actions as a colonialist became part of death's cycle. At the end of this tour of duty, he had served the colonial project and acquired enough wealth to secure his desired domestic conditions, but at what cost?

After Macário returns with his newfound wealth, he takes Luísa to choose an engagement ring. At the jewelry store, Luísa tries on a number of rings and settles on one that is too big for her finger. The store clerk gladly offers a readjustment and asks the couple to retrieve the ring at a later date. As they begin to leave, the attendant forcefully requests that they pay for another ring, which Luísa had taken without Macário's knowledge. Caught red-handed, she blushingly turns over the stolen ring. To avoid further embarrassment, Macário pays for the second ring, attributing the situation to a temporary distraction, a misunderstanding. In this third instance, though, Macário no longer rejects his own obliviousness and finally awakens to the truth. He confronts Luísa about her immoral behavior, calls her a thief, and sends her away, never to be heard from again. Eça's diplomatic poetics illustrate that while Portuguese colonialist endeavors sustain the decadence of bourgeois social rituals, ultimately the protagonist (and readers) have the choice to reject stolen wealth and the lifestyle that demands it.

Elsewhere in Eça's fiction, for instance, in the novella *O Mandarim* (1880), he engages moral philosophy with diplomatic poetics. The theme of the work again confronts his readers with ethical choices that must be made when colonialism and liberalism have merged: How far will one go to restrict the liberty of another to accumulate property, thus wealth? The protagonist of the novella, Teodoro, takes the reader on a journey into the interconnected networks of international trade, which intertwines the mores of European bourgeois decadence with the destruction of distant societies. Teodoro is a scribe at the Ministry for Internal Affairs and Education in Portugal who lives a simple and humble life, but he dreams of luxurious dinners and champagne at fancy hotels. One day, he is confronted with the option to ring a bell that will kill a mandarin in China; in return, he will receive the fortune of his dreams. Eça structures the plot based on an ethical dilemma that first appeared in Adam Smith's *Theory of Moral Sentiments* where Smith questioned if spatial distance determines the limits of one's moral responsibility.[15] Smith posited that a man in Europe might feel dreadful at hearing the news of a devastating earthquake in China, but would soon enough return to his normal business. Smith then posed an ethical dilemma that would reappear across numerous works for centuries to come: What if a man were to learn that he will lose his finger, but he could save it by sacrificing the lives of millions "he had never seen"?[16] Smith's ethical dilemma depends on constructing the Chinese Other as the hypothetical sacrifice. As Eric Hayot notes, by the nineteenth century, Smith's ethical inquiry, reliant on a hypothetical dispensable mandarin, appeared so frequently that the phrase "to kill the mandarin" earned a place in the *Littré* dictionary of 1874 to express commiting "an evil action in the hope that it will remain unknown."[17]

Eça engages the ethical conjecture "to kill a mandarin" to structure *O Mandarim*'s plot and develops a scenario in which, without hesitation, Teodoro rings the bell and indirectly kills a mandarin, a stranger in China. Teodoro is suddenly rich and famous, making headlines in contemporaneous journals that circulated in Portugal during the novella's publication. By naming these journals—periodicals such as *Gazeta das Locais* and *Figaro,* as well as the full-color foreign illustrated magazine, the *Illustration Française*—Eça creates an intersection between fiction and documentary planes of representation.

Teodoro is filled with guilt over his actions that killed someone on the other side of the world. The sense of culpability causes him to fall into a delusional state in which he sees apparitions of the "potbellied figure of the Mandarin" everywhere.[18] Monica Simas interprets the mandarin as a mirror that reflects the seduction of riches and power. The specter of the murdered mandarin haunts not only Teodoro, but the memory of Lisbon.[19] The ghosts of imperial exploits and their human costs haunt the material and symbolic ruins of memory. To atone for his immoral act, he decides to travel to China and turn over his newly acquired fortune to the mandarin's relatives.

A large portion of the novella is set in China, allowing *O Mandarim* to address the lack of economic and political infrastructure in China that contributed to the coolie trade. Teodoro arrives in China, but it is hardly the land of splendor he had anticipated. He describes the sight of "green and swollen corpses of beggars."[20] The full novella was published in 1884 but first appeared in serial form in the journal *Diário de Portugal* in 1880, six years after Eça's diplomatic mission to Havana. Eça spent his time in Cuba writing adamantly against the kinds of enslaved coolie labor that emerged from the practice of using unjust contracts, but some of his accounts were incorrect and he was unable to see Chinese laborers as more than wretched souls in need of liberation.[21] It is not surprising, then, that *O Mandarim*'s narrator also incorrectly uses the term *coolie* to describe a class of marginalized people in China. The discourse surrounding the "coolie race" emerged outside China, and the Chinese never referred to themselves that way.[22]

The narrator makes five fleeting references to coolies in the novella. Coolies receive no character development; instead, their purpose is solely to perform acts of servitude and blend into the background. At times, they appear among a list of mundane objects, as part of a list of possessions: "The next day I departed for Tien-Hó with my respectful interpreter Sá-Tó, a long caravan of carts, two Cossacks, and the rabble of coolies."[23] In other moments, they are an element that provides comfort by literally carrying the aristocracy on their backs. They have no interiority, no narrative consciousness; instead, they are inferior subjects, akin to wallpaper, relegated to the backdrop of a scene: "Then along comes a mandarin's sedan chair carried by coolies dressed all in blue, their queues flying, trotting along at a panting pace to the offices of the State."[24] The text serves as an instrument that both testifies to the existence of deep class stratifications and entrenched class hierarchy in China. In denying narrative interiority to this class of laborers and emphasizing a caricature, these depictions also affirm anti-Chinese sentiment, circulating around the globe at this time, that took shape in derogatory representations of the Chinese as a "coolie race."

The narrator expresses a vision that is critical of China by depicting the country in abject poverty, with lice-ridden children and beggars lying among piles of rags.[25] The 1927 edition of Eça's *O Mandarim* includes illustrations by Rachel Roque Gameiro, which visually render the narrator's description of poverty in China. Gameiro's illustration of impoverishment in China depicts the social and hierarchical stratification of Chinese society, juxtaposing starvation with extreme wealth (Figure 5.2). The image frames a group of people living in the streets in dire poverty, including an emaciated woman breastfeeding an equally gaunt baby. The illustration depicts a sensationalized scene of abject poverty. They are so poor that they do not even have clothes, and they huddle together for warmth. Some appear to be near death, while others sit among rags and gnaw on what appear to be bones. Behind the misery, people visit spectacular monuments that attest

FIGURE 5.2. "Impoverishment in China," by Rachel Roque Gameiro. Source: Eça de Queiroz, *O Mandarim* with illustrations by Rachel Roque Gameiro (Porto: Livraria Chardron, 1927): 69.

to China's great dynastic past, like the Hall of Prayer for Good Harvests located in the Temple of Heaven, a complex of religious buildings in Beijing. However, in Eça's China, two coolies pass in front of the temple, carrying a mandarin who is seated in a sedan chair and pays no attention to the corpse-like bodies surrounding him.

While in China, Teodoro decides that it would be proper for him to dress as a mandarin, a word that he learns does not actually exist in Chinese but comes from the Portuguese verb, to command or order, *mandar.*[26] Upon putting on the clothing of the "wealthy Chinaman of the literate classes," the mandarin's robes infuse him with "Chinese ideas and instincts—a love for meticulous ceremonies, a bureaucratic respect for formulations, a shrewd learned skepticism; and an abject terror of the emperor, a hatred of foreigners, a devotion to ancestral worship, a fanatic about tradition, and a taste for sweets."[27] Teodoro's mysterious transformation into a mandarin, depicted as having as much love for tradition as xenophobia, repeats the abolitionist rhetoric circulating widely in Brazil with the warning that Chineseness was a biological and cultural contagion—the Chinese would turn Brazil into a degenerate hybrid Brazil-China. In Eça's version, Teodoro's mysterious transformation facilitated a criticism of the decadence of Portuguese society and its dependence on colonial riches, but it also returns the gaze to the political and economic devastation occurring in China that was provoking emigration to the Americas. The imaginary of Chineseness in Eça's diplomatic poses and poetics negotiated a place for China in the Portuguese and Brazilian literary and national imaginary. In the context of Brazilian debates over Chinese immigration, Eça's body of work about China acts as a mode of diplomatic poetics that attempted to divest Brazil from accepting Chinese emigrants from this devastated China, spreading uncontainable Chineseness.

In 1897, seven years after Aluísio Azevedo published his highly successful novel, *O Cortiço* (*The Slum*)—a scathing and ironic assessment of rapid urbanization, immigration, and housing inequality in postslavery Rio de Janeiro—he visited Japan amid heated debates over the merits of Chinese versus Japanese immigrants. Brazilian politicians and elites favored Japanese immigration due to Japan's successes in the Sino-Japanese and Russo-Japanese wars, which marked its rise as an Asian superpower. Thus, Japanese agricultural immigration to Brazil represented a new alliance between Brazil and a powerful military and economic power.

Diplomat and author Aluísio Azevedo also wrote within the representational field where diplomacy and fiction converge, configuring knowledge about Japan for the interest of mediation and negotiation. The Treaty of Friendship, Commerce, and Navigation between Japan and Brazil began an official economic alliance. Two years after the treaty was signed on November 5, 1895, in Paris by Brazilian and Japanese plenipotentiaries, Azevedo embarked on a diplomatic mission to Yokohama, Japan, that lasted from 1897 to 1899. One of Azevedo's duties in Japan was serving in the role of an immigration agent or auxiliary, with the dual objectives of considering Japan as a source of inexpensive labor for Brazil's postslavery economy and examining the prospects for opening trade in agriculture.[28] As vice consul for Brazil, Azevedo's mission marked the beginning of the negotiations that led to Japanese immigration to Brazil in 1908. As a diplomat, his mission was tied to Brazilian government objectives and gaining intelligence about Japanese history and culture, which was in turn connected to questions of how Japanese settlement would affect Brazilian society.

The official start of Japanese immigration to Brazil began when the *Kasato-Maru* transported 781 individuals of 165 family units from Kobe, Japan, to the Port of Santos in Brazil, arriving on June 18, 1908.[29] By 1941, 188,615 people in Brazil claimed Japanese descent.[30] Today, there are an estimated 1.5 million Brazilians of Japanese descent, the largest Japanese population outside Japan.[31] However, regardless of an immigration history that spans over a century, popular culture and media representations of Brazilians of Japanese descent, and Asians writ large, continue to recycle Yellow Peril stereotypes that depict Asians as untrustworthy, harmful economic competitors and political threats—in sum, as perpetual outsiders to the Brazilian national body.

While in Japan, Azevedo wrote a series of notes about the history of Japan that he described as a "singela obra de impressões pessoais" ("a simple work of personal impressions"). His notes were discovered posthumously in 1984, and published as *O Japão* (Japan).[32] An alternate title for the manuscript was *The Agony of a Race*.[33] Since these were a collection of impressionistic notes about Japan, and perhaps Azevedo did not intend them to be published in this format, there are factual errors and the narrative is scattered. As Renato Ortiz has observed, Azevedo's information is at times incorrect, containing significant errors, including confusion with names and historical events. For example, Azevedo contends that the Portuguese accidentally discovered Japan when São Francisco Xavier disembarked at the port of Kagoshima in 1549 along with a group of Augustinians, Franciscans, and Dominicans. In fact, he arrived with Jesuit missionaries. In another example, Ortiz observes that Azevedo recounts Minamoto Yoritomo's establishment of the *bakufu* (shogunate), but he confuses *bakufu,* Japan's seven-hundred-year feudal military dictatorship, with *shogun,* the title of a military ruler. Nevertheless, as Ortiz argues, the errors do not indicate that Azevedo made assumptions about the homogeneity of Orientalism. Instead, he was attempting to make sense of Japan's new geopolitical and trade relationships with China, Korea, the United States, and Europe. The notes are written in a tone that expresses a mixture of fascination and anxiety toward Japan's open borders to trade and migration, which also opened the path to Japanese imperialist endeavors and gaining military intelligence from the West. Until then, Brazilians had understood the country through a series of Orientalist imaginings and negative stereotypes whose knowledge of Japan stopped at tea gardens and samurais. This Orientalist vision of Japan, as Azevedo and his contemporary diplomat-authors conveyed, was not only naive but dangerous, since it dismissed the actual political and economic threat or potential that Japan presented to Western civilization.

O Japão challenges the representation of a homogeneous and languid Orient. Without the pretension of having pursued a historical study or even achieved a work of fiction, Azevedo engages a diplomatic poetics about the Japanese cultural history of political representation, including the symbolic function of the Japanese emperor as a unifying emblem of Japanese nationalism. Recounting the origin story of Shintoism, which explains the Japanese imperial family's divine lineage to Amaterasu, the goddess of the sun and universe, Azevedo explains the belief in the imperial family's divine lineage; that the royal family is the divine embodiment of religion and politics is critical to understanding Japanese nationalism and political culture: "Amaterau's mirror, lovingly passed onto her offspring, is the symbol of the Shinto religion, which the Meiji could not deny without negating the divine quality of its own essence."[34] For Azevedo, gaining a deeper understanding of the Shinto religion was a way to build knowledge about the driving force behind Japanese militaristic nationalism that was driving Japanese imperial expansion in Asia. The primary mission of his diplomatic trip was to establish good relations with this growing Asian superpower vis-à-vis Japanese immigration. The turn to Japanese immigration was also a turn away from Chinese immigration, which would have aligned Brazil with a weak political and economic Chinese state.

Developing knowledge about Japanese culture as a means of understanding Japanese nationalism was also the focal point of the diplomatic poetics in which Luis Guimarães Filho (1878–1940) engaged. Like Eça de Queiroz and Machado de Assis, Guimarães Filho contributed crónicas to the *Gazeta de Notícias* and other journals published in Rio de Janeiro. He was also a member of the Academia Brasileira de Letras (Brazilian Academy of Letters), which Machado de Assis founded and served as the first president. Guimarães Filho began his diplomatic career in 1902, when he was named ambassador second secretary. He was subsequently sent on missions to Tokyo and Beijing, Europe, and the Americas. He was eventually promoted as the Brazilian ambassador to Madrid and Vatican City.[35] Drawing on the experience he gained during his missions, he published a collection of travel writing that was later republished as a book, *Samurais e mandarins* (1912). His work weaves together observations about economic and military affairs with fictional imaginings of China and Japan. These diplomatic fictions produce knowledge about China and Japan for unfamiliar readers. They created new ways of seeing Asia and Asians and mediated public opinion on Japanese and Chinese immigration. Guimarães Filho's writings expand on diplomatic and political views, transmitting them to a general readership to show how economic and political imperatives entered into Brazil's cultural spheres and structured interpersonal relations.

Samurais e mandarins is divided into two parts and is composed of a series of descriptive vignettes about Japan and China. Each vignette, or set of vignettes, is dedicated to presenting information the diplomat learned on his missions. Content includes descriptions of diplomatic meetings with Japanese and Chinese academics, missionaries, and other prominent figures, as well as other subject matter, such as Japanese and Chinese cultural traditions and histories.

Analyzing Guimarães Filho's writings about Japan and China yields insight into how diplomatic poetics translated into the private sphere, structuring new ways of imagining Asia and Asians. *Samurais e mandarins* assumes a female readership; Guimarães Filho's ideal reader is a housewife in her boudoir, absorbed in the labor-free tedium of a bourgeois life. He indulges his reader's fascination with exotic Japanese cultural objects to provide imaginative fodder for the bourgeois lady:

> I will send to your boudoirs single-plot chapters, oh naïve and curious reader, about the most interesting news of this land: lacquerware, fans, kimonos (oh! the languid, silk kimonos, pales, reds, blues, the color of ashes . . .), little wooden houses into which one enters without shoes, where storks fly in pairs on the paper walls of folding screens—a whole world that will delight your restless spirit like butterflies playing on lotus leaves.[36]

Descriptions of silk kimonos, biombos, and wooden homes with tatami flooring are not merely an exoticized distraction for a bored wife, however. Rather, Guimarães Filho explores the symbolic and political value of Japanese cultural objects in relation to how they support Japanese national unity. Disguised behind florid and ornate language, he criticizes the bourgeois household for its role as consumer and producer of incorrect Orientalist ideas about Asia. Then he seeks to persuade readers to form a new imaginary about Asia, which he has updated to be in line with the context of his contemporary period.

In keeping with the works of Eça de Queiroz and Aluísio Azevedo and their recurring critiques that their readers know Japan and China only through the European literary Orientalist lens, Guimarães Filho addresses his readers' misconceptions about the Orient, which he contends are largely a collection of erroneous impressions of Asian cultures. Recounting a conversation with a professor and director of foreign affairs at Gogakai University, Guimarães Filho quotes the professor's contention that tourists (mainly from England) write Orientalist novels of at least three hundred pages after having spent only one or two days in Japan's major cities. These impressionistic accounts have produced a market for an imagined Orient, composed of an abundance of false snapshots of Japan. However, the professor opined, the Japanese have the last laugh at the "colorless," "abundant," and "erroneous" depictions.[37] While Guimarães Filho is critical of his reader's false imaginings of Asia, he is aware of his public's attraction to Orientalist stories, and so he strategically uses Orientalist tropes to entice her to begin reading.

At least nine editions of *Samuaris e mandarins* were printed, attesting to the popularity of the book. First published in 1912, during the interim years between the First and Second Sino-Japanese Wars and preceding World War I, it is not surprising that the theme of warfare runs throughout the book. Gone are the Orientalist references that portray Japan and China as the subjugated lands of colonial dominion. At the beginning of the twentieth century, the Japanese imperial army began to gain power throughout Asia, while China was tied up in revolutionary, civil, and economic strife, involving the partition of the country among the United States, Europe, and Japan. In 1912, the same year as Guimarães Filho published his novel, Sun Yat Sen (1866–1925) led the revolutionary war that caused the Qing dynasty to collapse and founded the Republic of China.

Throughout the first section on Japan, Guimarães Filho explains the symbolic value of Japanese cultural objects and customs. He guides his readers to a new understanding of Japanese culture that relates to Japanese imperialism and the ideology of samurai warfare. He shows that samurais, flowers, and certain colors symbolize the ideology of Japanese purity that was driving Japanese military warfare. Biombos, cherry blossoms, and lotus flowers no longer provide the Orientalist imaginary habitat for the European bourgeois to play out fantasies. Instead, these symbols contribute to the rhetoric of war. The chapter titled "Cherry Blossom Trees" is thus replete with strong imagery and vivid descriptions of cherry blossoms that signify Japanese imperial power and purity. Cherry blossoms stand for the fallen soldiers of war, doubling as war memorials: "The time of war, between bombardment and the rattle of death, it is for her that the poetry of soldiers flutters its moribund wings."[38] Guimarães Filho repeatedly cites a line that associates fallen cherry blossoms with dying soldiers: "Spring has arrived and the cherry blossoms are in bloom. The time has also arrived for the soldiers to fall like the flowers!"[39] He continues, "The mountains, the trees, the rivers, the lotus, the glycine, the azaleas—like the cherry blossoms and stones—constitute the poetic notes of the militaristic lyre."[40]

He also uses descriptors normally used for flowers to portray the geisha, who, like the soldier, is first shown through Orientalist imaging—a docile and exotic handmaiden. However, Filho immediately transforms the geisha imagery into a critical vision of Japanese warfare and a critique of the treatment of women:

There is one species of flower that a powerful gardener cultivates for future business. . . . Some are able to captivate the infatuated heart and became grand mistresses or grand personalities: the majority, however, spend years experiencing life only through the illusory happiness of parties and the illusory madness of sake's vapors. Poor little dolls without any liberty.[41]

Guimarães Filho is clearly critical of Japanese patriarchy, but then he makes an abrupt reversal of his stance and configures Japan and Brazil as a shared and harmonious space by associating his memories and nostalgia for Brazil with Japanese cultural objects:

Who in actuality will stop contemplating the nature of the Orient? My eyes are still dazzled at the lofty panoramas of my land. Palm trees onto which the stars appear to rest, grand, blue mountains that redeem themselves into the tranquil bay, the crags and the waterfalls make Brazil a true heavenly paradise. . . . But here on my desk sits a bonsai tree. It does not reach two feet in height. It is a diverse spectacle of its own. All of Japan is minuscule, all of it, except its heroism, boldness, and courage of its children. The small tree reminds of the prickly shrubs that entertained the leisure of my childhood.[42]

He uses his nostalgia for Brazil as a rhetorical strategy; he repositions the harsh patriarchal military image of Japan into his longing for Brazil. By evoking the feelings of tenderness and yearning for childhood and home, he creates positive new ideas about Japanese people and culture. His descriptions encourage the notion that the rise of Japan as a superpower is a testament to the positive attributes that new generations of Japanese people could bring to Brazil.

While Guimarães Filho exhorts his public to perceive Japanese and Brazilian cultures through a similar lens, his writings on China portray it as vastly different from Japan. He rendered Japanese immigrants as a population that would improve Brazil, in contrast to the Chinese, who would bring a negative, retrograde effect to Enlightenment ideals of progress and civilization, leading Brazil toward backwardness and barbarism. In this, he is not alone. Guimarães Filho's images of the Chinese and Japanese were in line with the writings of earlier Brazilian diplomats, who were also working to make the case that Japanese immigrants would make a positive contribution to Brazilian society. Japanese immigrants would be civilized and Westernized, in contrast to the Chinese. In 1895, Brazilian diplomat José de Costa Azevedo, representing the president of the Republic of the United States of Brazil to the Ministry of Foreign Affairs, stated that the Japanese were able "to receive the civilization and customs of civilized people . . . [since they] have in general and naturally, qualities never considered in the Chinese."[43]

Guimarães Filho's writings on China follow a similar pattern to his writings on Japan. He begins by addressing readers' preconceived notions of China, predominantly created through Orientalist writings that arrived from Europe. Such notions would have been drawn from exaggerated accounts from sixteenth-century Portuguese voyager Fernão Mendes Pinto and Italian traveler Marco Polo, among others, who falsely painted China as a country of immense riches and marvels. Fernão Mendes's epic *Peregrinações* (*Pilgrimages*), posthumously published in 1614, had become a canonical Portuguese text. Filled with thrilling tales of adventure and exploration, the epic takes readers on a whirlwind journey to many different and distant lands. Its accounts are so astonishing and far-fetched that many have questioned its validity as a historical text; nevertheless, the epic tells a larger tale about the grand reaches of the Portuguese seaborne empire, a vision that Guimarães Filho unravels by comparing Fernão Mendes's accounts of the Orient with his own experiences, which were quite different.

Guimarães Filho's accounts of Asia are better understood as a mode of diplomatic poetics that debunks Portuguese Orientalist depictions of China. Fernão Mendes's accounts may be considered an example of Portuguese Orientalist literary expression. António Manuel Hespanha argues that Portuguese Orientalism was inextricably tied to the mode of discourse of Portuguese imperialist endeavor and expansion, which created a unified vision of the Portuguese seaborne empire.[44] Portuguese Orientalism was not concerned with the empirical differences of Portuguese settlements and the diversity of exchanges with local authorities that occurred in Portuguese entrepôts around the world. In Macau, for example, the Portuguese paid a fee to lease Macau from the Ming government, and although the Portuguese claimed sovereignty over Macau, the Ming did not recognize Portuguese rule.[45] Portuguese Orientalism simplified this complex history to produce a unified idea of the vast Portuguese empire, but as the diplomat-authors argued, such Orientalist depictions needed updating to advance the state goals that they were working to further.

Guimarães Filho complained that the China of *Peregrinações* no longer existed and perhaps had never existed at all. Fernão Mendes's epic invented China as a place of greatness, but when Guimarães Filho actually visited

China, he lamented that it was a grand disappointment: "Anyone who had read such an abundance of praise, sung by such clear understanding, would suffer a deep disappointment when stepping foot onto the land of Peking today."[46] In a fictional dialogue with Fernão Mendes, Guimarães Filho bemoans the absence of China's splendors and asks whether any of what Fernão Mendes wrote had even been true. Instead, based on his own visit, Guimarães Filho writes that China has become a land of mandarins covered in litter and bodily filth:

> Fernão Mendes! Why have you forsaken me, defunct Fernão Mendes?
> . . . Why did you not assist me with your holy zeal so that I could stay in the awning of my ship? Why did you not tell me that at the edge of this haughty Nanking, which together with the venomous Kiukiang, forms a giant sty? Is it possible that since you traveled here, the Chinamen have lost all of their greatness? That you indeed recounted what you saw? Because if the Nanking that you saw with your own eyes was a remarkable arrangement of castles with curuches that display a diversity of stylistic inventions, the Kiukiang that I saw with my own eyes is a mound of manure and excrement that scares me even to recount it. . . . From time to time, a mandarin covered in his own litter passes, while four hapless slaves carry him on their backs. The rest of the servants, on Mongol ponies, ride alongside the vehicle (where are, oh Fernão Mendes, the trumpets, the kettledrums, and the fifes?)—and two lackeys, covered in filth up to their noses, run ahead charged with the duty of removing the ragamuffins.[47]

His long lament to Fernão Mendes reconfigures Portuguese Orientalist visions of China to create new meanings in relation to his diplomatic mission and experiences in Chinese society. China is still a series of images and imaginative fictions the author invents to mediate and negotiate a new understanding of Chinese culture, architecture, and the natural landscape, with the aim of promoting Chinese exclusion. His literary accounts about the Chinese provide evidence to readers that in contrast to the Japanese, the Chinese have strong anti-Western views and thus would be unfit for assimilation in Brazilian society.

By the end of the nineteenth century, the United States, Europe, and Japan had forced the Qing dynasty to submit to trade policies that gave foreign control to China's economy. Anti-foreign and anti-Christian sentiment had been steadily growing in China, when the secret Society of the Righteous and Harmonious organized the Boxer Rebellion (also known as the

Boxer Uprising) and revolted against European and Japanese rule in China. In northwestern China, Boxers began to move against Chinese Christian missionaries and foreigners. In June 1900, the Qing imperial army joined with over 140,000 Boxer soldiers and moved into Beijing, where they burned down Christian churches, as well as the homes of foreigners. The Boxers laid siege on the foreign legations of the United States, France, Belgium, Great Britain, Russia, the Netherlands, and Japan, all located on the same city block near the Forbidden City. The international army of the Eight-Nation Alliance sent troops to lift the siege. After months of fighting, the troops forced the Qing court to flee the capital city. The Boxer Protocol, a peace treaty signed in September 1901, established commercial treaties in China, and China was forced to pay over $330 million in penalties for the uprising. Nevertheless, the Boxer Rebellion became a powerful symbol for revolution. In Brazil, news reports about the rebellion circulated the image of the Chinese with "yellow rage" as having the potential to act out in similar aggression and brutality.[48]

One of the goals of Guimarães Filho's diplomatic mission to China was to gather testimonies of US and European citizens about their experiences during the siege:

> The years have not erased this event from Europeans' memory (the "foreign devils" have, among other misdeeds, prevented the rain from falling on the land of China), the long series of crimes, betrayals, torture and despair that they fought off for eight weeks, when a few hundred foreigners were blockaded by a population avid for Christian flesh.[49]

His accounts include interviews with nuns who lived through the events. With an empathetic tone toward the Europeans who were held captive, Guimarães Filho portrays the Chinese as violently anti-Western and xenophobic. The revolt raised anti-Chinese sentiment in the United States, Europe, Japan, and Brazil. For example, Rio de Janeiro newspaper reporters fomented fear of the Chinese by referencing the Boxer Rebellion, without mentioning it by name, as a massacre of Europeans and Christians.[50] The image of uncontrollable Chinese fury and retaliation contributed to Yellow Peril tropes that were widely circulating in Brazil the idea that the Chinese were unsuitable candidates for nation building.

Shortly after meeting with the nuns who survived the siege, Guimarães Filho pays a visit to the residence of Monsignor Jarlin, vicar apostolic of Beijing, to interview him about the siege. Upon learning that Guimarães Filho is from Brazil, Jarlin becomes fixated on Brazil and adamantly attempts to convince him of the benefits that Chinese emigration would bring to Brazil. Out of sheer politeness, Guimarães Filho listens to Jarlin go on for over an hour, making argument after argument advocating for Chinese emigration, contending that the diligent work ethic of the Chinese would make them suitable settlers in Brazil. While Guimarães Filho diplomatically listens, he gives no response other than maintaining his silence as a sign of disinterest:

> Why not establish a stream of Chinese immigrants in Brazil? The China-men are good settlers, hardworking, humble. . . . It would be a great benefit for your country. Look, I know the Chinamen as well as the back of my hand! I have been trudging along with the likes of them since 1880. They are hard workers, yes sir, and easy to take with you. . . . During an hour's time, the zealous monsignor held me captive in his white beard while he made me listen to copious arguments in favor of Chinese emigration to our fields and farms.[51]

Guimarães Filho would later learn that the day after his visit with Monsignor Jarlin, a group of Boxers had murdered Jarlin, putting a bullet through his head. Then a few minutes later, they had set off a giant explosion that shook the ground like an earthquake. Everyone had thought that the Boxers had left Tientsin, but they had returned, and their newest victims were Catholic missionaries.[52]

The Boxer peasant revolts become a way for Guimarães Filho to advocate against Chinese agricultural labor immigration to Brazil through stirring fear that oppressed Chinese plantation workers would rebel and carry out similar attacks in Brazil. In his depictions of China, Guimarães Filho makes clear his anti-Chinese sentiment in his rhetoric that the Chinese will over-populate Brazil and consume all its resources and disturb the project of racial whitening. He expresses fear that the Chinese would devour everything, including the mulato.[53] Guimarães Filho categorizes the mulato within a lineage of animals consumed by the Chinese: "These people eat everything: veal, lamb, pork, goat, horse, buffalo, tiger, lion, dog, *mulato*, donkey, zebra, tapir, otter, badger and, finally, any animal that can be given a name."[54] The term *mulato* is pejorative. It was commonly used to refer to mixed-race descendants of European and African parentage. *Mulato* referred to the off-spring of a horse and donkey; its meaning had been coterminous with the notion of "the stallion impregnating the she-ass . . . to be *a priori* analogous with the Portuguese male impregnating non-white women (to produce *mulatos*)."[55] The word therefore drew an analogy between mixed-race children and animals that were the product of different species and were thus sexually inadequate or sterile. In configuring the racial term *mulato* within a list of animals that compose part of the Chinese diet, Guimarães Filho rehashes popular ideas that if the mulato was to be the bridge between the black and white races, the Chinese would cannibalize them and that role. Ultimately the Chinese would not allow Brazil to become white. Instead, they would turn Brazil yellow.[56] To be sure, there is a long cultural tradition, evoked by whites and blacks alike in Brazil, particularly in sambas, that reclaims the term so that its use can have a neutral or even positive connotation.[57]

However, in stating that the Chinese would eat any kind of animal, along with the *mulato*, Guimarães Filho amplifies the pejorative meaning of the word. This situated his depiction of Chinese laborers within both contemporaneous debates over Chinese immigration and the discourse of miscegenation, recalling the *Revista Illustrada* cartoon that depicted the Chinese as bringing an unfavorable yellow hue to Brazil.[58] By situating mulatos among a list of domesticated and wild animals, he evokes social Darwinism and scientific racism—the idea that mixed-race people fit into an evolutionary stage between black and white, in which white defines the top of the racial pyramid.

Guimarães Filho's diplomatic poetics reiterated the trope that the Chinese were a biological contagion to Western civilization, considered to be ravenous, consuming even the mulato, the symbolic and biological bridge that could whiten the nation. This anti-Chinese rhetoric evoked the fearful question of what would happen to the project of racial whitening and the dominance of European virility if Chinese laborers invaded white liberal European and American cities. Accounts about the Boxer rebellion had made Chinese peasant workers into a force to be reckoned with, echoing Eça de Queiroz's crónicas about China that addressed the general fear that Chinese immigration would lead to a silent and passive invasion of Brazil, in which the Chinese would slowly but surely consume the Brazilian economy. Most of all, the goods yielded from their labor would go back to China. Guimarães Filho's accounts present a much more ferocious side of Chinese peasants. While both images portray the Chinese in different ways, they share the idea that Chinese laborers are an unbridled force that would degrade humanity and elevate it to a new level of savagery.

Guimarães Filho symbolically puts a stop to China's power. He describes the numerous stopped clocks in the ravaged Summer Palace to illustrate that Chinese time has reached an end. The grandeur of China's past centuries would remain in the ashes of defeat:

> I close my eyes and evoke these palaces from a thousand years ago! I recall the lakes and see them lucid and diaphanous! I see the galleys of the emperors sailing noiseless on the waters. . . . I hear the poets of the court as they celebrate the transparency of the currents. . . . I find Jade Island to be even more verdant and mysterious. . . . And I am filled with love for the China that has disappeared into the dust of bygone centuries! . . . Alas! The countless watches of the Summer Palace rest in peaceful stillness in the obscurity of the rooms, but mockingly Time ticks, ticks, ticks.[59]

In Guimarães Filho's diplomatic poetics, Asianness gains meaning within a larger economy of racial labor, in which the labor of Chinese and Japanese immigrants becomes the primary mode of negotiating Brazil's new geopolitical alliances and economic future. Diplomatic and fictional negotiations over racial laboring bodies are ultimately tied to economic discussions about the labor and the wealth of nations. The diplomatic poetics in play shows the fluid passages among political, economic, cultural, and literary spheres.

Ideas about Chineseness and Japaneseness that fluctuated in relation to blackness and whiteness demonstrated the complex intersections of geopolitics, race relations, and the cultural transmission of these ideas. In these diplomatic poetics, constructions of Japaneseness and Chineseness acquired additional layers of meaning in accordance with new geopolitical alignments in an unstable atmosphere of economic uncertainty and looming war. Circumoceanic memories of race require consistent and renewed mediation. In the mid-twentieth century in the lead-up to World War II, when imperial Japan and the Axis powers threatened the Allied powers and China joined forces with Brazil and the United States, Chinese and Japanese people and cultures were once again tarred with the same brush as the one that had painted them as the obstacle to or possibility for Brazil's future. These common perceptions entered into Brazilian popular music wherein miscegenation with the Chinese became the content of sonorous landscapes as vocalists and musicians delighted mass audiences and shaped public opinion about Brazil's wartime ally with notes about Brazilian alien citizens and permanent foreignness.

SIX

The Yellow Peril in Brazilian Popular Music

Brazilian popular music production functions as a specific regime of representation and declaration, sharing social, political and economic realities, and playing a critical role in staging new imaginaries of citizenship.[1] Twentieth-century racial representations of China and the Chinese in Brazilian popular music reformulated the pseudoscience of eugenics and the branqueamento (racial whitening) project that had accompanied abolition in 1888, and the turn to a new labor source via immigration from Europe, the Middle East, and Japan. Debates over Brazilian nation building were inseparable from discussions over labor, sexual procreation, and miscegenation in defining the racial makeup of the first Brazilian republic, established in 1889.[2] Politicians and agriculturalists projected these desires onto the bodies of newly arriving immigrants. "Constructive" miscegenation signified the desired road to whiteness, but whiteness was a relational concept that depended on constructing notions about "degenerative" miscegenation. Racial mixing with liberty's antithetical Others, often personified through racial representations of the black slave or yellow laborer, signified the road back to slavery and colonialism. The topic of miscegenation was a common theme in Brazilian music of the 1930s and 1940s and acted as a response to these earlier views. Samba, marchas, and other music genres that developed in Brazil as the result of intercultural exchanges via circumoceanic encounters played to lyrics about the positive or negative effects of racial mixing with the Chinese in a new context concerned with trade relations and geopolitical alliances during World War II. Lyrics and melodies transmitted recycled ideas about Chineseness within discourses about Brazilian national identity and *mestiço* (mixed-race) nationalism.

While few Chinese people lived in Rio de Janeiro during the early twentieth century, musicians and composers produced a number of sambas and marchas about the Chinese.[3] Composers may not have been intentionally referencing nineteenth-century stereotypes about the unsuitability of Chinese migrants for white liberal nations, but their songs reveal the powerful role that racial representations and cultural production played in establishing conceptual boundaries around Brazilian mestiço nationalism.[4]

As I have demonstrated throughout this book, racial representations are relationally constituted and may function as a mode of governance rooted in violent racial regimes' desire for dominance. Cultural expressions of race are critical sites for the struggle for memory and political contestation and therefore replete with contradictions. In the songs I discuss in this chapter, Chineseness is never simply about Chinese people. Instead, Chineseness reveals the cultural work of racial representations in mediating conflicting Brazilian nationalisms. They also signal shifting geopolitical dynamics and the collision of oppositional and interwoven ideologies and political subjectivities. Racial representations are not simply a product of aesthetics; rather, they have sociohistorical context since their origins are rooted in violent racial regimes that orient a way of looking and being hypervisible while always being seen through.[5] Racial representations thus are better understood as contested cultural memory sites that play a crucial role in upholding, recasting, or interrupting national allegories and political mythologies. Racialized national categories, then, are critical spaces that reveal how colonial racial hierarchies were reformulated into new relationships between race, territory, and national identity, often with the purpose of producing recognition and inclusion into the ethical boundaries of the state.

Brazilian popular music has played an important role in shaping new imaginaries of race and nation. Music is often thought of as a utopian space or a means of resisting or subverting dominant power. It may also work to encourage nationalist assimilation by normalizing gender binaries and heterosexuality and associating racial identity with national identity.[6] Replete with tension and contradictions, in some instances, constructions of Chineseness serve to cohere Brazilian mestiço nationalism through staging Chineseness as a site of racial and cultural difference that cannot enter into the tightly woven notion of mixed-race national identity. In other instances, they are critical sites for claiming memory and representation, which is also a claim to political inclusion. Brazilian music, to recast the words of Jacques Rancière, is the embodied expression of the political and aesthetic at once.[7] During the twentieth century, songwriters created racialized and gendered notions about Chineseness to shape public opinion about the Chinese, appropriating the racial identities that were constructed out of nineteenth-century debates about unfree "yellow labor." However, the consistency of these renderings—across the nineteenth and twentieth centuries to the present—allows us to observe that while racial regimes may lie dormant for some time, they may be activated or triggered for presentist needs.

Since the nineteenth century, popular culture and mass media in Anglo-America and the British Empire circulated the Yellow Peril discourse to portray the threat of Asian domination over the West. This discourse included ideas that the Chinese failed to meet heteronormative Anglo standards of patriarchal order. The songs that I examine in this chapter depict Chinese sexuality as inadequate, bizarre, or threatening in some way, which repeats the same negative opinions that were circulating in the nineteenth century during the worldwide debates about the Chinese question.[8]

While negative portrayals of Asians served the global reaches of the US propaganda machine and influenced Brazilian perspectives, the meaning of Chineseness did not remain static across national boundaries. In Brazil, beliefs about the Chinese acquired a different form in relation to discrete strands of Brazilian nationalist movements. Different branches of Brazilian nationalism diverged in their attitudes about how to address the racial legacy of colonialism. This legacy was apparent in continuing forms of racial violence and the exclusion of black and Indigenous people, as well as in the ways in which new immigrant populations in Brazil were received or reproached. The shifting meanings associated with Chineseness allow us to examine the viewpoints of different sociocultural movements that occurred between 1930 and 1945, years marked by Getúlio Vargas's rise to power and Brazil's involvement in World War II. These racial depictions about the Chinese persisted after World War II's end and are still ingrained in the contemporary popular-cultural imaginary.

Under President Getúlio Vargas (1930–1945; 1951–1954), the Brazilian state exerted increasing control over the arts, cultural production, and mass-media programming.[9] Some of these plans included introducing musical education into school curricula. In 1932, composer Heitor Villa-Lobos was invited to lead musical education in schools. His pedagogical philosophy was driven by the idea that music was not merely an artistic skills-based education but was also a medium for providing civic training that would foster patriotism and appreciation for the diverse cultures of Brazil.[10] Brazilian popular music thus became a contested site for constructing cultural citizenship.[11] It served the state-sponsored function of building patriotism and civic duty, but cultural producers had their own ideas about how to use music to sway conceptions of race, sexuality, and gender as they related to cultural citizenship and inclusion. During this period, Vargas advanced his populist politics and cultural nationalism by elevating samba, representative of African diasporic culture, to the status of national popular music.[12] The discourse of miscegenation and the project of *brasilidade* (Brazilianization) functioned in parallel but in contradiction, abetting the elite project of whitening at the same time as it affirmed African diasporic cultures and black agency.[13]

Cultural exchange with the United States also strengthened during this time. Growing military tensions between Europe and Asia had led Franklin Roosevelt to institute the Good Neighbor Policy in the 1930s. Presented as a form of cultural diplomacy meant to promote education, cultural exchange, friendship, and mutual defense within the hemispheric Americas, the Good Neighbor Policy established US hegemony through cultural and peaceful means, including economic expansion by way of tourism and artistic and cultural exchanges, of which music was a component.[14] While the Good Neighbor Policy resulted in new forms of US cultural hegemony, it also brought great visibility to Latin American music and dance, introducing Brazilian musical rhythms such as samba to ballroom three-step dances and bringing bossa nova into contact with jazz.[15]

Under Vargas, musicians and composers used radio and popular entertainment to share multivalent perspectives about their contemporary context. The results demonstrate how the aural realm disseminated its own constellation and moral codes for circulating ideas about race, gender, national identity, and geopolitics. The 1930s and 1940s were the golden age of Brazilian radio, and President Vargas mobilized radio for his brasilidade campaign. Brasilidade aimed at producing a unified Brazilian national identity through forging mestiço nationalism. The brasilidade campaign was arguably a rebuttal to white supremacist ideologies driving Nazism and European fascism as well as Jim Crow laws in the United States. Mestiço nationalism inverted negative representations about racial hybridization; instead, the celebration of mixed-race Brazilian identity was tied to new ideas about modernization and industrial production.[16] Vargas's industrialization policies promoted the formation of a multiracial working class that lived in close proximity to one another in urban centers. However, although his policies that promoted brasilidade refused extremist racial purity ideologies, Vargas-era debates about cultural and racial heterogeneity or homogeneity did not fully break from the existing terms of eugenics ideology.[17]

Vargas instituted immigration restriction policies in line with US policies.[18] In 1924, the United States had passed the Johnson-Reed Act, excluding "Chinese, Japanese, Indians, and other Asians on the grounds that they were racially ineligible for naturalized citizenship . . . that simultaneously solidified the legal boundaries of the 'white race.'"[19] Following the United States, Vargas's government passed similar prohibitions against Japanese and non-European immigration, including a new quota system, in the Brazilian Constitution of 1934, which set in place a nationwide immigration restriction policy and established restrictions on Japanese immigration by mandating an 80 percent reduction in entrance from 1924 to 1934.[20] Lesser notes that the "Constitution of 1934 reflected the xenophobia that had become widespread in urban Brazil."[21] In 1937, Vargas created the Estado Novo (New State), officially introducing a new corporatist state and industrial era in Brazil, taking a turn toward authoritarianism with fascist doctrines. In 1938, Vargas's policies targeted unassimilated immigrants by prohibiting ethnic institutions, language schools, and foreign-language press. With the advent of World War II, the government placed restrictions on people with Axis citizenship or affiliation, including in São Paulo and southern parts of Brazil, areas with heavy concentrations of Italian, German, and Japanese populations. In 1942, a delegate from Penápolis, São Paulo, made the provocative statement that Nikkei who could not speak Portuguese should not speak at all.[22] Vargas's brasilidade project, as Paulina Alberto observes, transformed the "once prized immigrants" into "interloping foreigners" who threatened national security.[23]

During the 1930s and 1940s, musicians and songwriters created a large trove of marchas and sambas that incorporated racialized ideas about Chineseness. Representations of Chinese gender and sexuality, in particular, served as allegories for Brazil's relationship to China and other Allied powers, but they also reveal anxieties about Chinese economic competition. These works circulated the discourse of the Yellow Peril. The songs convey moralistic views about miscegenation with the Chinese, and they repeatedly depict deviant Chinese sexuality. The moral values assigned to Chinese sexuality show a power dynamic between Brazil and China that related fluctuating periods of either economic insecurity or competition, political alliance or instability.

China in Brazilian Popular Music in the 1930s and 1940s

A number of songs released during Vargas's governance expressed conflicting attitudes about the Chinese.[24] Under his leadership, Brazil joined the Allied Powers in World War II on August 22, 1942. Prior to officially entering the war, Brazil had aided both Axis and Allied powers, allowing the United States to build military air bases along the northeastern coast in cities like Recife and Natal, while continuing trade relations with Germany and Italy. Brazil was the first Latin American government to declare war on the Axis powers and the only one to contribute troops to fight alongside the Allies in Europe. While it may seem logical that Brazil's geopolitical alliance with the Allied powers would influence popular Brazilian cultural representations of Asians to be in line with the war propaganda circulating in the United States and around the rest of the Allied world, Brazilian references to China and the Chinese were contradictory at times and thus give an indication of Brazil's shifting geopolitical position in relation to the United States and China. References to the Chinese had a number of functions. They were the unassimilable and inscrutable Other in relation to Brazilian racial democracy and mixed-race nationalist project of brasilidade. They were an expression of economic anxiety and the perceived threat of Chinese economic competition to Brazilian markets. At times, we can observe recurring themes in the lyrics that construct Chineseness as a stand-in for economic efficiency or deficit, or even Sino-Japanese geopolitical conflict. It follows that depictions of Chinese migrants in Brazilian society fluctuate: the Chinese are strong and trustworthy when they are fighting with Brazil against the Japanese in World War II, yet they are sexually impotent when the topic turns to Chinese economic competition with Brazil.

Brazilian popular music written and produced during the Vargas years rehearsed the nineteenth-century discourses on the Yellow Peril, which represented Chinese laborers as a threateningly endless flow of people who would crowd out the economic and moral livelihoods of a white, Protestant United States.[25] Playful melodies and Orientally accented marchas were composed with seemingly innocuous musical tones and catchy tunes, but their lyrics circulated ambivalent portrayals of Chinese sexuality. Anti-Chinese sentiment in music depicted Chinese immigrants as shrewd, emasculated, conniving, and sexually impotent or immoral, harkening back to late nineteenth-century illustrated portrayals that circulated around the globe, which, in racial and gendered terms, deemed Chinese immigrant laborers unfit for white liberal nations. The songs rehearsed the tropes of unbeatable and threatening Chinese competition in economic and labor markets by expressing anxiety about sexual and cultural intermixing with Chinese immigrants. On the flip side, in some lyrics, China offers an alternative to US imperialism and capitalism. Some songs portray the Chinese as powerful allies, indexing the important role that China played for the Allied powers in the fight against the Imperial Japanese Army during World War II.

Representations of Asian male sexuality range from emasculated to threatening, while depictions of Asian female sexuality created gendered ideas of women as submissive and exotic. While mestiço nationalism embraced the myth of racial democracy and Chinese people are depicted in the lyrics as existing within Brazilian national borders, they are never fully integrated into Brazilian mestiço national identity. Lyrics about the "Chinaman" portray male Chinese sexuality as abnormal, perverse, or immoral—Chinese men are gendered effeminate or impotent, and Asian women are objectified as small, childlike, exotic objects who could be bought and sold. Indeed, a character named Butterfly appears in a number of Brazilian songs and functions as an Orientalist, homogenizing symbol for Asian female sexuality and gender. Butterfly is a likely reference to Giacomo Puccini's *Madame Butterfly*, an opera that premiered in Milan in 1904 and drew largely from Pierre Loti's novel *Madame Chrysanthème* (1888), whose protagonist goes to Japan in search of a bride who will be a "little yellow skinned woman with black hair and cat's eyes. She must be pretty. Not much bigger than a doll."[26] Puccini's opera presents an encounter between the West and Japan, allegorized in the romantic relationship between a US naval officer named

Pinkerton and an adolescent Japanese girl nicknamed "Madame Butterfly," a geisha who is included with his rental property, along with views of Nagasaki Harbor. In this allegory, Butterfly is an exotic object who is destined to sacrifice her life for Western triumph.[27] Pinkerton weds Butterfly, a fifteen-year-old girl who became a geisha because her family lost its fortune. Act I ends with Pinkerton and Butterfly in the garden where they consummate their marriage. However, it is clear that Pinkerton never took the marriage seriously; for him, Japanese traditions and ceremonies, and taking Butterfly's virginity, were only playful activities that helped pass the time during his sojourn in Japan. At the end of his tour, he leaves Japan and Butterfly, only to return three years later with his new American wife to take the son he had conceived with Butterfly. Upon facing the devastating news that Pinkerton has remarried, Butterfly agrees to give him her child in exchange for seeing him one last time. To mark their last encounter, she commits suicide and thus conveniently rids him of the problem of having to confront her or the memory of his whimsical actions that did not affect his livelihood but destroyed another. While Butterfly is depicted as a Japanese woman, this story is not about Japan or Japanese people. It stages the mind's Japan by dramatizing distance and difference to shape the perception and form of encounter between East and West.[28] The story transforms Japan into an Orientalist stage wherein Japan may be substituted for any place where such an encounter is desired. For example, Alain Boublil and Claude-Michel Schönberg's *Miss Saigon*, which opened on Broadway in 1999 and had a revival in 2017, reproduced Puccini's Japan in their narrative structure that set Vietnam on the Orientalist stage.

While Brazilian depictions of Butterfly may share characteristics with Puccini's Butterfly, they belong to another "semiotics of representation."[29] Rather, Asian female sexuality gains meaning in relation to the *mulata*—the iconic symbol of mixed-race female sexuality whose figure serves as a bridge for forging Brazilian mestiço nationalism. By comparing the mulata trope with portrayals of Asian sexuality in Brazilian popular music, we can examine how gender and racial formation are relationally constituted and instrumentalized for the purposes of nationalist historiography.

In Brazilian cultural expressions, the mulata figure functions as a symbol of a racial continuum—a spectrum of race—whose racial identity is not determinable in black or white terms. While the mulata figure symbolizes Brazilian national identity as a spectrum of racial identities, her sexualized figure adheres strictly to heterosexual binary.[30] Antonio Herculano Lopes observes that the invention of the hypervisible and sexualized mulata originates in Brazil's patriarchal slave society, in which mixed-race relations were often the result of sexual violence of slaveholders toward enslaved women. In this sense, cultural expressions of the mulata exemplify a mode of circumoceanic forgetting and invention that replaces the malice of the violent histories of slavery with a sanitized and sensuous version of the past.[31] The mulata figure gives insight into the ways in which the Chinese were assigned racial difference within a Brazilian circumoceanic memory of race and its transmissions of blackness and whiteness.

A number of Brazilian carnival marcha and samba songs addressed Chinese sexuality in ways that allow us to examine the entangled logics of race, gender, and sexuality in the construction of Brazilian mestiço nationalism, a political response that condemned extremist nationalist racial ideology circulating during the 1930s in the form of European fascism, Nazism, and US segregation policies.[32] During the 1930s and 1940s, the celebration of a mixed-race Brazil, mestiço nationalism, became a common theme in carnival marcha songs as a political gesture against white supremacist ideology. The marcha "Hymn of Brazilian Carnival" (1938), composed by Almirante, stands as the most famous statement of Brazil's mestiço nationalism. It also provides an example of circumoceanic cultural transmission that forgets the mulata figure's violent past to glorify Brazil's mixed-race heritage. It extolls Brazilian women as commoditized racial bodies to be admired and consumed like fruit and spices. The lyrics include lines like, "Brazil has 500,000 morenas, 100,000 blondes, the color of oranges, and the mulata, the color of cinnamon, is Brazil's greatest production."

Brazilian song lyrics about Chinese female sexuality rehearse a larger discourse about Chinese female docility in which women are depicted as objects of sexual desire, as commodity, or as slavelike and generally subordinate to white patriarchal power. The lyrics of the songs I discuss here often refer to people from China as *china* or *chim*, derogatory terms that rehearse the anti-Chinese rhetoric of the nineteenth century for a new generation. The lyrics allow us to observe how racial terms and concepts are diachronic and localize circumoceanic cultures within a Brazilian historiography. In Portuguese, the word for Chinese is *chinês* for someone perceived as male and *chinesa* for someone read as female. *China* refers to the country. In Rio Grande do Sul, in the southern region of Brazil, *china* is a slang word for prostitute, referring to Indigenous and Indian girls. In the 1935 song "Aquela china" ("That China"), the song conveys the singer's nostalgia for his *china* or *chinoca* who tastes of yerba mate tea, commonly drunk in southern Brazil, Argentina, and Uruguay.[33] The song begins, "The milk of that *china* is very pretty," and then escalates by calling "that china" a "chinoca," a derogatory term that refers to a young prostitute or to a Chinese, Indian, or Indigenous girl.[34] The song harnesses political and cultural angst about Chinese female sexuality as related to the project of miscegenation, which underlies the discourse of mestiço nationalism. Chinese women are treated as objects of economic transactions. They are commodities and thus do not enter into the spheres of normative domestic relations.

Composer João de Barro had a profound influence on Brazilian music and popular culture. In addition to his international visibility as artistic director for Columbia Records, he recorded over five hundred songs during his career, writing a carnival song every year from 1930 to the late 1970s.[35] In 1935, João de Barro wrote a marcha about a Chinese girl called "Linda Mimi" ("Pretty Mimi"), recorded by early twentieth-century sambista Mário Reis.[36] Then in 1936, João de Barro and Alberto Ribeiro wrote another carnival marcha, titled "Cadê Mimi" ("Where Is Mimi").[37] "Where Is Mimi" and "Pretty Mimi" are both about Mimi, a Chinese girl whom the lyrics describe as a small possession who can be locked up. The famous sambista Mário Reis recorded both songs. The lyrics of "Where Is Mimi" express longing for a Chinese girl who has escaped to Shanghai. Mimi is a precious object the singer found and then lost, and no one knows where she has gone. If he ever finds Mimi again, he will lock her up inside his heart. In "Pretty Mimi," a little crystal doll named Mimi lives inside the singer's heart. Mimi is a rare sight; Brazil does not have her type; Mimi must have escaped from a fan or a teacup. The lyrics to these love songs seem silly and sexist; Mimi is an exotic object of male desire and the reincarnation of Puccini's Butterfly. Mimi has no place in this Brazil except to symbolize and reinforce the stance that brasilidade will stand beside white patriarchal dominance over Asia.

A number of songs portray Chinese masculinity in a way that is allegorical of political and economic issues, including military conflict, economic competition, and negative views of racial mixing. Chinese male sexuality is shown as emasculated, hypersexual, or perverted in ways that recall colonial portrayals of Chinese laborers and the accordant fears that Chinese immigration would spread the yellow race to Brazilian society's biological and cultural DNA. For example, in the marcha "Grau dez" ("Perfect Ten") (1935) composed by Ari Barroso and Lamartine Babo, men of various nationalities confess their love for a *morena* (bronze-skinned girl) whose beauty captivates men from many nations including Spain, England, Germany, France, and Argentina.[38] They express their desire for her in multilingual catcalls: The Englishman says, "Yes, my baby"; the Frenchman coos, "Bonjour, mon amour, très bien, très bien." The Argentine man plays a tango and calls out "Milonguita." While these men act out their masculinity by trying to catch the attention of the perfect girl, the Chinese man cannot perform masculinity in this way. He tries to make similar sexual whistles but does not produce sound. He "talks the talk, but he bluffs." He clearly does not prefer women. He has a secret that requires he keep his sexual preferences to himself.

Portrayals of Chineseness are allegorical for economic competition in the 1936 carnival marcha song titled "Lig, lig, lig, lé," written by Santiago Osvaldo and Paulo Barbosa, performed by famous Brazilian singers such as Castro Barbosa and Carmen Miranda.[39] The lyrics state that the Chinaman will not return to Shanghai to find his Butterfly; instead he will remain in Brazil with his *morena*. As previously mentioned, *morena* refers to a woman with tanned or bronze skin, but the history of the word can be traced to the complex colonial hierarchy of racial categories, in which *morena* alluded to any number of racial tones that resulted from African, Indigenous, and European miscegenation: "Will go no / more to Shanghai/To find a Butterfly / And here, with the bronze skin girl / He will make his faith).

While the lyrics tell us that the Chinese man will stay in Brazil and find his "faith" with his morena, his sexuality threatens Brazil's racial makeup, and his cunning economic skills destabilize the local economy as well. The song goes on to rehearse nineteenth-century anti-Chinese rhetoric that the Chinese cannot be fully trusted because their political and economic loyalties are with China. The Chinese man also silently and sneakily undercuts his competition by selling Brazilian products, such as bananas and coffee, at rates unbeatable even by Brazilians: "Here comes your Chinaman / On tiptoe / Ten coppers, twenty plates / Banana and coffee." The song goes on to state that the Chinese offer unbeatable prices because they only need to eat once a month: "The Chinese/ Only eat / Once a month." The song assigns meaning to the Chinese as subhuman or even nonhuman. They do not have the same dietary needs that sustain human life, which gives them a competitive edge in Brazil's banana and coffee industries, two great sources of national wealth. The song warns that the Brazilian economy cannot compete with the Chinese merchants' exorbitantly low prices, and Brazilian society has no room for the Chinese. In this version, the Chinese merchant will wipe out the local Brazilian economy and transform society's racial makeup. Here the Chinese man has decided to stay in Brazil with "his morena." But he is a perpetual outsider, residing in a country with growing xenophobic attitudes and government policies that had recently tightened immigration restrictions. His presence infringes on the imagined space of brasilidade, even as the lyrics convey that he resides within the territorial national space.

In 1944, Brazilian composers Arnaldo Passos and Ari Monteiro wrote the song "China," in which they cited the lines from the 1936 carnival marcha, "Lig lig, lig, lé." [40] The lyrics expressly create a distinction between Chinese and Japanese residents of Brazil but show that they still align in some aspects. First, the song expresses that the Chinese are now civilized, but the lyrics also refer to the Chinese as monolith, a "China" that eats everything. They may eat with spoons, but they are also consuming everything and leaving nothing for "us both": "China, China, lig, lig, lé / Eat everything, everything, everything all at once." The song is ambiguous; some lines can be interpreted as either the imperative "Eat everything," or as addressing the third person plural pronoun: "Chinese / They eat everything." Thus, it is unclear if the song is addressing habits in China or if it is aimed at the Chinese in Brazil. The song conveys that there is scarcity of food and resources in both China and Brazil, but it explicitly states that the competitive Chinese will always take more than their fair share.

Next, the song also depicts the Japanese as a common enemy. While the Chinese eat everything, they will save the bones to use as weapons against the Japanese: "[The Chinese] only leave the bones for skewering the Japanese." However, although China and Brazil were allies and shared common enemies during World War II, the song says that China is also not to be fully trusted—the Chinese may consume all the resources of Brazil: "China, China, now, ask for more rice / With or without chopsticks, there has to be enough for us both."

In the 1948 song "Serenata chinesa" ("Chinese Serenade"), written by João de Barro, Chinese masculinity is again rendered effeminate, and female sexuality is the object that determines assimilation or segregation. [41] The

Chinese flute player is nicknamed "Patchouli," and although he is depicted as a delicate, fairy-like figure—a flower playing a bamboo flute—the singer, presumably a Brazilian, cannot compete with him for the Chinese woman's attention. She prefers the sounds of her Chinaman: "I prefer the sound of the flute of my Chinaman / That plays fi-fi-rin-fin-fin." That the Chinese woman prefers the Chinese man indicates her ultimate loyalty to China and its men. The song expresses anxiety about the prospect for Chinese assimilation and miscegenation in Brazilian society.

A number of other marchas constructed Chineseness and Japaneseness in overlapping forms of racialization. These songs are ostensibly about Sino-Japanese military conflict, using sexuality to allegorize concerns over national security and economic issues—war and trade. In 1943, one year after Brazil entered World War II, João de Barro wrote the carnival song "China pau" ("China Wood"), recorded by Columbia Records.[42] Across his many songs, Barro frequently used cultural and racial references to create allegories for contemporary political and economic context. Likewise, this song diminishes and ridicules Japanese power while extolling China, making clear reference to the Sino-Japanese War in the phrase "if Chiang Kai Chek continues this way, he will make tambourines with the enemy's skin."

References to Chinese male sexuality stand in for military power. *Pau* or *wood* colloquially refers to male sexuality, and in the song "China Wood," Chinese masculinity is strong, unbreakable, and undefeatable: "It is China wood / China is hard to crack." The song is clearly juxtaposing strong Chinese masculinity with Chinese military strength over Japan. The Japanese military invasion of Nanjing in 1937 had forced China to enter World War II and unite with the Allied powers. Chinese troops went on to fight an arduous eight-year war against Japan (1937–1945) and suffered the largest number of military and civilian casualties during World War II. Diverse sources cite vastly different numbers that range from approximately 20 million to 50 million civilian and military deaths in China alone.[43]

On December 13, 1937, in what has since become known as the Nanjing Massacre or the Rape of Nanjing, Japanese imperial soldiers entered Nanjing, marking the beginning of the Second Sino-Japanese War and China's entrance into World War II. The lyrics to "China pau" make reference to these Japanese military actions and invoke the Yellow Peril discourse to convey the fear of Japanese military invasion that could take shape as racial domination.

The song makes an allegory for a Japanese military invasion via the figure of a Japanese woman; her voracious sexual appetite has birthed seven mixed-race children with "pixaim" hair: "And a Japanese woman / that took Nanking / Had seven children / with *pixaim* (frizzy/nappy) hair." The colloquial expression *pixaim* carries a negative and racialized connotation about black hair. In this song, the Japanese woman's mixed-race "seven children" have "frizzy" hair, extending the allegory of Japanese sexuality to include a portrayal of miscegenation with the Japanese that overlaps with a derogatory reference about blackness. In this song, the Japanese are no longer the desired "white" immigrants who will improve Brazil; instead, Japaneseness and blackness are racialized together as citizen aliens. The song recycles the racist eugenic rhetoric of the whitening project and teaches the message that only certain kinds of miscegenation yield positive results for Brazil, and mixing with the Japanese is no longer one of them.

The song then goes on to make a reference to *pé-de-moleque* (peanut brittle) in a way that is similar to a reference in the foxtrot "Salada chinesa" ("Chinese Salad").[44] "Chinese Salad, " like "China Wood," addresses war and scarcity. Common themes in marcha songs during World War II dealt with war and the rationing of food and natural resources, including water, wheat, and gasoline.[45] In 1932, Carolina Cardoso de Menezes and Vitório Lattari composed "Chinese Salad," and over two decades later, in 1956, Odeon Records rereleased the song, attesting to its ongoing popularity. The lyrics of "Chinese Salad" discuss food shortage in a slapstick manner: "I read the fan / of a mandarin's woman / That peanut brittle / No longer has peanuts." The song portrays the chim (Chinaman) as a shrewd character who skimps on ingredients and thus cheats his Brazilian customers out of quality products, a characterization that is repeated across many songs: "There is no shrimp [instead of *camarão*, the Portuguese word for shrimp, the lyrics state, "camaló," to poke fun at the Chinese accent] in the seafood stewed calulu water from Vichy."[46] The lyrics fearfully contend the Chinese have depleted Brazilian resources to the extent that Brazilian peanut brittle no longer has peanuts, seafood stews are missing the seafood, and its abundant sources of mineral water are now imported from France.

The song warns that China has co-opted Brazil, but the Chinese cannot replicate what is quintessentially Brazilian. The song's surreal and slapstick lyrics jump between Chinese and Brazilian contexts. The song tells of a resource-depleted and conflict-ridden China, referred to as "Shanghai-

Peking, the Chinaman's zone," where there is no more fish and the mandarin has no more satin. That is, the Chinese tendency to consume is too great; all the fish and the fine textiles of China are already gone, and so the Chinese have headed to Brazil: "The mandarin has no more satin-in-in," the lyrics say. The next line switches the scene to a restaurant in Brazil, to the neighborhood of "Jardim Leblon" ("Leblon Garden") where a Chinese waiter serves "Chinese breaded beef cutlet salad."

The lyrics make explicit that what was once Brazilian is no longer; even the Jardim Leblón neighborhood has been renamed *Conchinchina*, and traditional Brazilian desserts such as peanut brittle now come from China: "Over in Conchinchina / The peanut brittle is from China." The word *Conchinchina* can be traced to sixteenth-century Portuguese traders, who gave the name to what is today the southern region of Vietnam.[47] Its contemporary colloquial use in Portuguese and Spanish gives the sense that the speaker is referring to a remote and far-flung place without a specific location. In this way, the song casts the Chinese-run restaurant in Brazil as an alien place. The Chinese restaurant is here in Brazil, yet at the same time it is far away in Conchinchina, an imagined geography that operates similarly to Chinatown (or Japantown), spaces that are both semimythical and racialized.[48]

The song ends with a reference to a contemporaneous conflict in Tsingtao, China, the main port of Shantung Province: "In Tsingtao, things are bad / They are striking blows, they are striking blows." In January 1932, the same year the song was released, Japanese troops had besieged Tsingtao in response to the Min Kuo *Daily News* lamenting the failed attempt to assassinate Emperor Hirohito of Japan. In response to the defamation of the emperor, Japanese vigilantes from the Japanese quarter of the city retaliated violently against the *Daily News* offices and burned down the headquarters of the Kuomintang Party. Within twenty-four hours, Japanese troops and ships had occupied the city, and Chinese local officials were forced to apologize for anti-Japanese behavior.[49] People in Brazil were taking notes of these events, and it added to their discomfort about the Chinese in Brazil. These sentiments showed themselves in song lyrics.

Performing Fu Manchu and the Yellow Peril

Hollywood played a critical role in spreading images of the Yellow Peril, the threat of Asian economic and political domination over the West, to Brazil.[50] The London-based author Arthur Henry Ward, under the pen name Sax Rohmer, serialized and popularized the anxiety of the Yellow Peril in thirteen novels about Fu Manchu that were published between 1913 and 1959. The worldwide depictions of Fu Manchu, "the Yellow Peril incarnate in one man," as Rohmer described him, embodied the anxieties about a Chinese invasion and domination over British and Anglo-American power.[51] Multifarious depictions of Fu Manchu exploded around the world in all forms from 1913 to the 1970s.[52] He represented a geopolitical and economic threat; however, cartoons and illustrations sought to allay that fear and anxiety through mockery and ridicule, conveying instead that Fu Manchu's love for decadence and opium would impede his rise and weaken any power he might possess. Fu Manchu drew on and extended nineteenth-century negative views about Chinese laborers, who represented the threateningly endless flow of people who would crowd out the economic and moral livelihood of a white Protestant United States.[53] The figure appeared in radio performances, on board games, and in kitsch marginalia such as on candy and in coloring books, and it circulated across more than thirty countries, including Argentina, Brazil, Burma, Japan, Malaysia, Thailand, and the Ukraine.[54] The figure of Fu Manchu formed part of a transnational discourse that gave way to xenophobic and exclusionary policies against Asians and other non-Europeans in the service of white supremacist ideology.[55]

Whereas the figure of Fu Manchu and his female equivalent, the Dragon Lady (first played by Anna May Wong in the 1931 film *Daughter of the Dragon*), expressed political and economic threat to Anglo-American and British imperial expansion, they also represented fears of interracial sexual reproduction.[56] In the Brazilian context, Fu Manchu personified a complex and uneven multilateral relationship between Brazil and the threat of new forms of colonialism. Negative portrayals of Chinese people were not simply a repetition of US-driven anti-Chinese sentiment. Rather, authors and songwriters created and circulated a different semiotics of representation, for which they appropriated and reformulated Fu Manchu tropes for new cultural expressions of Brazilian nationalism that were at odds with US goals for hemispheric domination.

Fu Manchu made a number of appearances in works that had a significant impact on Brazilian cultural and aesthetic movements of the early twentieth century. In 1927, author Théo-Filho (Manuel Theotonio de Lacerda Freire Filho) published the highly popular book *Praia de Ipanema* (*Ipanema Beach*), considered an example of Brazilian literary naturalism because of its treatment of the marginalized aspects of Rio de Janeiro society. While Brazilian literary history may have forgotten Théo-Filho or not considered his work serious enough to enter the canon, he was a prolific and influential writer who published twenty-three books during his career. As Ruy Castro notes in the Preface to the 2000 edition, the first edition of *Praia de Ipanema*, published in 1927, sold over eight thousand copies, and there were subsequent editions. Written decades before the 1960s and 1970s, when high-rises began to grow on the now-famous beachfront neighborhood, *Ipanema Beach* was the first book written about and set in Ipanema. It played an important yet relatively unknown role in putting Ipanema on the map as a luxurious tourist destination that could rival US resort developments like Miami and Newport Beach.[57] The novel's main characters, Otto O'Kennutchy Guimarães, twenty-six-year-old wealthy son of jewelry dealers, and Paulo Correia, twenty-year-old heir to a cabinet seat in the Ministry of Agriculture, are part of Rio de Janeiro's haute-bourgeois society. Apart from spending their time at the country club, they indulge in Rio's underworld, demarcated as sites where "the Blacks and the Yellows dictated the mode of their bizarre and chaotic music and toxic vices imported from the Far East."[58] The Far East does not refer to an actual geographical location, but it is the racialized site where the "yellows" and "blacks" together determine the immoral order of the city's criminal world, in which jazz music is as threatening as Fu Manchu's opium den. Indeed, the Far East is located in the backstreets of Ipanema, in a kind of mystical and menacing Chinatown known by the street name Prudente de Moraes, where Hong-Lao-Tchao, the novel's stock Fu Manchu character, the "most sinister Chinese who ever penetrated the city's capital," runs an elaborate drug-trafficking trade in opium, cocaine, heroin, and other dealings.[59] Portrayed as a folkloric figure, Hong-Lao-Tchao arrives in Rio de Janerio in 1920 as the manager of an acrobatic troupe with the circus. He brings the "refined civility of his race that is older than all of the Western races and the most dainty of all the continents."[60] Hong-Lao-Tchao is the "most perfect and admirable Chinese drug trafficker."[61] Otto enjoys frequenting his *fum-*

erie to smoke opium and seek his Far Eastern wisdom derived from a state of opium-induced delirium.

Fu Manchu also made an appearance in the radical and experimental theatrical piece *O homem e o cavalo* (*The Man and the Horse*) (1933) by Oswald de Andrade, who was at the inaugural forefront of Brazilian modernism. Oswald used the stage to publicly portray and then destroy symbols of imperialism, racism, and fascism, depicted in characters such as Fu Manchu, Hitler, and Chiang Kai-shek. Through these characters, Oswald presents a complex portrait of racial ideologies circulating during the interwar period that culminated in World War II's ethnic cleansings and genocides. A pastiche of cultural and political referents composed of nine tableaux, *The Man and the Horse* called for a cast of nearly fifty characters portraying political and religious leaders, philosophers, and popular culture icons from several different millennia as well as from diverse geographical, extraterrestrial, and spiritual realms.

Oswald's Fu Manchu retained characteristics of what one scholar observes is a "throwback" to the "Mandarin of imperial China" who "sought retribution against those who humiliated and degraded the Chinese."[62] It bears noting that Oswald's version takes a different tack from those representations reiterating fears of Asian domination personified by the Yellow Peril. In a departure from those depictions, Oswald's Fu Manchu's identity is fluid, and he plays contradictory roles. Fu Manchu is Chang Kai-shek, and he is also the last hope against Western imperialism. Yet he is called a slave and rendered powerless. Fu Manchu is the last one standing, but he is also the figuration of "graceful death."[63] In a monologue, Fu Manchu stands on the stage and proclaims that he fought against subservience to Western imperialism to the bitter end. Oswald's Fu Manchu was not simply a reiteration of anti-Asian Yellow Peril discourse, but Oswald used the stage to perform postcolonial critiques that inverted tropes like Fu Manchu. The stage became the site to challenge imperialist discourse and reconfigure colonial legacies of race.

The trope of Fu Manchu circulated across the Brazilian cultural milieu during the first half of the twentieth century, including in Brazilian popular music, wherein musicians and songwriters took it into their own hands to infuse these racial representations with new meaning. In the song "Negócio da China" ("Chinese Business"), composers Afonso Teixeira and Peterpan begin the song with Butterfly and Fu Manchu: "I'm going to China to see how it's going / A Butterfly with Fu Manchu."[64] In Portuguese, the colloquial expression *negócio da China* connotes a lucrative business, but the song's lyrics convey the opposite message. The lyrics portray the Chinaman who was once yellow as now red with shame, an allusion in racialized terms to the idea that the Chinese economic system is dysfunctional and corrupt: "Because he is involved in a swindle / He is embarrassed. / Well now, one grain of rice that was not enough for one has to provide for two." "Negócio da China" connects China's weak economy to a frail economic alliance between Brazil and China.

Other songs about China released during World War II portray uneasiness about forging economic alliances with the Chinese, even though a military alliance was already in place. These songs depict Chineseness as too different to allow for full assimilation into Brazilian cultural traditions like carnival. Brazilian carnival uses strategies of satire, inversion, and revelry to express political critique. It has a long historical and political tradition, whose origins can be traced to the carnivals of Catholic Europe. In 1940, André Filho and Durval Melo composed "Carnaval na China" ("Carnival in China"),[65] which describes a carnival parade that the Chinese get all wrong.[66] "Carnival in China" recounts a list of missing elements necessary for carnival; clearly the Chinese efforts lack the carnival essence, the festivity, the music, and the organizational structure for a truly Brazilian event: "My first carnival in China / Over there, they don't have confetti and ribbon / Over there, they don't have tambourines or guitars / And also in China, they don't make carnival lines." Carnival in this song draws the cultural line between Brazilian and Chinese identity as being so incompatible that the speaker rejects intercultural mixing. The speaker tells us that carnival in China is a big disappointment. All of the traditional elements of Brazilian carnival are absent, and he cannot put up with those cultural differences "não aturei." The composer uses carnival and its attendant political and cultural traditions as one example of how China and the Chinese would misconstrue Brazilian culture and politics, and thus not assimilate well.

"Na China" ("In China"), composed by Haroldo Lobo and Milton de Oliveira in 1941, describes irreconcilable differences between Chinese and Brazilian culture: "There, in China / No one is named John / The Chinese eat / Seated on the ground / He has a Chinese name / That's too funny."[67] The differences range from the small—in China, no one is named John and the Chinese eat seated on the ground—to the large and incomprehensible.

The lyrics create grammatically confusing sentences and imagery as a metaphor for unexplainable cultural differences. The melody and lyrics have a playful musical quality, but they have no logical meaning. For example, in reference to a jackfruit wedge, the lyrics state, "É goma na jaca" ("it's wedge in the jackfruit"), which would be like stating "a slice in an orange" rather than simply "an orange slice." Even more puzzling, the lyric's pronouns are unclear, so we are left wondering to whom or what the verb belongs. For example, the line "É cata caju" sounds odd because it inserts the conjugated form of the verb *ser* (to be) in front of the verb *catar* (to collect/gather). The translation to English would be something like, "It is/He is collects *caju* [fruit that grows from the cashew tree]." The lyrics describe his actions, but the word order does not make sense. The strange grammatical structure makes the Chinese man's actions into something that is literally indecipherable and implicitly offers a common stereotype about the inscrutable Chinese other.

In 1945, composers Benedito Lacerda and Haroldo Lobo wrote "Pagode na China" ("Pagode in China").[68] The song depicts a Chinaman jumping like Saci Pererê. In Brazilian folklore, Saci is portrayed as a one-legged black or mixed-race prankster, embodying a mixture of Indigenous, European, and African traits. The folklore of Saci has many versions. It is believed to have originated from a Tupi-Guaraní legend.[69] Saci's figure carries a number of representations that express Brazil's history of colonialism and slavery. In one version, Saci was a slave who had cut off his leg in order to escape. In another version, he is one-legged because he is the deformed offspring of a slave master and enslaved woman. Saci not only misbehaves and causes much disorder; he also has the ability to multiply quickly. He is permanently childlike and magical; he loves mischief and grants wishes to those who capture him. The lyrics liken the caricature of the Chinaman to Saci. Both jump in a magical, funny way, and the Chinaman, like Saci, cannot be taken too seriously.

Despite the cartoon-like characteristics of the jumping Chinaman, the song suddenly takes a solemn tone, describing how a neighbor has lowered the flag to half-mast: "In the neighbor's house, there is a flag at half-mast / In the Chinaman's house, now there is carnival." While the song does not specify the neighbor, the historical context makes it likely that the reference is to China's neighbor Japan's defeat in World War II in 1945. The neighbor lowers the flag to half-mast, a public gesture that signals a commemoration, mourning, or death, usually for a politically influential figure or event. Meanwhile, the Chinese man celebrates in his house with a carnival. Yet, the song cautions, he is not naive about this victory. He knows that while the Japanese have been defeated, that does not imply that the Chinese will be held in better standing: "And the Chinaman, he is no fool to avoid more problems / He put a zipper on the dragon's mouth." The colloquial expression "to zip up the dragon's mouth" implies that he conceals his illicit dealings. This song rehearses the recurring theme of mistrust about transactions with the Chinese.

Even after the end of World War II, similar sentiments about the Chinese pervaded Brazilian popular music. In line with previous songs that portrayed Chinese sexuality to symbolize Chinese competition or Chinese military power, the 1953 song titled "Dança chinesa" ("Chinese Dance"), composed by Haroldo Lobo and Nestor de Holanda, depicts Chinese sexuality as impotent and not normative.[70] The song brings back the figure of the jumping Chinaman, but this time he leaps to and fro in vain, for he does not go anywhere: "He leaps a little, here and there, but stays put." There is leaping, teasing, and leading each other on, but nothing happens: "In Peking everything goes / Girls dance with girls / Men with men / It's Chinaman here / It's Chinaman there / It's Chinaman here / It's Chinaman there / And it goes on in this teasing way." The song describes that in Beijing, anything goes—girls go with girls and men go with men; sexual preferences are not heteronormative.

The metaphor of the jumping Chinaman as unreliable, unstable, and fickle persisted across time. Decades later, in 1974, Brasinha wrote "Marcha do Kung Fu" ("Kung Fu March").[71] The song seems to be about a heroic man who has an excess of masculinity, expressed in the colloquial expression *homem para chuchu*, meaning "manly in abundance." The song actually means the opposite: Chinese masculinity is not in abundance; rather, it is lacking. Soon enough, the lyrics resort to old stereotypes about Chinese men as ambiguously gendered with animal-like features and inadequate male sexuality: "When he fights / He jumps more than a kangaroo." The lyrics refer to the Chinese as "Kung," short for Kung Fu: "His philosophy / Is to do good for whomever he can / Kung is only wrong / Because he is not into women / Go for it Kung!" The song thus parodies Chinese masculinity as unfit for heteronormative domestic relations.

In 2004, Brazilian popular music singer Adriana Calcanhotto released a children's album titled *Adriana Partimpim*. She included the song "Lig, lig, lig, lé," discussed earlier in this chapter. In a music video of Calcanhotto and her band members performing the song for children, they wear origami hats made to resemble dragons, and when she sings the line, "Here comes your Chinaman on tiptoe . . . The Chinese eat only once a month," she pulls back her eyes to make them look squinty and slanted.[72] Singing and performing anti-Chinese gestures, whose histories are replete with racial profiling and exclusion, reproduces for children the project of whitening. "Lig, lig, lig, lé" was popular in the early twentieth century, and clearly still popular in the twenty-first century. That it has also become a popular children's song ingrains racial ideas into children at a young age. These entrenched modes of racialization fortify feelings of racial superiority and inferiority that sit on opposite sides of the same coin, depending on how individuals are made conscious of their position to race and nation.

The cultural production and consumption of Chineseness can be observed today in the popular Brazilian Chinese fast food chain Lig-Lig. Its name plays on the verb *to telephone* (*ligar*), and repurposes the title of the popular song "Lig, lig, lig, lé" (Figure 6.1). In 1992, its founder and CEO, Thomas Liu, a descendant of Chinese immigrants, brought the US concept of Chinese food delivery to Brazil when he opened the first Lig-Lig.[73] The restaurant chain has since expanded to approximately thirty-one cities across five states. The brand logo features a caricature with slanted eyes, a knot button shirt, and rice field hat. The caricature is holding chopsticks and a square Chinese food take-out box. The restaurant's slogan is "Authentic Chinese Food." That the highly popular Chinese fast food restaurant chain has embraced this caricature as its brand exemplifies this stereotype's market appeal. The image indexes cultural expressions of anti-Chinese sentiment in Brazilian popular culture, but it also shows how racial representations are appropriated, commodified, and turned into profit.

Throughout the twentieth century, songs about China and the Chinese aided in fortifying Brazilian nationalism during times of geopolitical

FIGURE 6.1. Lig-Lig restaurant website.

conflict. In some cases, state-sponsored war propaganda circulating in the United States, and among Allied powers, entered into Brazilian cultural expressions to reinforce geopolitical alliances. In other instances, various actors actively unraveled state projects of cultural citizenship and appropriated discourses of Chineseness for their own enterprises.

CONCLUSION

Imaginative Geographies
of Brazil and China

Racial representations have played a critical role in structuring Brazilian emancipation narratives of liberty and citizenship. This book's archives of Chinese racialization—whether in Brazilian popular music, vaudeville, poetry, porcelain, or graffiti—allow us to trace how signifiers of race get bound to emotions, bodies, and geographies. Mapping cultural production about Chineseness across political borders reveals the processual and relational structure of racial formation across time and space. These cultural constructions have also challenged and reorganized the cartographic concepts of East/West and North/South. As constructions of Chineseness move across space and time and shift in value, they expose the imperialist and nationalist imaginative geographies that orient ideas about self/Other, proximity and distance. Imaginative geographies have been a keystone for forging notions of racial, political, and moral superiority over a region.[1] Spatial designators are epistemological because they assign notions of social and political systems as well as economic dynamism to landmass.[2] They have been critical for visualizing the modern world as a structured totality with Euro-America (the West) at the unified center.[3] Imaginative geographies that constructed ideas of the Américas, the *Indies* or a "New World," for example, have been crucial for justifying imperialist expansion, Indigenous land expropriation, colonist extraction of natural resources, and racialized exploitative labor. Prominent twentieth-century Brazilian intellectuals, such as Gilberto Freyre and his contemporary Antônio Gomes do Carmo, in their analyses of Brazilian society and culture, took on the task of reordering imperialist and capitalist cartographic imaginaries that created the Americas as a stage for enacting Euro-American political and economic projects. Freyre and Carmo framed Brazil and China as sharing connected histories. They produced a conceptual nearness between these two geographically distant places to perform a critique of imperialist geographical imaginaries and global capitalist expansion through uneven trade and exploitative labor. Robert Stam and Ella Shohat observe that Freyre's writings about the Orient reveal how "in the Ibero-American context," Orientalism and de-Orientalization have always been a postcolonial critique wherein the Orient performs "opposite intellectual meanings and emotional affects" that disrupt European cultural hegemony and geographic consciousness.[4] Freyre and Carmo create proximity between China and Brazil to perform anti-imperialist and anti-capitalist encounters that expose continuing forms of colonialism, including the persistence of racial purity ideologies and racialized exploitative labor. Their writings reveal how Asian racialization helped to shape Brazil's image as a racial democracy.

A Chinese History of Brazil

Antônio Gomes do Carmo, who wrote under the pseudonym of Simão de Mantua, worked as an agronomist for the Ministry of Agriculture during the first decades of the twentieth century. He published a number of studies about Brazilian culture, society, and agriculture.[5] Among his works are *Cartas de um Chinez do Brasil para a China* (1923) (*Letters from a Chinaman from Brazil to China*), a highly important book that has nearly disappeared from history.[6] The so-called Chinese history of Brazil is a political-satirical analysis of Brazilian history, economics, and society as told from a supposed Chinese man's perspective.

The book purports to be a collection of nine letters about Brazil written by a Chinese man named Ho-He Dgent to his friend, Ling-Ling, in China. The titles of the letters include such topics as "The history of Brazil as told by a Chinaman," "Social aspects of Brazil as described by a Chinaman," "Political and social aspects of Brazil as noted by a Chinaman" and other topics, including the economy, religion, divorce, the penitentiary system, and the branches of the government, all as observed by the so-called chim, Ho-He Dgent. The book presents itself as a collection of historical documents, claiming that they first appeared in the Chinese gazette *Tomh-Ha-Pao*. The *Changhaian Times* distributed the letters, and Simão de Mantua translated them into the "vernacular." The book begins with a "Necessary Explanation," a preface of sorts, that explains the curious origins of the letters written by a Chinese man from Brazil. This prompts the translator to wonder if Brazil had not really been colonized by the Chinese and their descendants.[7]

The first letter includes a critical portrayal of Portuguese colonial history in Brazil, and it is replete with anti-Portuguese terminology. The letter's scathing tone condemns Brazil's colonial history, which the author marks as beginning in the year 1500, when the Portuguese, referred to as "demons from the West,"[8] first arrived in Brazil, introducing wars, disease, starvation, and other sufferings for centuries to come.[9] Addressing a fictional Chinese public, Ho-He Dgent explains the Brazilian expressions and culture that would have been familiar to a Brazilian reading public. However, the strategy of addressing a Chinese audience allows him to defamiliarize well-known historical, political, and social customs, allowing for a critique of Brazil's odd, hypocritical, and absurd laws and cultural habits. In this way, *Cartas de um Chinez*, as told from the guise of a Chinese man from Brazil, provides a critical interpretation of Brazilian politics, economics, laws, and social customs. The critiques range from condemning the incorrect naming of Rio de Janeiro (January River), whose waters were never a river, to explaining the expression *for the English to see*, which means that it is a Brazilian custom to do things "on paper" but without any intention of doing them in actuality.[10]

Ho-He Dgent tells his readers that miscegenation with the local population is a key method for the Portuguese to establish dominion in new territories.[11] Using the pseudoscientific eugenics-based rhetoric of miscegenation, he describes the actions of the *bandeirantes*, whom he calls the "neo-lusos"—the barbarous, profiteering exploiters—as the product of the racial mixing between Portuguese and Indigenous parents, also referred to as *mamelucos* or *caboclos*.[12] His anti-Portuguese statements offer a nuanced understanding about branqueamento, Brazil's racial whitening project that aimed to transition the population from blacker to whiter. As I have discussed throughout this book, *whiteness* and *blackness* were relational terms that gained meaning through circumoceanic cultural expressions rather than skin color. For Carmo, the mixed-race offspring of Portuguese and

Indigenous parents would not bridge civilization and barbarism, as others imagined.[13] Rather, he used eugenic ideology to negatively portray the mixed-race descendants of the Portuguese, and in the process he threw a wrench at racial whitening ideology. His Chinese history of Brazil turns the critical gaze inward at both the legacy of Portuguese imperialism and Brazilian actors whose actions and policies kept colonialist practices going.

Gilberto Freyre's Brazilian Orients

Gilberto Freyre, an international figure and one of the leading Brazilian intellectuals of the twentieth century, advanced a number of political projects through conceptualizing Brazil as the site where many Orients converged.[14] His literary constructions of plural Brazilian Orients are foundational to understanding his work in crafting Brazil's myth of a racial democracy, which sold Brazil's image on the world stage as a harmonious, mixed-race nation.[15]

His prolific writings that spanned much of the twentieth century are replete with celebratory ideas about interracial relations that has had lasting impact in defining Brazilian national identity and the policies that attempt to craft it. His seminal work, *Casa grande and senzala* (*The Masters and the Slaves*) (1933), arguably a pseudosociological study of the intimacies of nineteenth-century Brazilian plantation life that intertwined memoir with historical and sociological research, marked a foundational moment in the construction of Brazil's national myth of racial democracy, though Freyre did not specifically use the term *racial democracy* until the 1960s.[16] Freyre's views of Portuguese colonists—slave drivers though they were—fluctuated from celebratory to condemning in his prolific writings that spanned well-over half a century. In his earlier writings published in the 1930s, he contended that Portuguese colonizers had "social plasticity" in their ability to racially cross with "exotic women," he asserted they left a legacy rooted in "ineptitude, stupidity, and salaciousness."[17] This tongue-in-cheek portrait suggested that while the Portuguese willingly accepted mixed-race unions with "exotic women," they were blundering colonizers.

Freyre's *Casa grande* rewrote slavery's histories of sexual and racialized violence in a nostalgic manner, as romanticized remembrances of plantation life.[18] Enslaved black, Indigenous, and mixed-race women's sexual intimacies and reproductive abilities were regulated by the whims of the men and women of the *casa grande* (master's house or big house), intertwining with the market logic of capitalism. Perverse cruelty transformed sexual abuse into capital. Enslaved women were turned into breeders and forced to have sexual relations with the strongest male slaves to reproduce more laborers at low cost. Forcing women to serve as *amas-de-leite* (wet nurses) transformed breast milk into a commodity.[19] Scholars have widely critiqued his work for its overwhelming nostalgic and sentimental tone that erases such violent colonial histories and sexual violence committed against enslaved and Indigenous women.

His celebratory rhetoric about mixed-race relationships was also a critical intervention in and denouncement of early twentieth-century white supremacy movements that were gaining steam on a worldwide level. European fascism and the rise of Nazism had cleared the way for systemic ethnic cleansing; in the United States, Jim Crow laws mandated racial segregation in public facilities and institutes, disenfranchising those considered racial minorities; and the National Party of South Africa moved toward institutionalizing racial segregation into policy in apartheid laws. Within this complex political constellation, Freyre recast Brazil's violent past to reformulate eugenic-based ideas about degenerative miscegenation into a celebration of Brazil's Oriental heritage. The Orient, for Freyre, referred to everything but Anglo-America and Western Europe—the Occident.

Freyre's *Sobrados e mucambos* (*Mansions and Shanties*) (1936) is a study about the complex continuum of the master/slave social and economic structure of the plantation economy. It traces this continuum into urban development, housing inequality, and race- and class-based segregation. His chapter "Orient and Occident" provides a backdrop against which to reflect on his analysis of urbanization, modernization, and racial difference in Brazilian perspective. Freyre's Orient recast European Orientalist fantasies of Western triumph over Asia. His idea of the Orient represented places where the Portuguese had settled and set up trade. It also signified a strong Islamic and Jewish influence, owing to seven centuries of coexistence among Christians, Jews, and Muslims on the Iberian Peninsula, as well as the strong African influence, which Brazil "assimilated" and "converted" into "its own patrimony."[20] Brazil, for Freyre, had a hybrid and Oriental cultural essence due to Islamic, African, and Asian influences in Brazilian architecture and cultural traditions.[21] Freyre framed the Orient as Brazil's founding matrix, Silva argues, one that embraced non-European as well as anti-Europeans values.[22]

Freyre created multiple Orients in Brazil, a rhetorical strategy that inverted and rearranged European racial mythologies and cartographic knowledge to disrupt the idea that Europeanization or Occidentalization, necessarily precedes modernization. Freyre was not reconceptualizing the formation of continental landmasses so much as he was inverting the positive and negative symbols of East and West, deliberately aligning Brazil with the Orient to criticize the processes of "modernization" that Brazil had been suffering through since the nineteenth century.[23] *Modernization* was a bad word in Freyre's view, since it referred to the ethnic cleansing of Brazil's multicultural, non-Northern Protestant European heritage. His celebratory tone of Brazil's multiethnic cultures was a strategy to critique and condemn Anglo-French imperialism in Brazil—including the ethnic cleansing that contributed to the destruction of non-European cultural patrimony.

While Brazilian civilization had once been very diverse, the nineteenth century had ushered in an era of Anglo-French imperialism and racial and ethnic cleansing, what Freyre denounced as *"desassombrando-se"* (unshadowing).[24] He used the phrase *unshadowing* not as a critique of Portuguese imperialism or Brazil's Oriental features, but rather to refer to the negative influence of Northern European racism in Brazil. Freyre blamed English and French cultural hegemony for removing Oriental influence in customs and architecture from Brazilian society. "Unshadowing" referred to the forced elimination—ethnic cleansing of material culture and cultural patrimony—of Oriental, or *shadowed,* aspects of the multicultural past, which he referred to as *Orientalism, Asianism,* or *Africanism.* He asserted that the process of unshadowing Brazil's Oriental features was part of the ideological campaign of Aryan racial purity and white supremacist ideology:

> The surviving characteristics of Asia and Africa among us, the Aryanists believed, only served to humiliate us in European eyes. We should completely free ourselves of them instead of encouraging or revitalizing them by introducing into the country new Asianisms and Africanisms, alongside new Africans and Asians in grand numbers who would embarrassingly accentuate the black, mulato, and yellow stain on the face of the population and preserve in Brazilian culture and landscape scandalous reds and screaming yellows that no longer correspond to European taste in color, decoration, and composition that developed here.[25]

Freyre's symbolic use of unshadowing and shadowing subverts European philosophical symbols commonly used in writings about the Enlightenment, wherein light is a metaphor for knowledge, maturity, and freedom. In Freyre's use, the symbols of lightness and darkness, shadowing and unshadowing, are actually a critique of the Western European intellectual tradition and the negative effects European ideologies of racial superiority had had on Brazil. In the Greco-Roman Christian tradition, the dualism between light and dark conveys a series of binary relationships that could essentially be broken down into ideas about good and bad, knowledge and ignorance. For example, in biblical terms, light is a consistent symbol that conveys the goodness of God: "And God saw that the light was good; and God separated the light from the darkness."[26] The analogy between light and creation of the world is, significantly, also a way of naming and producing knowledge about the world. Light, as a metonym for creation and knowledge, is consistent across the European philosophical tradition, readily observable in Kant's writings about the Enlightenment, a state in which man emerges from nonage toward freedom—the attainment of understanding through one's own reasoning.[27] Kant crafts his meaning of enlightenment by creating the dichotomy between a mature and immature state. The enlightened man has reached a full level of maturity.

The idea that an enlightened state is synonymous with maturity is also observable in the work of political economist John Stuart Mill, whose famous essays on liberty defined maturity in racial terms when he contended that certain races were not yet ready for freedom due to their nonage (immature state), and so his doctrines on liberty "apply only to human beings in the maturity of their faculties. . . . We may leave out of consideration those backward states of society in which the race itself may be considered as in its nonage."[28] While Mill, like Kant, advocated autonomy and opposed paternalism, these ideas of racial superiority still entered into their rationales when it came to defining who constituted the fully mature political subject capable of self-rule, and thus who did or did not have access to the inalienable rights of liberty. Mill rehearsed Aristotle's philosophy of natural freedom in racial terms when he indicated that some races were not suited for deliberation and rational thinking. Freyre's essays reacted against the mythical hierarchy of the enlightened technological and philosophical advancements of Northern Europe when he asserted and appropriated the symbols of Brazil's shadowed, backward Oriental heritage.

In emphasizing Brazil's Oriental heritage, Freyre was able to discuss relational forms of racialization that Asians and Africans in Brazil experienced. His writings show that yellow and black labor was symbolic of racial categories assigned to semifeudal and unfree laborers. In Freyre's view, through centuries of trade, Brazil and the Orient were already culturally and economically linked: "Brazil and the Orient had been brought so close together that the regular and irregular commerce between them during the colonial era constituted one of the firmest bases of the Brazilian agrarian and patriarchal system."[29] Brazil shared characteristics with Eastern (semifeudal) modes of production and maintained rural and patriarchal qualities that had resisted modernization. Those who advocated for Asiatic (Chinese) and African labor immigration as a means to offset the labor shortage that had occurred with the end of slavery believed that Chinese and African laborers would be familiar with Brazil's feudal conditions. They rationalized that since African and Chinese laborers were already accustomed to serving as serfs in their home countries, they would "effortlessly" adapt to Brazil's slave and semi-slave labor conditions.[30] Within the new context of the formation of the nation-state and waves of immigration labor that accompanied the end of slavery, those against Asian and African immigration spoke of the threat that ongoing modes of unfree labor would mean to progress, development, patriotism, and enlightenment. Adding the presence of these semi-slaves to Brazil's climate of inequality and unfree labor conditions would produce a highly "disagreeable effect" on "free men," European laborers, including "workman of England or France, a peasant of Germany or Switzerland, or even of Spain and Portugal."[31]

Freyre condemned ideologies of white supremacy that upheld Chinese and Africans' slave and slave-like statuses, which had qualities that made them unfit citizens for the emerging nation endeavoring to approximate European standards of civilization measured in the nation's ability to whiten the population. In subverting the language of light and dark, Freyre reinterpreted the founding symbols of Enlightenment temporality that held European civilization to have reached a level of full maturity, while so-called barbaric and savage races were still in the dark, immature and thus better off being ruled, and relegated to lower racial and social hierarchical categories. Freyre celebrated Brazil's Oriental, thus shadowed, characteristics, and in doing so, he critiqued European Enlightenment and its symbols of lightness and knowledge. These, for him, had produced the ideology of ethnic cleansing and white supremacy that had forced Brazil to unshadow and thereby whiten its past.

Freyre's writings on the Oriental influences in Brazilian culture not only advanced the idea that the Portuguese seaborne imperial history had produced new kinds of ethnic mixing. He also used Portuguese trade and colonial histories in Asia and Africa to highlight how Portuguese imperial expansion facilitated the global slave trade and new modes of unfree labor that followed abolition. Freyre showed that Asiatic—by which he meant Chinese—and African laborers were relationally racialized: yellow and black labor both signified unfree labor and serfdom. He attributed Brazilian racism to European ideologies of racial superiority that deemed yellow and black labor symbolic of semi-feudalism. He condemned the white supremacist attitude that Chinese and African laborers embodied the undesirable ethnic and racial qualities that would keep the Brazilian nation in a backward economic state. Instead, he created a spatial proximity between Brazil and the Orient to emphasize their historical connections that came out of imperialist and capitalist expansion. In configuring Brazil as the Orient, he created a global space, connected by transoceanic circuits of exploitative racialized labor. He configured a new *mapamundi* where racialized nationalisms and overlapping forms of racialization between Chineseness and blackness were bound to an imperialist and global capitalist imaginary rather than to a national space.

Freyre attempted to grapple with Brazil's geopolitical positioning as both Latin *and* American in *New World in the Tropics* (1960), which he intended for an international audience, and where he called on Brazil to advocate for a new kind of national culture, one that would move away from the facade of political independence and toward economic independence.[32] To address concerns about loosening Brazil's economic dependency on the United States, Freyre asserted that Brazil could become as powerful and vast as China because it could inherit the seat of Portuguese governance over colonial territories in Africa and Asia, which, according to him, were already united through a shared Lusophone heritage in language and religion. He put forth the notion that the Brazilian economic and political state shared more commonalities with Eastern (Chinese and African) systems than Western ones (Northern European and the United States). In emphasizing this difference, he created a conceptual space in the Orient for positing Brazilian economic autonomy from the United States and Northern Europe.

Although US hemispheric domination favored Brazil, granting it economic, military, and diplomatic privileges, the United States was using Brazil as a bridge to Spanish America to secure a stronghold in Latin America.[33] This relationship changed by the mid-1970s when Brazil aligned with Spanish American countries and led Latin American resistance against US policies. To find a common ground, Freyre recommended reciprocal exchange, a "two-way cultural policy" between North and South America, and opined that if the United States forced Brazil to conform to American standardization, it should close itself off from further trade, to the "point of appearing Chinese," that is, following suit with China in restricting trade relations with the United States.[34] For him, China signified different alignments Brazil could take during the Cold War and a source of "anti-Yankee" power and "aggressive resistance" against US regional domination in Latin America.[35] Solidarity with China also signified "receptive tolerance towards Soviet Russia, the only rival power of the United States at present."[36] Aligning with China would mean that Brazil would be stronger, since, as he contended, China and Brazil were each larger than the continental United States in landmass alone.

His declaration that Brazil had the ability to absorb Oriental traits offers another dimension to understanding his large body of work regarding Lusotropicalism, which asserted that the Portuguese overseas empire produced a uniquely multicultural empire, a "Portuguese-tropical, civilization that would be a vast civilization more widespread even than that of China—in America, Africa, the Orient, islands of the Atlantic, and Europe itself, in spaces either tropical or quasi-tropical."[37] Lusotropicalism was among other things an attempt to justify continuing Portuguese imperialism in Africa and Asia after World War II. Freyre drew on Brazil's Oriental past to advance a multiculturalist agenda that could sanitize the history of Portuguese imperialism in Africa. Rewriting this history served Brazil politically and economically and also opened the way for Brazilian imperialism in former Portuguese colonies. He emphasized the notion of an Oriental heritage to portray Brazil as a multicultural nation ready to enter the world stage and position the country as the rightful and able inheritor of the vast and diverse Lusotropical Portuguese imperial legacy, namely, Portugal's existing colonies in tropical regions in Asia and Africa. In the 1970s, he began advancing the idea that Portuguese imperialism was not as disastrous as other regimes of colonization. He emphasized that Portuguese colonists had the unique ability to adapt well in semitropical and tropical climates, as well as in integrating local customs with Lusophone culture: "By their [Portuguese] genius in combining civilized and Indigenous values, they had been able, perhaps better than any other people of predominantly European origin, to adapt a European civilization to the tropics."[38] In the context of Portugal's dissolution of its African colonies in the mid-1970s, as Jerry Dávila observes, white Brazilians leveraged Brazil as a racial democracy to assert their blackness or Africanness to establish relations with Africa and claim a place as an emerging world power.[39]

Shifting geopolitical dynamics shaped Freyre's writings about Brazil and the interpretations he assigned to the Orient. His celebration of Brazil's multicultural past as a means of establishing the possibility of a new form of Brazilian imperialism in Asia and Africa produced an additional layer in the processual and polycentric structures of racial formation and representation that founded the Brazilian nation, and allows us to observe the prismatic contours of circumoceanic memory.

Ruins of Race

Imaginative geographies of an Oriental Brazil are still relevant today; they map a story about the international division of labor, wherein global capitalism has distributed extreme exploitative and slave-like labor to the Global South. The condition of some newly arriving Chinese immigrants to contemporary Brazil too readily resembles the nineteenth-century cases of the Chinese "coolies" discussed in earlier chapters. Recent investigations have uncovered a Chinese mafia–led network of human labor trafficking between Brazil and China. In 2013, the Ministry of Public Labor Prosecution (MPT) and the Ministry of Labor and Employment (MTE) began discovering a string of cases of Chinese enslavement in Brazil: undocumented Chinese migrants arrived in Brazil and were forced into conditions of exploitative captive labor.[40] Since September 2015, the MPT and MTE have uncovered four cases alone in the state of Rio de Janeiro. Other cases have also appeared in São Paulo. Labor inspectors have found undocumented Chinese migrants working in slave-labor conditions in Chinese-owned pastry shops and other small commercial businesses, such as jewelry and accessory stores. The investigations discovered shared patterns among these cases, leading labor inspectors and the police to believe there is a Chinese mafia–led network facilitating the transportation of Chinese youth to precarious labor conditions in Brazil.[41] Chinese headmen lure Chinese youth from southern Chinese provinces with promises of riches and adventure. They pay their voyage to Brazil and provide them with falsified documents. In exchange, the young men and women agree to work in Brazil until their debt is paid off. However, in many cases, once they arrive in Brazil, employers withhold their passports, place them in captivity, and force them to live and work in storage rooms hidden in the backrooms of stores. Employers withhold pay or pay measly wages, reasoning that the workers are paying off their debts. In 2013, in Mangaratiba, a city located in Rio de Janeiro State, a labor inspector found a minor working daily from 5:00 a.m. to 10:00 p.m. His employer had physically abused and tortured him with cigarette burns. He was able to escape and filed a denouncement with the MPT.[42] He testified against his employer, who was subsequently arrested, and the young man entered into a witness protection program.[43] In 2014, the MPT and the federal police rescued a twenty-three-year-old Chinese woman who was working in a condition analogous to slavery in a jewelry and fashion accessories store, located in Araçatuba, São Paulo.[44] The woman could not leave the store without authorization. She slept in the storage room. The owners served food to her on the floor, and she drank water from a bucket.[45]

In another case, labor inspectors rescued two Chinese men whom agents had found working in slave-labor conditions. Two months following their rescue, the men returned to their old jobs. Journalists Eliane Lobato and Helena Borges interviewed one of the workers about his current conditions, and he contended that conditions had improved: he now goes out to drink beer and visits the mall. Most of all, however, he did not want to return to China.[46] His response complicates the news story about slavery, since he states that he works willingly, and even indicates that he enjoys leisure time and middle-class consumption. It is impossible to assess from this news story the true nature of his response. Regardless, these stories give a sense of the kinds of labor insecurity that newly arriving Chinese immigrants face in Brazil. Marcia Albernaz, a labor inspector who works on cases of Chinese slavery in Brazil, has made public statements about Brazilian labor rights. Victims of slavery are protected under the law. In a partnership between the MPT and the Rio de Janeiro superintendent for human rights promotion, a number of rights have been granted to undocumented victims of slavery, including immediate rights to work permits, Portuguese-language classes, and professional training.[47] In addition, the government may prosecute criminal behavior, and fine employers to pay indemnity and severance to the exploited workers. Unfortunately, many of the undocumented Chinese who are working in slave and slave-like conditions may not know that they have labor rights, and they may fear that denouncing their employers will lead to deportation.[48] These contemporary stories of labor trafficking uncannily recall the dystopic views that writers of the late nineteenth century had about Brazil's future, where a hybrid Brazil-China could mean a new era of slavery in the form of despotic Chinese labor.

Old stereotypes about the Chinese as antithetical to liberty are still present in contemporary society, attesting to ongoing cultural transmissions of circumoceanic memory. On a trip to Rio de Janeiro in December 2015, I spotted a street mural in the Lapa neighborhood that depicted a taxi driver driving a Hawaiian-shirt-sporting tourist to the Maracanã stadium (Figure C.1). On the street, on either side of the taxi, are caricatures of coolies riding on bicycles. On one side, one caricature represents one ambiguously gendered Chinese bicyclist wearing a cone-shaped rice paddy field hat. The facial profile reveals slanted eyes, buck teeth, and a long braid, a likely reference to the Qing queue—a men's hairstyle that the Qing dynasty forced on Han men that symbolized loyalty to the Qing. The caricaturized features too easily recall the constructions of Chineseness as a yellow race that circulated during the height of worldwide anti-Chinese sentiment in the nineteenth century. But the Chinese are insiders in this mural of Brazilian society; they are extras in the background. They are a symbolic representation of unfreedom and as quotidian as Rio's traffic. The outsider in the scene is the white foreign tourist who is visually depicted as getting taken for a ride. The taxi driver smiles cunningly. The words above his head state that he will take the tourist down the best route, but the tourist stares back at him with alarm. Perhaps he fears that the taxi driver will pull a scam by taking him on a longer and more expensive ride. In allegorical fashion, the mural depicts a complex structural interplay of geopolitical and economic relations. Brazil and China are on the same side, easily recalling the economic bloc BRICS (Brazil, Russia, India, China, South Africa). Yet as Freyre deconstructed Western cartographic knowledge between East/West, North/South, and capitalist distributions between economic centers and peripheries, the swindle on the tourist portrays the foreigner as the gullible and vulnerable center in the hands of Brazil's internal corruption. The mural also suggests

FIGURE C.1. Street mural in Lapa, Rio de Janeiro, December 15, 2015. Source: Photograph by the author.

the view that the coolie is not the inassimilable Chinese Other; instead, the coolie is Brazilian, as ordinary as traffic, and symbolizes a pessimistic, postcolonial critique of global capitalism and the global neoliberal regime that depends on producing states of invisible, insecure, and precarious labor as an unexceptional condition. In this mural's bleak view, Brazil's contemporary political and economic situation is retrograde and peripheral.

While racial ideology may reinforce state power—essentially a global phenomenon—circumoceanic memories of race demand site-specific study, owing to the way that racial regimes hang together but get deployed for different localized objectives. In turn, it is essential to recognize the quotidian practices of the individuals who have carved out their own social spaces and cultural memories. Historians who have conducted studies about Chinese diaspora to Latin America have pieced together intergenerational familial histories about Chinese Panamanians, Chinese Mexicans, and Chinese Cubans.[49] People who self-identify with Asian ancestry in Brazil have fought against longstanding forms of racialization, still very present today. Contemporarily, the Asian feminist collective Lótus PWR organizes a platform to advance discussions about intersectionality and antiracism to combat gender and racial stereotypes that fixate ideas of Asians as perpetual outsiders and as inscrutably Other.[50] These studies and activism provide a social history of individuals whose complexities and contradictions refuse narratives that pin them between warring racial and national ideals.

Sigmund Freud, in *Civilization and its Discontents* (1930), created an analogy between the ruins of a city and memory, illustrating the idea that history does not remain in the past; it survives in the material and symbolic realms of memory. The analogy between the ruins of memory and the material remnants of the past ultimately speaks to the material, symbolic, imaginative, and enacted dimensions of cultural memory. Circumoceanic memories of racialization occupy a place like the material residue buried in the soil beneath the newest modern buildings, which constitutes the elements of its foundation. The remnants may belong to an earlier phase of history that has since been renovated, buried, demolished, and yet they "continue to exist alongside the latest one."[51] How histories of racialization perform, create, destroy, transpose, and suture the physical and symbolic realms of memory that exist as an aspect of us require that we recognize and interrupt their disciplinary power. How we construct futures for these memories is an ongoing pursuit.

Notes

PREFACE

1. I thank Jeffrey Lesser for providing a history of the church during a walking tour of Liberdade.

2. *Nippo* 1999; Lammardo 2016.

3. Guimarães 1979, 91.

4. "Temas Anteriores" (previous themes), *Festival do Japão* website.

5. Ide 2014, 28.

6. Weinstein 2015, 6.

7. My investigation of Asian racialization in the historically contingent context of Chinese diaspora to Brazil and the formation of the Brazilian nation expands on previous scholarship in Luso-Hispanic Orientalism. As scholars have observed, Edward Said's work dealt mainly with representations of the Islamic world and the Middle East in French, British, and (US) American literary production; he only briefly considered the special cases of Portugal, Spain, and the imperial rivalries that existed among European colonial interests. Scholarship on Luso-Hispanic Orientalism has argued that studies about the Iberian empires require a different lens that can account for multilateral economic imperatives, as well as the distinct religious and racial relations that formed among the Iberian empires, the Middle East, Asia, Africa, and the Americas (Kushigian 1999; Tinajero 2004; López-Calvo 2008).

8. Saito 1959, 1961; Saito and Maeyama 1973; Lesser 1995, 1999, 2002, 2013; Dezem 2005; Fausto 2009; Takeuchi 2009; Shizuno 2010.

INTRODUCTION

1. Beatriz Basto da Silva's (1994, 45) study of coolie emigration from Macau observes that the city's toponyms provide material evidence of the coolie trade's logistics. Toponyms are spatial mnemonics that help us imagine human activities that occurred at a specific location. Along these lines, Jeremy Tambling and Louis Lo's (2009, 4) beautifully written *Walking Macao, Reading the Baroque* takes readers on a walk through Macau's obscure and forgotten places to explore baroque and colonial elements in its architectural forms.

2. Macarena Gómez-Barris (2008, 7–8) offers a valuable way to conceive of memoryscapes and what she calls "memory symbolics," the spatial and material dimensions of cultural memory. A region's physical features, including the architectural and material remnants of authoritarian pasts, are productive sites for representing, contesting, and struggling over memory.

3. I thank Brent Edwards for pushing me to consider the complex memory fields that exist beyond erasure, remembrance, and disremembrance.

4. Hsu 2004.

5. For an excellent study about the history of coolie women, sexuality, and labor, see Bahadur (2014).

6. "Shanghai" (*Dictionary.com Unabridged* 2017).

7. Hu-Dehart 1993a, 258.

8. Meagher 2008, 99.

9. Meagher 2008, 99.

10. Yun 2008; Jung 2009; Young 2014; Ngai 2015; Lowe 2015.

11. Tinker 1974; Meagher 2008, 25.

12. Ngai 2015, 1084; Chang, K. 2015, 37.

13. Hu-DeHart 1992; Lai 1993; Yun 2008; Young 2014; Lowe 2015.

14. Costa 1996; Conrad 1974; Skidmore 1993; Lesser 1995, 1999; Dezem 2005.

15. Jung 2006, 38.

16. Yun 2008, 5.

17. Yun 2008, 5; Young 2014, 28.

18. Conrad 1975, 48.

19. Conrad 1975; Leite 1999. See chapter 1 for more on this topic.

20. Conrad 1975; Lesser 2013, 20.

21. Lesser 1999.

22. "História Nosso Jardim." Jardim Botánico do Rio de Janeiro. http://jbrj.gov.br/jardim/historia.

23. Lesser 1999.

24. Lesser 1995.

25. After the founding of the First Republic, it was renamed the Estrada de Ferro Central do Brasil.

26. Rodriguez 2004, 21.

27. Elias 1973, 698; Meagher 2008, 263–266.

28. The Origin of the Name Queimados (A origem do nome Queimados), http://www.queimados.rj.gov.br/prefeitura_publicacao.asp?idArea=1&idSecao=8.

29. Schwarcz 2006, 306.

30. Conrad 1975, 43–44.

31. Conrad 1975, 42.

32. Skidmore 1993, 25.

33. Skidmore 1993, 26.

34. Skidmore 1993, 26.

35. Louie 2004, 7–8.

36. Artist Beatrice Glow has a satirical performance piece, *Spanish Lesson on How to Speak Chino,* in which she teaches audiences about the various uses of the word *chino* in different Spanish-speaking countries.

37. Individual memory is an aspect of collective memory, since it must pass through symbolic systems like language that is socially bound (Halbwachs 1992, 53).

38. Taylor 2013, 10.

39. Paul Taylor, in his elaboration of Omi and Winant's work on racial formation, argues that racial projects are "binary constructions with parallel semantic and structural aspects. When we decide on or debate which meanings to assign to human bodies and bloodlines—which, as Omi and Winant put it, is to interpret the concept of race—we occupy the semantic side of a racial project. And when we distribute social goods along racial lines—which is to say, when we offer a racialized proposal for organizing our practical affairs—we occupy the structural side of a racial project" (Taylor 2013, 24). I thank Robert Gooding-Williams for suggesting this connection to Taylor's work.

40. Taylor 2013, 5.

41. Mignolo and Ennis 2001, 28.

42. Silva's *Toward a Global Idea of Race* (2009) provides a critical foundation for understanding race as an analytic in her study about the global dimensions of racism. Lipsitz (1998, 49) observes that racialized exploitative labor and attendant racism exist as a continuum in his example of the efforts of large corporations and small business employers alike that demonize undocumented workers as "illegal aliens" to "escape their own legal obligations and moral responsibilities to obey statutes mandating safe working conditions, a living wage, and dignified relations between employers and employees."

43. Roach 1996, 2–7. I am also responding to Kandice Chuh's call to extend Roach's concept to include an Asian Americanist Hemispheric perspective (2006).

44. Silva 2014, 132.

45. Silva 2014, 159–160.

46. Silva 2014, 159–160.

47. Silva 2014, 159–160.

48. Lee 1999, 2.

49. Ngai 2004, 2.

50. Chang, G. 2015, 80.

51. Wong 2015, 5.

52. Scholars of Asian diasporic histories in the Americas caution against attributing too much power to the US historiography of racialized discourses, which would superimpose US racial histories onto other places and thus obscure different ways in which race has been used for individual state needs (Delgado 2016; Siu 2016). In his examination of Chinese immigrants in Cuban literary and cultural imaginary, literary scholar Ignacio López-Calvo contends that elites and politicians perceived Chinese subjects as a threat to national homogeneity. Yet regardless of these exclusionary attitudes, Chinese and Chinese Cubans carved unique spaces within Cuban society, and in turn produced new cultural and social changes. Cuban and Chinese Cuban writers and artists have demonstrated that identity is always malleable and contestable. One such site of contestation is Cuba's mestizo nationalism. His study underscores moments of "(mis)representation and erasure" of the Chinese in Cuban literary and cultural production in order to emphasize the role that Chinese diasporic history and attendant "ethnic difference" have played in offering a counterpoint to "official black-and-white" national narratives (2008, 20).

53. Quijano 1998, 2000; Quijano and Wallerstein 1992; Mignolo 2008. Coloniality is heterogeneous, historically situated and contingent, different but connected (Lowe 2015, 8).

54. Bosi 2015, 196.

55. "História Nosso Jardim." Jardim Botánico do Rio de Janeiro. http://jbrj.gov. br/jardim/historia.

56. Bosi 2015, 167.

57. Holanda 2012, 129.

58. Bosi 2015, 163.

59. Bosi 2015, 168.

60. Bosi 2015, 163.

61. Bosi 2015, 197.

62. Schwarz 2000, 14.

63. Schwarz 1992, 22.

64. Schwarz 2000, 14.

65. Moog 1955; Ribeiro 1995, 120–21.

66. Martínez 2008. See chapter 1 for a discussion on sistema de casta.

67. Lesser 2013, 13. Lamarckian eugenic theory proposed that cultural traits developed according to environmental conditions.

68. Lesser 2013.

69. Lipsitz 1998, 3; Weinstein 2015, 6.

70. Rebecca Karl (2002, 17) argues that to understand the historical and global-spatial logic of national imaginaries, and the deterritorialized logic of nationalism, one must disentangle nationalism from nation-statism, "the purely functional pursuit and institutional elaboration of state power."

71. Skidmore 1993, 24.

72. By analyzing race alongside the sociopolitical and cultural processes of national memory making, this book complicates Benedict Anderson's conception of the nation as imagined communities (Anderson 2006).

73. hooks 1992, 2.

CHAPTER 1

1. Findlay and O'Rourke 2007.

2. Findlay and O'Rourke 2007.

3. Lewis and Wigen 1997.

4. Ahmed 2006, 112.

5. Mignolo 2005.

6. Wills 2010; Boxer 1975, 63.

7. Loureiro 2000, 543–545; Wills 2010, 38.

8. The Ming had unsurpassed naval technology during the early fifteenth century, but that had waned by 1525. Between 1405 and 1433, Admiral Zheng He led seven oceanic voyages that stretched from China to Southeast Asia, India, the Persian Gulf, and the Swahili coast of Africa. The high monetary and human cost of the voyages, consisting of thousands of men and hundreds of ships, led the Ming to order the destruction of all oceangoing vessels, totaling about 3,500 ships, therein bringing an end to expansionism. Had the Ming continued to develop their navy, the Portuguese expeditions might have been ended quickly (Gronewald 2015).

9. Meagher 2008, 117; Wills 2010, 36–37.

10. Wills 2010, 24.

11. Findlay and O'Rourke 2007, 170.

12. McNeil 1963, 574–8.

13. Madsen and White 2011, 8–11.

14. Cheung 2008, 2010.

15. I thank Dominic Cheung for this and many other insights about the history of Chinese porcelain.

16. Castro 1987, 68.

17. Said 1978.

18. Augustus the Strong (1670–1733), elector of Saxony King of Poland, invested heavily in porcelain research. He was a great collector of porcelain and nearly bankrupted his kingdom to increase his collection. Discovering the secret to making porcelain would symbolize Poland's scientific and industrial advancement as well as high culture. Porcelain manufacture was of such importance to Augustus that he imprisoned the alchemist Johann Friedrich Böttger (1682–1719) until he could produce a recipe for porcelain. In 1708, Böttger accidentally, and luckily, uncovered the secret to making hard-paste clay, marking that year as the first time that true porcelain was made in Europe. In 1710, the Royal Saxon Porcelain Manufactory was established in Meissen, marking the beginning of European porcelain manufacture.

19. Hochstrasser 2010, 46.

20. Hochstrasser 2010, 46.

21. Hochstrasser 2010, 45.

22. Freyre 1987, 280.

23. Clarence-Smith 1985, vii-2.

24. "Estrada Real," Instituto Estrada Real, http://www.institutoestradareal.com.br/estradareal.

25. Due to numerous pirate attacks, the road was later rerouted to Rio de Janeiro. "Estrada Real," Instituto Estrada Real. Accessed July 14, 2017. http://www.institutoestradareal.com.br/estradareal.

26. Mata 2007, 2–3.

27. Longobardi 2011.

28. Hansen 2006, 5.

29. Hansen 1995, 2001.

30. Schmidt 2015, 232.

31. Lee 2012.

32. Martínez 2008, 342.

33. Slack 2009, 38.

34. Slack 2009, 41.

35. Seijas 2014, 50.

36. Leite 1999, 19.

37. Leite 1999, 19.

38. Novembro 25, 1715, Macau, Carta [cópia] do provincial da província do Japão, Miguel de Amaral, para o governador e capitão-geral de Macau [D. Francisco de Alarcão Soto Maior?]. [Correspondence from Miguel de Amaral, stationed

in the province of Japan to the governor and captain-general of Macau] Ms. Av. 54-X-19, n1. Biblioteca da Ajuda, Lisboa.

39. Leite 1999, 20.
40. Leite 1999, 19.
41. Boxer 1975, 52–53.
42. Gupta 1999.
43. Mata 2007, 3.
44. Martínez 2008, 143.
45. Martínez 2008, 163.
46. Martínez 2008, 142.
47. Martínez 2008.
48. Martínez 2008, 148.
49. Martínez 2008, 166.
50. Plato 1992, 91.
51. Aristotle 1998, 74–80.
52. Aristotle 1998, 74.
53. Hanke 1970; Tierney 2001.
54. Sepulveda 1960.
55. Casas 1960.
56. Klein and Luna 2010, 190.
57. Klein and Luna 2010, 190.
58. Martínez 2008, 144.

59. For an excellent study about the lives of children affected by the Free Womb Law, see Chalhoub 1990, 2003.

60. Spillers 1997, 393.

61. Nearly fifteen years later, another gradual emancipation law went into effect on September 28, 1885, *Lei dos Sexagenários* (Law of Sexagenarians), which liberated people who were sixty years old and older. While this law "retired" people from slavery, it also relieved slave owners from the financial obligation of tending to an aging labor force.

62. A number of scholars have also made this observation, including Gilberto Freyre.

63. Chalhoub 2011, 424.
64. Bosi 1992, 165.
65. Chalhoub 2011, 424.
66. Chalhoub 2011, 430.
67. Chalhoub 2011, 409.
68. Caldeira, Carvalho, Marcondes, and Paula 1999, 200.
69. Caldeira, Carvalho, Marcondes, and Paula 1999, 201.

70. See Gikandi (2014) for an excellent study about the high cultures of modernity, in which he argues that the tastes and consuming practices of elite British eighteenth-century society were produced in the same register as the African slave trade wherein the production of whiteness necessitated blackness and difference as its counterpoint.

71. Schwarz 2001, 21.

72. See Guénif-Souilamas (2017) for a discussion about the sexualized and gendered lines of restrained equality.

CHAPTER 2

1. Skidmore 1993, 24; Lesser 2013, 23.

2. Lesser 2013, 10.

3. Skidmore 1993, 25.

4. Skidmore 1993, 25.

5. Lesser 1995, 1999; Dezem 2005.

6. Tocqueville 2003, 418.

7. Tocqueville 2003, 386.

8. Torres 1914, 62.

9. Lesser 1999, 15.

10. "Darwin's Theory Illustration—The Creation of Chinaman and Pig," *Wasp*, January 6, 1877, 217, reprinted in Choy, Dong, and Hom 1994, 111.

11. Ngai 2015, 1084.

12. Here I place Micol Seigel's work on the geopolitics of racialized national categories in conversation with Rebecca Karl's call to understand nationalism globally within the context of global asymmetries and inequality (Seigel 2009, 27; Karl 2002, 24).

13. Young 2014, 98.

14. Decreto nº 528, June 28, 1890, http://www2.camara.leg.br/legin/fed/decret/1824–1899/decreto-528-28-junho-1890-506935-publicacaooriginal-1-pe.html. While the Chinese were not explicitly mentioned, debates at the time of the ban made it clear they were the focus. I thank Jeffrey Lesser for this insight.

15. Shah 2011, 38.

16. Moon 2005, 115.

17. Wang 2001, 40.

18. Wang 2001, 40.

19. Wang 2001, 45.

20. Azuma 2005, 20.

21. I thank Eugenia Lean for pointing this out.

22. Azuma 2005, 18.

23. Lee and Cho 2012, 605.

24. Dower 1993, 6.
25. Dower 1993, 204-205.
26. Dower 1993, 8.
27. Yoneyama 1999, 6.
28. Dower 1993, 11.
29. Tchen 2012, 489.
30. Dower 1993, 9.
31. Lesser 1995, 1999; Dezem 2005.
32. Lesser 2003, 5.
33. Lesser 2013, Ch. 6.
34. Akio 2000, 4.
35. Akio 2000, 4.
36. Lesser 2013, Ch. 6.
37. Lesser 2013, Ch. 6.
38. Lesser 2013, Ch. 6.
39. Not all Japanese migrants acted on behalf of Japanese state goals. Many voyaged abroad in search of adventure and to acquire personal riches. In the late 1880s, groups of Japanese laborers, mainly young, penniless bachelors with dreams of riches and adventure, went abroad as *dekasegi* (temporary overseas laborers) or *shosei* (working students). They first headed to the sugar cane plantations of Hawaii and the Pacific Coast of North America (Sakata 2004, 16). Private Japanese immigration companies (*imingaisha*) facilitated Japanese emigration labor (Moriyama 1985).
40. Shouyi and Yanjing 1995, 18.
41. Karl 2002, 80.
42. Shouyi and Yanjing 1995, 21.
43. Fu Yunlong [1892] 2005, 387–388.
44. Wang 2001, 41.
45. Bussche 2016.
46. Bussche 2016.
47. Fu Yunlong 1901.
48. Fu Yunlong 1901.
49. Fu Yunlong [1892] 2005, 387-388.
50. Fu Yunlong 1901.
51. See Rebecca Karl's *Staging the World* for an excellent analysis of emerging views of "the people" (guomin/minzu) and the efforts to transform them into an "active national people" in late Qing discourses (2002, 117–148).
52. Adam McKeown (2001, 3–7) argues that Chinese migration must be understood from a global perspective that integrates transnational dynamics and patterns

with localized research. He refutes nation-centered studies that locate narratives of migration as "monodirectional" with "locally conditioned transformation."

53. Fu Yunlong [1889] 2005, 212–215.

54. Siu 2012.

55. Fu Yunlong [1889] 2005, 212–215.

56. Wang 2001, 43.

57. Liang 2016, 142–147.

58. Liang 2016, 142–147.

59. By the early twentieth century, the bleak conditions of plantation life and meager earnings forced the Japanese government to reformulate its emigration plans (Nakamaki 2004, 23). Rather than sending out dekasegi, the Japanese government began to invest in permanent settlements in Brazil invested in cultivating individuals. In the 1920s, with the aid of prefectural emigration associations and the private organization Rikkō Kai, Japanese migrants from Nagano, Tottori, and Toyama prefectures set up the Aliança Colony in São Paulo State with the slogan, "cultivating capable individuals rather than cultivating coffee plants" (Nakamaki 2004, 23).

60. Qi Yaolin 1918, 3–6.

61. Moura 2011, 33.

62. Qi Yaolin 1918, 3–6.

63. Order of Chief Executive Office of Jiangsu Province (No. 381), "Permit the Ministry of the Interior's Promotion of Immigration-Plantation Project after It (The Ministry of the Interior) Consults Our Representative to Brazil, Who Sent Letters to Ask for Migrant Worker to Meet the Need of Labor That Results from the European War [World War I]," January 29, 1918. Translated by Wang Siwei.

64. Machado 2014.

65. Karl 2002, 118.

66. Sun Yat-sen, quoted in Scott 2008, 216.

67. Li Dazhao, quoted in Scott 2008, 217.

68. Keevak 2011, 3–8.

69. Lisboa 1888, 275.

70. Pratt 2007.

71. Appadurai 1997, para. 4.

72. Lisboa 1888, 333.

73. Lisboa 1888, 370–371.

74. The *Revista Illustrada* totaled approximately 740 numbered editions, with additional publications that were not numbered.

75. Lisa Lowe (2015, 8) argues that the "safekeeping and preservation of liberal political society and the placement of peoples at various distances from liberal

humanity—"'Indian,'" "'black,'" "'Negro,'" "'Chinese,'" "'coolie,'" and so forth—are thus integral parts of the genealogy of modern liberalism."

76. Immediately after Brazil declared independence in 1889, artists began to allegorize Brazil in the likeness of New York's Statue of Liberty.

77. Sommer 1991, 139.

78. Wolfe 2006, 387.

79. Between 1867 and 1868, Alencar wrote a series of political texts in defense of slavery.

80. Alencar 2007, 87.

81. Bosi 2015, 163; Lowe 2015, 8.

82. 1888. *Revista Illustrada*, no. 523.

CHAPTER 3

1. Azevedo 1901, n.p.

2. Lane 2008, 1730.

3. Hartman 1997, 21.

4. Lott 1992, 23.

5. Monteiro 2008, 24.

6. Neto 2008, 41.

7. Jette Barnholt Hansen (2012) explains that the revue is a specific form of rhetorical discourse that must capture the immediacy of the current times as directly related to spectators' lives.

8. Taylor 2003, 6.

9. Antonio Herculano Lopes, personal communication, February 1, 2016.

10. Veneziano 1996, 128.

11. Eric Hayot, in *The Hypothetical Mandarin: Sympathy, Modernity, and Chinese Pain* (2009), analyzes the metaphoric value of China in Western political philosophy. In my analysis, I examine the symbolic place of China in the Brazilian context of modernity/coloniality (Quijano 1998, 2000; Mignolo 2008).

12. "Mandarin" (*Merriam-Webster* 2008).

13. "Mandarin" (*Oxford Dictionaries* 2016).

14. Corominas 1987, 377.

15. Conrad 1975; Lesser 1995, 1999; Leite 1999.

16. Bolton 2006, 177.

17. Conrad 1975.

18. "Tong King Sing," *Correio Paulistano*, October 19, 1883.

19. "Tong King Sing," *Correio Paulistano*, October 19, 1883.

20. Laërne 1885, 148.

21. Laërne 1885, 149.

22. Laërne 1885, 150.

23. See chapter 2.

24. Karl Von Koseritz was a playwright, journalist, and provincial deputy of Rio Grande do Sul. Hermann Blumenau founded the German colony of Blumenau, located in Santa Catarina, and Hugo Gruber was the editor of *Allgemeine Deutsche Zeitung* in Rio de Janeiro (Brasil 2015).

25. *A Imigração Orgão da Sociedade Central de Imigração*, bulletins 1–4 (December 1883–August 1884), Biblioteca Nacional do Rio de Janeiro.

26. See chapters 2 and 4.

27. Lee 2007a, 2007b.

28. *A Imigração Orgão da Sociedade Central de Imigração*, bulletins 1–4 (December 1883–August 1884), Biblioteca Nacional do Rio de Janeiro.

29. In 1883, the theater had 14 box seats, 465 seats, 60 spots in the noble gallery, and 150 spots in the general gallery (*Teatros do Centro Histórico do Rio de Janeiro* 1997).

30. The Fundação Biblioteca Nacional in Rio de Janeiro holds two musical scores for *O Mandarim*: a mazurka by J. Alves Leite Successor and a tango composed by José Simões Junior.

31. Veneziano 1991, 40.

32. Veneziano 1991, 40.

33. Azevedo and Sampaio 1883, 1021.

34. Azevedo and Moreira 1883, 1021.

35. See chapter 4 for a discussion of Machado de Assis and the Chinese question.

36. Azevedo and Moreira 1883, 1021.

37. Azevedo and Moreira 1883, 1022.

38. See chapter 2.

39. Azevedo and Moreira 1883, 1046.

40. Azevedo and Moreira 1883, 1026.

41. Azevedo and Moreira 1883, 1037.

42. Sean Metzger's (2014) cultural study of US–China relations and performances of Chineseness in theater and film argues that clothing and accessories convey aspects of Chinese history and culture as "surfaces" that produce the "skein of race." Performances of the skein of race have shaped audience understandings of China as an "embodied perception" during different moments in US–China relations (20).

43. Azevedo and Moreira 1883, 1037–1038.

44. Azevedo and Moreira 1883, 1030–1031.

45. Azevedo and Moreira 1883, 1041.

46. "Chronica," *Gazeta de Notícias,* July 22, 1900.

47. "Chronica," *Gazeta de Notícias,* July 22, 1900.

48. "Chronica," *Gazeta de Notícias,* July 22, 1900.

49. According to Sidney Chalhoub (1996), the rise of precarious and overcrowded housing conditions in Rio de Janeiro in the late nineteenth and early twentieth centuries coincided with the intensification of black struggles for liberty. Furthermore, the *cortiços,* or so-called beehives, often served as a haven for fugitive slaves. While located in central locations such as the neighborhood of Botafogo, the cortiços were nevertheless spatially and socially marginalized areas of the city. In fact, beginning in the 1870s, the officials of Rio de Janeiro began to demolish the homes, often while people were still living inside them. The most famous example occurred on January 26, 1893, with the destruction of Cabeça de Porco (pig's head tenement), which housed between two thousand and four thousand people. The destruction of these settlements displaced thousands of people from their homes, forcing them to build on the landslide-prone hillsides of the city and sparking the rise of favelas.

50. Azevedo 2000, 13.

51. "Salamaleque" (Priberam Dicionário 2015).

52. Azevedo 1959, 100.

53. "O riso encontra eco." (*Veja* 1889).

54. "O riso encontra eco."

55. "O riso encontra eco."

56. "Theatro Variedades Dramáticas (1888)," *Teatros do Centro Histório do Rio de Janeiro,* http://www.ctac.gov.br/centrohistorico/TeatroXPeriodo. asp?cod=120&cdP=17.

57. Azevedo and Azevedo 1888, act III, scene IV.

58. See chapter 2.

59. Azevedo and Azevedo 1888, act III, scene IV.

CHAPTER 4

1. Skidmore 1993; Lesser, 1999; Dezem 2005; Oliva 2008; Lee 2014; Suárez 2015; Roncador 2016.

2. In a critical study about the global history of anti-Asian racism, Erika Lee (2007a, 2007b) observes that national policies regarding immigration exclusion were not insular cases; rather, they connected Chinese immigration and exclusion in the United States, Canada, Hawaii, Mexico, the Caribbean, and other parts of Latin America. Anti-Asian expressions that circulated during the nineteenth century in the United States were a response to industrialization and US continental frontier expansion (Lye 2004). Furthermore, national immigration restriction policies like the Chinese Exclusion Act of 1882 actually originated in Caribbean sugarcane fields, where, as Moon-Ho Jung contends, "slavery's death generated a planter demand for Asian coolies in the [US] South" (2009, 40).

3. Ngai 2015.

4. Lee 1999; Moon 2005.

5. Chang, G., 2015, 80.

6. Chang, G., 2015, 80.

7. Young 2014; Lee-Loy 2015; Chang 2017.

8. Adler 2008.

9. Adler 2008.

10. "The Chinese Question," *Harper's Weekly*, February 18, 1871, http://www.harp-week.com/09Cartoon/BrowseByDateCartoon.asp?Month=February&Date=18.

11. Chalhoub 2005, 87.

12. Chalhoub 2005, 102.

13. Bosi 1992, 216.

14. Bosi 1992, 207.

15. Lesser 1999, 22.

16. Lesser 1999, 22.

17. For recent studies about Machado de Assis's writings about Chinese labor, see Lee 2014 and Roncador 2016.

18. Nietzsche 1967, 28.

19. Machado de Assis 1878.

20. "John Chinaman" (*Merriam-Webster* 2017).

21. Machado de Assis 1994.

22. Machado de Assis 1994.

23. According to Joanna Richardson's (1986) biography of Gautier, Monseigneur Callery, bishop of Macau, sponsored Dunling's trip to Paris to produce a Chinese-French dictionary. Soon after arriving, Callery died, leaving Dunling unemployed until he received an offer from the famed French Orientalist Théophile Gautier to teach his daughter Chinese, as well as give her the opportunity to—in the words of Théophile—"study a country that is still unknown, and seems prodigious" (23). Another account of Dunling's arrival in Paris revealed that he was an assistant teacher to Stanislas Julien at the Collège de France. One day, an argument broke out when Dunling accused Professor Julien of not knowing any Chinese, even though he was teaching it, leading to Dunling's dismissal. Dunling was a minor character who made a major impact on the publication of Gautier's *Le Livre de Jade* and on the larger history of French Orientalism. However, accounts of his life are known only through others' pens. The fact that his actions are understood through the curious, lost-in-translation descriptions of Gautier and her contemporaries converts the actual man Dunling into a fictional character based on a historical figure. References to the Chinese scholar gave Gautier credibility and in turn placed Dunling in a prominent position that gave validity to *Le Livre de Jade*. Yet

the actual Chinese scholar is displaced, appearing more as bright shadows against Gautier's light. *Le Livre de Jade* is dedicated to "Tin-Tun-Ling Poete chinois," and some of the poems are written by him but translated by Gautier.

24. For an informative study on Judith Gautier's work, including an analysis of the validity of her translations, in introducing Chinese poetry to Europe and in particular its impact on French literary traditions, see Yu 2007.

25. For a comparative study of Machado and Gautier's translations, see Knowlton 1976.

26. Ishimatsu 1984, 74.

27. "Falena" (*Michaelis Dicionário Online* 2017).

28. "Falena" (*Dicionário Online de Português* 2017).

29. "Falena" (*Dicionario informal, Radio e Televisão* 2016; *Trecanni La Cultural Italiana*).

30. Nabuco [1879] 2010, 127–128.

31. Nabuco [1879] 2010, 127–128.

32. Nabuco quoted in Lesser 1999, 28

33. See chapter 2.

34. See chapter 3.

35. Emphasis mine; Machado de Assis 1870, 119–120.

36. Gautier 1867, 41.

37. Chalhoub 2001, 178.

38. Chalhoub 2001, 178.

39. Schwarz 2001, 37.

40. Gledson 2001, xvii.

41. Machado de Assis 1880, 363.

42. *Academia Brasileira de Letras*, "Fundação." http://www.academia.org.br/academia/fundacao.

43. *Academia Brasileira de Letras*, "Fundação." http://www.academia.org.br/academia/fundacao.

44. Castro 1880, 251.

45. Luca 1998, 20–21.

46. Luca 1998, 22.

47. Luca 1998, 22.

48. Hashimoto 2009.

49. Machado de Assis 1998, 69.

50. Machado de Assis 1998, 69.

51. Abreu 2015, 379.

52. Machado de Assis 1998, 71

53. Machado de Assis 1994.

54. Machado de Assis 1994.
55. Machado de Assis 1896, scene VII.
56. Machado de Assis 1896, scene VII.
57. Hu DeHart 1993b, 64.
58. DeHart 1992; Yun 2008.
59. Young 2014, 53.
60. I thank Evelyn Hu DeHart for this information.
61. Suárez 2015, 67.
62. Suárez 2015, 67.
63. Eça de Queiroz 2000, 165.
64. Eça de Queiroz 1994, 6.
65. I thank Evelyn Hu DeHart for this insight.
66. Eça de Queiroz 1994, 6.
67. Eça de Queiroz 1994, 6.
68. Eça de Queiroz 1994, 5.
69. Eça de Queiroz 1994, 5.
70. Eça de Queiroz 1994, 5.
71. For a detailed record of the *Cuban Commission Report*, see Helly 1993.
72. Eça de Queiroz 1900, 54.
73. Eça de Queiroz 1900, 50.
74. Eça de Queiroz 1900, 62.
75. Eça de Queiroz 1900, 65.
76. Eça de Queiroz 1900, 70.
77. Eça de Queiroz 1900, 50.
78. Eça de Queiroz 1900, 22.

CHAPTER 5
1. Hampton 2009, 4.
2. See chapter 2 for a discussion on unfree labor.
3. Fialho 2012, 10. The cabaia de mandarim that Eça is wearing was a gift from Conde d'Arnoso (Filho 1984).
4. Molloy 1998, 184.
5. Here, I am referencing Roland Barthes's (1982) discussion of the punctum to explain the effect that documentary photography has on a viewing subject. It indexes a history that bruises, wounds, and arrests a particular viewing subject. The punctum does not restore "what has been abolished (by time, by distance), but [it] attest[s] that what I see has indeed existed" (80–81).
6. Molloy 1998, 184.
7. See chapter 4.
8. Mónica 2005, 106.

9. Eça de Queiroz 1874, 7.

10. Eça de Queiroz 1874, 5–6.

11. Eça de Queiroz 1874, 7.

12. Eça de Queiroz 1874, 9.

13. Eça de Queiroz 1874, 9–10.

14. Eça de Queiroz 1874, 14.

15. Eric Hayot's excellent study about the "hypothetical mandarin" examines the relationship between the Western philosophical tradition of sympathy and representations of the Chinese other, expressed through depictions of pain, disease, torture, and death (Hayot 2009, 5).

16. Smith 1790, III.I.46. For more on moral philosophy and distance, see Ginzburg 1994; Landau 2005.

17. Hayot 2009, 5.

18. Eça de Queiroz 1927, 37.

19. Simas 1999, 6.

20. Eça de Queiroz 1927, 55.

21. See chapter 4.

22. See Introduction and chapter 4.

23. Eça de Queiroz 1927, 47.

24. Eça de Queiroz 1927, 36.

25. Eça de Queiroz 1927, 54.

26. Eça de Queiroz 1927, 58.

27. Eça de Queiroz 1927, 61.

28. Vejmelka 2013, 404.

29. Akio 2000.

30. Saito 1961, 50.

31. Brazil and China established a similar treaty on October 3, 1881, decreed on August 24, 1882. One year later, Rio de Janeiro received the official visit from Tong Jing Xing and his African American assistant, G. C. Butler, who ultimately declared Brazil unsuitable for Chinese emigration, although, as discussed in chapter 3, Qing diplomats advocated for immigration to Brazil.

32. Azevedo 1984, Preface.

33. The manuscript remained at the Academia Brasileira de Letras, where Azevedo was a founding member in 1897, for nearly a century until researcher Luiz Dantas uncovered the novel and published it in 1984.

34. Azevedo 1984, chap. 1.

35. Luis Guimarães Filho, biography, http://www.academia.org.br/academicos/luis-guimaraes-filho/biografia.

36. Guimarães Filho 1925, 25.

37. Guimarães Filho 1925, 21.

38. Guimarães Filho 1925, 15.

39. Guimarães Filho 1925, 30.

40. Guimarães Filho 1925, 30.

41. Guimarães Filho 1925, 36–37.

42. Guimarães Filho 1925, 23.

43. Lesser 1999, 83.

44. Hespanha 1999, 15.

45. See chapter 1 for a discussion of Sino-Portuguese history.

46. Guimarães Filho 1925, 311.

47. Guimarães Filho 1925, 372–373.

48. "Chronica," *Gazeta de Notícias,* July 22, 1900.

49. Guimarães Filho 1925, 373.

50. "Chronica," *Gazeta de Notícias,* July 22, 1900.

51. Guimarães Filho 1925, 343.

52. Guimarães Filho 1925, 356–357.

53. This recalls the racial rhetoric described in the *Revista Illustrada,* in which a caption stated that the yellow hue of the Chinese threatened the status of the mulato. See chapter 2.

54. Emphasis added, Guimarães Filho 1925, 312.

55. Forbes 1993, 138.

56. See chapters 2 and 3.

57. I thank Christopher Dunn for this insight.

58. See chapter 2.

59. Guimarães Filho 1925, 407.

CHAPTER 6

1. Avelar and Dunn 2011.

2. See Stephan (1991) for an excellent study about eugenics, national identity, and racial transformation in Latin America.

3. Fausto 2009, 32.

4. See Chang (2017) for an analysis of Chinese exclusion in forging Mexican mestiço national identity.

5. Here I am referencing Viet Thanh Nguyen's (2016, 63) prose when he states, "Disremembering is not simply the failure to remember. Disremembering is the unethical and paradoxical mode of forgetting at the same time as remembering, or, from the perspective of the other who is disremembered, of being simultaneously seen and not seen."

6. Seigel 2009, 27.

7. Rancière 2004, 12.

8. See chapter 4.

9. Hertzman 2013, 173.

10. Peppercorn 1941, 689–690.

11. Avelar and Dunn 2011.

12. Avelar and Dunn 2011, 12.

13. Lima 2011, 269.

14. Guerrant 1950, 36.

15. Guerrant 1950, 36.

16. Ortiz 1985, 36–44.

17. Stephan 1991, 166–167.

18. Lesser 2013, 138.

19. Ngai 2004, 7.

20. Lesser 1999, 116–20.

21. Lesser 2013, 138.

22. Shizuno 2010, 117.

23. Alberto 2011, 129.

24. I thank Christopher Dunn for helping me find the lyrics to many of these songs.

25. Tchen 2010, 263.

26. Loti 2006, 9.

27. Kondo 1990, 9.

28. Said 1978, 55; 58.

29. Avelar and Dunn 2011, 4.

30. Corrêa 1996.

31. Lopes 2001.

32. Dunn 2006, 39.

33. Luiz Cosme and Neto Vargas. 1935. "Aquela china." Victor, 78 rpm. Instituto Moreira Salles.

34. "Chinoca" (*Priberam Dicionário* 2013).

35. Neder 2016.

36. Alberto Ribeiro and João de Barro. 1935. "Cadê Mimi." Odeon, 78 rpm. Instituto Moreira Salles.

37. João de Barro. 1935. "Linda Mimi." Victor [Records]. 78 rpm. Instituto Moreira Salles.

38. Ary Barroso and Lamartine Babo. 1934. "Grau dez . . ." Victor, 78 rpm. Instituto Moreira Salles.

39. Osvaldo Santiago and Paulo Barbosa. 1930. "Lig, lig, lig, lé." Victor, 78 rpm. Instituto Moreira Salles.

40. Arnaldo Passos and Ary Monteiro. 1944. "China." Continental. 78 rpm. Instituto Moreira Salles.

41. João de Barro. 1948. "Serenata chinesa." Continental, 78 rpm. Instituto Moreira Salles.

42. Neder 2016. Alberto Ribeiro and João de Barro. 1943. "China pau." Continental, 78 rpm. Instituto Moreira Salles.

43. National WWII Museum, New Orleans, http://www.nationalww2museum.org/learn/education/for-students/ww2-history/ww2-by-the-numbers/world-wide-deaths.html.

44. Carolina Cardoso Menezes and Vitório Lattari. 1932/1956. "Salada chinesa." Odeon, 78 rpm. Instituto Moreira Salles.

45. Paranhos 2011, 39.

46. This kind of mockery recalls the way Azevedo and Moreira portrayed the *chim* shrimp seller in their 1883 *O Mandarim*. See chapter 3.

47. "Cochinchina" (*Diccionario panhispánico de dudas* Real Academia Española 2005).

48. Moon 2005, 119.

49. Jordon 2001, 13.

50. Fausto 2009, 30.

51. Rohmer 1913, 25.

52. While images of Fu Manchu circulated across popular culture and mass media, the figure also haunts the imperial archive. According to James Hevia, the British archive contributed to and shaped knowledge about the Chinese and China for the purpose of protecting the interests of the British Empire and containing the expansion of other empires, namely, Imperial Russia. The production of knowledge about China was part of British military operations that prioritized information gathering (deterritorializing) over tactics that demanded physical force. Intelligence gathering enabled the establishment of new British institutes (reterritorializing) within China, through which Britain could "interface." Hevia's (1998) study of Fu Manchu figurations provokes a reading of the archive that accounts for the military and colonizing strategies of colonial administration, in which the paperwork and bureaucratic dealings of empire define and incorporate new subjects. He contends that administrative procedures "are absolutely critical for understanding the relation between the real and the fictional, between the archives and imaginings of empire" (237–241).

53. Tchen 2010, 263.

54. Lawrence Knapp, "The Page of Fu-Man-Chu" (New Jersey Intercampus Network), 1997, http://www.njedge.net/~knapp/FuFrames.htm).

55. Tchen 2012, 489.

56. Moon 2005, 117.

57. Castro in preface to Théo-Filho's *Praia de Ipanema* 2000, 10–13

58. Théo-Filho 2000, 51.

59. Théo-Filho 2000, 53.

60. Théo-Filho 2000, 53.

61. Théo-Filho 2000, 106.

62. Hevia 1998, 251.

63. Andrade 1973, 212.

64. Afonso Teixeira and Peterpan. N.d. "Negócio da China." Continental, 78 rpm. Instituto Moreira Salles.

65. André Filho and Durval Melo. 1940. "Carnaval na China." Odeon, 78 rpm. Instituto Moreira Salles.

66. Filho is most known for composing *Cidade maravilhosa* (*Marvelous City*), which has since become the unofficial anthem song of Rio de Janeiro.

67. Haroldo Lobo and Milton de Oliveira. 1941. "Na China." Marchinas de Carnaval. V9. MNR Media, release date: August 30, 2011.

68. Pagode is a musical subgenre of samba that originated in Rio de Janeiro and a dance that is accompanied by percussion, guitar, and the cavaquinho (related to the ukulele). Benedito Lacerda and Haroldo Lobo, "Pagode na China." 1945. RCA Victor, Disc 78 rpm. Instituto Moreira Salles.

69. Anthropologist Renato da Silva Queiroz (1987) shows that prior to the arrival of European settlers, Saci was present in the Indigenous imagination in a plurality of forms usually associated with nature and explanations of natural phenomena. For the Tupinambá, Saci was also known as "Matintapereira" and acted as a sacred medium of communication between the living and the dead. For the Tupi Guaraní, Saci was a playful elf, a childlike trickster. Upon the arrival of the colonists and Christian missionaries, Saci received a radical transformation and took on Christian traits; for example, Saci could be captured with a rosary or a cross. For a collection of Saci Pererê stories, see Lobato 1917.

70. Dilermando Reis. 1944. "Dança chinesa." Continental, 78 rpm. Instituto Moreira Salles.

71. Brasinha, "Marcha do Kung-Fu. Carnival 1975," https://www.youtube.com/watch?v=JnQVSohdoak.

72. Adriana Calcanhotto, "Adriana Partimpim," https://www.youtube.com/watch?v=c7TnUY7bdaA.

73. "Como tudo começou" (How it all started). Lig-Lig restaurant website: http://www.liglig.com.br/liglig.

CONCLUSION

1. Said 1978, 67.

2. Lewis and Wigen 1997, 75.

3. Karl 2002, 4.

4. Shohat and Stam 2016, 20.

5. Simão de Mantua [pseudonym of Antonio Gomes Carmo] wrote a number of studies about Brazilian society. Among his titles are *O estado moderno e a agricultura* (1908), *A cultural do trigo* (1918), *Figurões vistos por dentro: Estudo de psychologia social brasileira* (1921), *Exemplos e problemas* (1936), and *Considerações históricas sobre a agricultura no Brasil* (1939).

6. I thank Christopher Dunn for bringing my attention to the existence of *Cartas de um Chinez.* Monteiro Lobato & Cia. published *Cartas de um Chinez.* Monteiro Lobato, among Brazil's most influential authors—a municipality in São Paulo is even named after him—founded one of Brazil's first publishing houses and played an instrumental role in establishing a tradition of Brazilian children's literature. Through children's stories, he created national folkloric characters and forged a sense of Brazilian national identity.

7. Simão de Mantua 1923, 8.

8. Simão de Mantua 1923, 14–19.

9. Simão de Mantua 1923, 15.

10. Simão de Mantua 1923, 38.

11. Simão de Mantua 1923, 21.

12. Simão de Mantua 1923, 22–23.

13. See chapter 2.

14. Edson Nery da Fonseca (2003) brings together the corpus of Freyre's writings on the Orient.

15. Freyre earned his BA at Baylor University in Waco, Texas, in 1921, and went on to complete an MA in anthropology at Columbia University (1921–1922), where he studied under Franz Boas. He also lived in Europe and traveled extensively throughout Africa.

16. I thank Jerry Dávila for pointing out the timeline of Freyre's use of "racial democracy."

17. Freyre [1933] 1971, 185–6.

18. Silva 2007, 233.

19. Leite 1984, 91–95.

20. Freyre [1936] 1987, 297.

21. For more on Freyre and Islam, see Isfahani-Hammond 2014. For Freyre and the Moorish-Sephardi Atlantic, see Shohat and Stam 2014, 2016.

22. Silva 2011, 45.

23. Silva 2011, 18–19.

24. Freyre [1936] 1987, 278.

25. Freyre [1936] 2003, 39.

26. Genesis 1:4.

27. Kant 1784.

28. Mill 1991, 14.

29. Freyre [1936] 1987, 297.

30. Freyre [1936] 1987, 280.

31. Freyre [1936] 1987, 281.

32. Freyre [1971] 2012, 299.

33. Hilton 1981, 599.

34. Freyre [1971] 2012, 260.

35. Freyre [1971] 2012, 305.

36. Freyre [1971] 2012, 305.

37. Freyre [1971] 2012, 311.

38. Freyre [1971] 2012, 34.

39. Dávila 2010, 2–8.

40. "MPT e MTE flagram trabalho escravo em pastelaria do RJ," *MPT Notícias,* Ministério Público do Trabalho Procuradoria-Geral, July 9, 2015.

41. Eliane Lobato and Helena Borges, "Escravos chineses," *Istoé,* February 12, 2015. http://istoe.com.br/441647_ESCRAVOS+CHINESES/.

42. "Chineses eram escravizados em pastelaria de Copacabana," *MPT Notícias,* Ministério Público do Trabalho Procuradoria-Geral, April 14, 2015.

43. "MPT e MTE resgatam chineses de trabalho escravo no Rio de Janeiro," Ministério Público do Trabalho no Rio de Janeiro, April 13, 2015.

44. "Chinesa é resgatada de trabalho escravo em SP," *MPT Notícias*, Ministério Público do Trabalho Procuradoria-Gera, September 24, 2014.

45. "Chinesa é resgatada de trabalho escravo em SP."

46. Eliane Lobato and Helena Borges, "Escravos chineses," *Istoé*, February 12, 2015. http://istoe.com.br/441647_ESCRAVOS+CHINESES/.

47. "Chineses são resgatados de escravidão em pastelaria," *MPT Notícias*, Ministério Público do Trabalho Procuradoria-Geral. December 1, 2015.

48. Eliane Lobato and Helena Borges, "Escravos chineses," *Istoé*, February 12, 2015. http://istoe.com.br/441647_ESCRAVOS+CHINESES/.

49. Siu 2005; Delgado 2013; López 2013.

50. The feminist collective, Lótus PWR, has an active social media presence, including the Facebook group "LÓTUS Feminismo Asiático." The Lótus Platform has also received the attention of major media outlets. For example, on March 30, 2017, the *Estadão* ran an article spotlighting leaders of the collective: "Você já ouviu falar do feminismo asiástico?" (http://emais.estadao.com.br/blogs/nana-soares/voce-ja-ouviu-falar-de-feminismo-asiatico/).

51. Freud 1989, 726.

Bibliography

Abreu, Marcelo de Paiva. 2015. *Anglo-Brazilian Economic Relations and the Consolidation of American Pre-Eminence in Brazil, 1930–1945*. New York: Bloomsburg.

Adams, Rachel. 2009. *Continental Divides: Remapping the Cultures of North America*. Chicago: University of Chicago Press.

Adler, John. 2008. "Background: Harper's Weekly." *Harper's Weekly*. http://www.harpweek.com/02About/about.asp.

Ahmed, Sara. 2006. *Queer Phenomenology: Orientations, Objects, Others*. Durham, NC: Duke University Press.

Akio, Armando. 2000. "Kasato-Maru, o navio da esperança." *Imigração japonesa: Museus, história e depoimentos*. http://www.imigracaojaponesa.com.br/?page_id=261.

Alberto, Paulina. 2011. *Terms of Inclusion: Black Intellectuals in Twentieth-Century Brazil*. Chapel Hill: University of North Carolina Press.

Alencar, José. 2007. *Iracema*. São Paulo. Editora Martin Claret.

Alonso, Carlos. 1990. *The Spanish American Regional Novel: Modernity and Autochtony*. Cambridge: Cambridge University Press.

Althusser, Louis. 1971. "Ideology and Ideological State Apparatuses" *Lenin and Philosophy and Other Essays*. New York: Monthly Review Press.

Anderson, Benedict. 2006. *Imagined Communities*. New York: Verso.

Andrade, Oswald de. 1973. *Obras completas 8*. Rio de Janeiro: Editora Civilização Brasileira.

Appadurai, Arjun. 1997. "The Colonial Backdrop." *Afterimage* 24, no. 5.

Aristotle. (c. 350 BC) 1998. *Politics*. Cambridge: Hackett.

Armitage, David. 2004. "John Locke, Carolina, and the Two Treatises of Government." *Political Theory* 32, no. 5: 602–627.

Arneil, Barbara. 1996. *John Locke and America: The Defense of English Colonization.* New York: Clarendon Press.

Avelar, Idelber, and Christopher Dunn. 2011. *Brazilian Popular Music and Citizenship.* Durham, NC: Duke University Press.

Azevedo, Aluísio. 1901. *Palestra.* Rio de Janeiro, March 20.

———. 1959. *O Cortiço.* São Paulo: Livraria Martins.

———. 1984. *O Japão.* São Paulo: Roswitha Kempf. Kindle.

Azevedo, Aluísio, and Arthur Azevedo. 1888. *Fritzmac.* Kindle.

———. 2000. *The Slum.* Translated by David H. Rosenthal. Oxford: Oxford University Press.

Azevedo, Arthur. 1876. "O Jardim." *Revista Illustrada* 45.

Azevedo, Arthur, and Sampaio Moreira. (1883) 2002. *O Mandarim. Teatro de Artur Azevedo.* Rio de Janeiro: Funarte.

Azuma, Eiichiro. 2005. *Between Two Empires: Race, History, and Transnationalism in Japanese America.* Oxford: Oxford University Press.

Bahadur, Gaiutur. 2013. *Coolie Woman: The Odyssey of Indenture.* Chicago: Chicago University Press.

Bailey, Steven. 2007. *Strolling in Macau.* San Francisco: Things Asian Press.

Barthes, Roland. 1982. *Camera Lucida: Reflections on Photography.* Translated by Richard Howard. New York: Hill and Wang.

Bederman, David. 2010. *International Law Frameworks.* New York: Foundation Press.

Bell, Caryn Cossé. 1997. *Revolution, Romanticism, and the Afro-Creole Protest Tradition in Louisiana, 1718–1868.* Baton Rouge: Louisiana State University Press.

Bergard, Laird. 2007. *The Comparative Histories of Slavery in Brazil, Cuba, and the United States.* Cambridge: Cambridge University Press.

Bethencourt, Francisco. 1993. "A Igreja." In *Historia de Portugal: No alvorcer da modernidade (1480–1620),* edited by J. Romero-Magalhões, 3:149–164. Estampa: Lisbon.

———. 2013. *Racisms: From the Crusades to the Twentieth Century.* Princeton, NJ: Princeton University Press.

Bhabha, Homi. 1994. *The Location of Culture.* New York: Routledge.

Bletz, May. 2007. "Race and Modernity in *O Cortiço* by Aluísio de Azevedo." *LL Journal* 2, no. 1. http://ojs.gc.cuny.edu/index.php/lljournal/article/view/231/198.

Bolton, Kingley. 2006. *Chinese Englishes: A Sociolinguistic History.* Cambridge: Cambridge University Press.

Bosi, Alfredo. 1992. *Dialética da Colonização*. São Paulo: Campanhia das Letras.
———. 2015. *Brazil and the Dialectic of Colonization*. Urbana: University of Illinois Press.

Boxer, Charles. 1975. *The Portuguese Seaborne Empire, 1415–1825*. New York: Knopf.

Brasil, Bruno. 2015. "Sociedade Central de Immigração." *Biblioteca Nacional do Rio de Janeiro*. https://bndigital.bn.gov.br/artigos/sociedade-central-de-immigracao/.

Briggs, Ronald. *The Moral Electricity of Print: Transatlantic Education and the Lima Women's Circuit, 1876–1910*. Nashville, TN: Vanderbilt University Press.

Bussche, Eric Vanden. 2016. "Travel Literature and the Transformation of Qing China's Perceptions of Brazil during the Late Nineteenth Century." Paper presented at the 34th Annual Meeting of the Latin American Studies Association, New York.

Byrd, Jodi. 2011. *The Transit of Empire: Indigenous Critiques of Colonialism*. Minneapolis: University of Minnesota Press.

Caldeira, Jorge, Flavio de Carvalho, Claudio Marcondes, and Sergio Goes de Paula. 1999. *História do Brasil*. São Paulo: Campanhia das Letras.

Campos, Haroldo de. 1983. "Da razão antropofágica: diálogo e diferença na cultural brasileira." *Boletim Biblioteca Mária de Andrade* 44:107–125.

Carvalho, Bruno. 2013. *Porous City: A Cultural History of Rio de Janeiro*. Liverpool: Liverpool University Press.

Castro, Antonio Maria de Miranda e. 1880. Review of "*Trabalhadores asiáticos*." *Revista Brazileira*. Rio de Janeiro: N. Midosi.

Castro, Nuno de. 1987. *A porcelana chinesa ao tempo do Império*. Portugal and Brazil: ACD Editores.

Chalhoub, Sidney. 1990. *Visões da liberdade: Uma historia das últimas décadas da escravidão na corte*. São Paulo: Companhia das Letras.
———. 1996. *Cidade febril: Cortiços e epidemias na corte imperial*. São Paulo: Campanhia das Letras.
———. 2001. "What Are Noses For? Paternalism, Social Darwinism and Race Science in Machado de Assis." *Journal of Latin American Cultural Studies* 10, no. 2: 171–191.
———. 2003. *Machado de Assis, historiador*. São Paulo: Campanhia das Letras.
———. 2005. "Interpreting Machado de Assis: Paternalism, Slavery and the Free Womb Law." In *Honor, Status and Law in Modern Latin America*, edited by Sueann Caulfield, 87–108. Durham, NC: Duke University Press.
———. 2011. "The Precariousness of Freedom in a Slave Society: Brazil in the Nineteenth Century." *International Review of Social History* 56:405–439.

————. 2015. "The Politics of Ambiguity: Conditional Manumissions, Labor Contracts, and Slave Emancipation in Brazil (1850s–1888)." *International Review of Social History* 60: 161–191.

Chang, Gordon. 2015. *Fateful Ties: A History of America's Preoccupation with China.* Cambridge, MA: Harvard University Press.

Chang, Jason Oliver. 2017. *Chino: Anti-Chinese Racism in Mexico, 1880–1940.* Urbana- Champaign: University of Illinois Press.

Chang, Kornel. 2015. "Coolie." In *Keywords for Asian American Studies,* edited by Cathy J. Schlund-Vials, Linda Trinh Võ, and K. Scott Wong, 37–39. New York: New York University Press.

Chang-sheng, Shu. 2009. "Imigrantes e imigração chinesa no Rio de Janeiro (1910–90)." *Leituras da História* 17: 44–53.

Cheung, Dominic. 2008. *As Grandiose as the Ru Wares: Essays on Chinese Bronze, Porcelain and Paintings.* Taipei: Artist Publisher, 2008.

————. 2010. *A Heart for Porcelain—from Monochrome Wares to Famille Rose.* Taipei: Artist Publisher.

"Chinoca." 2013. *Priberam Dicionário.* Accessed December 29, 2017, at http://www.priberam.pt/dlpo/chinoca.

Choy, Philip P., Lorraine Dong, and Marlon K. Hom. 1994. *The Coming Man: 19th Century American Perceptions of the Chinese.* Seattle: University of Washington Press.

Chuh, Kandice. 2006. "Of Hemispheres and Other Spheres: Navigating Karen Tei Yamashita's Literary World." *American Literary History* 18, no. 3: 618–37.

Clarence-Smith, Gervase. 1985. *The Third Portuguese Empire, 1825–1975: A Study of Economic Imperialism.* Manchester: Manchester University Press.

"Cochinchina." 2005. *Diccionario panhispánico de dudas.* Real Academia Española. http://lema.rae.es/dpd/srv/search?key=Cochinchina.

Connerton, Paul. 1989. *How Societies Remember.* Cambridge: Cambridge University Press.

Conrad, Robert. 1975. "The Planter Class and the Debate over Chinese Immigration to Brazil, 1850–1893." *International Migration Review* 9, no. 1: 41–55.

Corominas, Joan. 1987. *Breve diccionario etimológico de la lengua castellana.* Madrid: Editorial Gredos.

Corrêa, Mariza. 1996. "Sobre a invenção da mulata." *Cadernos Pagu* 6–7: 35–50.

Costa, Emilia Viotti da. 1966. *Da senzala à colônia.* São Paulo: Difel.

Cowling, Camillia. 2013. *Conceiving Freedom: Women of Color, Gender, and the Abolition of Slavery in Havana and Rio de Janeiro.* Chapel Hill: University of North Carolina Press.

Creet, Julia, and Andreas Kitzman. 2011. *Memory and Migration: Multidisciplinary Approaches to Memory Studies.* Toronto: University of Toronto Press.

Dantas, Luiz. 2011. "Chaves para compreender *O Japão* de Aluísio Azevedo." In *O Japão*, edited by Aluísio Azevedo. Brasilia: Fundação Alexandre de Gusmão.

Darwin, Charles. 2001. "The Descent of Man [1871]." In *Darwin*, edited by Phillip Appleman, 175–254. New York: Norton.

Dávila, Jerry. 2003. *Diploma of Whiteness: Race and Social Policy in Brazil, 1917–1945*. Durham, NC: Duke University Press.

———. 2010. *Hotel Trópico: Brazil and the Challenge of African Decolonization, 1950–1980*. Durham: Duke University Press.

Debord, Guy. (1967) 1977. *Society of the Spectacle*. Detroit: Black & Red.

Delgado, Grace Peña. 2013. *Making the Chinese Mexican: Global Migration, Localism and Exclusion in the U.S. Mexico Borderlands*. Stanford: Stanford University Press.

———. 2016. "Globalizing Asias: A Multiscalar Approach to Immigration and Inter-Ethnic History in the Americas." Comments presented at the annual meeting of the Pacific Coast Branch of the American Historical Society, Waikoloa Beach, Hawaii, August 7.

Dezem, Rogério. 2005. *Matizes do "Amarelo" A gênese dos discursos sobre os orientais no Brasil (1878–1908)*. São Paulo: Editorial Humanitas.

Díaz, Roberto Ignacio. 2002. *Unhomely Rooms: Foreign Tongues and Spanish American Literature*. Lewisburg, PA: Bucknell University Press.

Dirlik, Arif. 1993. "Introduction: Pacific Contradictions." In *What Is in a Rim? Critical Perspectives on the Pacific Region Idea*, edited by Arif Dirlik, 3–15. Boulder, CO: Westview Press.

Dower, John. 1993. *War with Mercy: Race and Power in the Pacific War*. New York: American Council of Learned Societies.

Du Bois, W. E. B. 1939. *Black Then and Now*. New York: Holt.

———. 1999. *The Souls of Black Folk*. New York: Norton.

Dunn, Christopher. 2001. *Brutality Garden*. Chapel Hill: University of North Carolina Press.

———. 2006. "A retomada freyreana." In *Gilberto Freyre e os estudos latino-americanos*, edited by Joshua Lund and Malcom McNee. Pittsburgh: University of Pittsburgh Press.

———. 2014. "Mapping Tropicália." In *The Global Sixties in Sound and Vision*, edited by Timothy Scott, 29–42. New York: Palgrave Macmillan.

Eça de Queiroz, José Maria de. N.d. *Eça de Queiroz diplomata*. Compiled by Archer de Lima. Lisboa: Portugália.

———. 1874. *Singularidades de uma rapariga loira*. Belém: Universidade da Amazônia. http://www.dominiopublico.gov.br/download/texto/ua00088a.pdf.

———. 1900. *Cartas familiares*. Porto: Livraria Chardron De Lello & Irmão.

———. 1927. *O Mandarim*. Illustrations by Rachel Roque Gameiro. Porto: Livraria Chardron.

———. 1980. *O nosso cônsul em Havana: Eça de Queiroz*. Edited by Joaquim Palminha Silva. Lisboa: A Regra do Jogo Edições.

———. 1994. *Eça de Queiroz, correspondência consular, 1872–1874*. Compiled by Alan Freeland. Lisbon: Edições Cosmos.

———. 2000. *A emigração como força civilizadora*. Edited by Raul Rêgo. Lisbon: Publições Dom Quixote.

Edwards, Brent Hayes. 2003. *The Practice of Diaspora: Literature, Translation, and the Rise of Black Internationalism*. Cambridge, MA: Harvard University Press.

Elias, Maria José. 1973. "Os debates sobre o trabalho dos chins e o problema de mão-de-obra no Brasil durante o século XIX." In *Trabalho livre e trabalho escravo*, edited by Eurípedes Simões de Paula, 697–715. Goiânia: Anais do VI Simpósio Nacional dos Professores Universitários de História, ANPUH.

"Falena." 2017. Michaelis Dicionário Online. São Paulo: Editora Melhoramentos. Accessed December 1, 2017, at http://michaelis.uol.com.br/moderno-ingles/busca/portugues-ingles-moderno/falena/.

"Falena." 2017. Dicionário Online de Português. Accessed December 1, 2017, at https://www.dicio.com.br/falena/

"Falena." 2016. Dicionario informal, Radio e Televisão. http://www.dicionarioinformal.com.br/falena/.

"Falena." Trecanni La Cultural Italiana. Accessed November 30, 2017, at http://www.treccani.it/vocabolario/falena/.

Fausto, Boris. 2009. *O crime do restaurante chinês: carnaval, futebol e justiça na São Paulo dos anos 30*. São Paulo: Campanhia das Letras.

Festival do Japão. "Temas Anteriores." Accessed December 15, 2017, at http://festivaldojapao.com/temas-anteriores/

Fialho, Irene. 2012. *Eça de Queiroz entre os seus: Apresentada por sua filha: Cartas íntimas Maria de Eça de Queirós, José Maria Eça de Queiroz*. Lisboa, Portugal: Leya.

Findlay, Ronald, and Kevin H. O'Rourke. 2007. *Power and Plenty: Trade, War, and the World Economy in the Second Millennium*. Princeton, NJ: Princeton University Press.

Fishkin, Shelley Fisher. 1988. *From Fact to Fiction: Journalism and Imaginative Writing in America*. Oxford: Oxford University Press.

Forbes, Jack. 1993. *Africans and Native Americas: The Language of Race and the Evolution in Red Black Peoples*. Urbana: University of Illinois.

Freud, Sigmund. 1989. *The Freud Reader*. New York: Norton.

Freyre, Gilberto. 1933. *Casa grande e senzala*. São Paulo: Global Editora.

———. 1936. *Sobrados e mucambos.* São Paulo: Global Editora.

———. 1958. *Integração portuguesa nos trópicos.* Lisbon: Ministério do Ultramar.

———. 1961. *Talvez poesía.* Rio de Janeiro: Livraria José Olympio.

———. (1933) 1971. *The Masters and the Slaves: A Study in the Development of Brazilian Civilization.* Translated by Samuel Putnam. Berkeley: University of California Press.

———. (1936) 1987. *The Mansions and the Shanties: The Making of Modern Brazil.* Translated by Helen Caldwell. Los Angeles: University of California Press.

———. (1936) 2003. *A China tropical: E outros escritos sobre a influencia do Oriente na cultura luso-brasileira.* Compiled by Edson Nery da Fonseca. Brasilia: Editora University de Brasilia.

———. (1971) 2012. *New World in the Tropics.* Brasília: Federal Republic of Brazil, Ministry of Sport, International Advisory.

Fu Yunlong. 1901. "Baxi feng su [Customs in Brazil]." *Baxi tu jing [Brazil Travel Map],* V4. [China]: N.p.

Fu Yunlong. [1889] 2005. *Fu Yunlong Riji.* [Fu Yunlong's Diary], compiled by Fu Xuncheng. Hangzhou, Zhejiang guji chu ban she.

Fu Yunlong. [1892] 2005. *Fu Yunlong Riji.* [Fu Yunlong's Diary], compiled by Fu Xuncheng. Hangzhou: Zhejiang guji chu ban she.

Gautier, Judith. 1867. *Le Livre de Jade.* Paris: Alphonse Lemerre.

Ginzburg, Carlo. 1994. "Killing a Chinese Mandarin: The Moral Implications of Distance." *Critical Inquiry* 21.

Gledson, John. 2001. Introduction to Roberto Schwarz's *A Master on the Periphery of Capitalism.* Durham, NC: Duke University Press.

Glynn, Irial, and J. Olaf Kleist. 2012. "Memory and Migration Nexus: An Overview." In *History, Memory and Migration: Perceptions of the Past and the Politics of Incorporation,* edited by Irial Glynn and J. Olaf Kleist, 3–29. New York: Palgrave Macmillan.

Gómez-Barris, Macarena. 2008. *Where Memory Dwells: Culture and State Violence in Chile.* Berkeley: University of California Press.

Gooding-Williams, Robert. 2005. *Look, a Negro! Philosophical Essays on Race, Culture, and Politics.* New York: Routledge.

Gordon, Avery, 2008. *Ghostly Matters: Haunting and the Sociological Imagination.* Minneapolis: University of Minnesota Press.

Gronewald, Sue. 2015. "The Ming Voyages." http://afe.easia.columbia.edu/special/china_1000ce_mingvoyages.htm#introduction.

Guénif-Souilamas, Nacira. 2017. "Restrained Equality: A Sexualized and Gendered Color Line." In *Austere Histories in European Societies: Social Exclusion and the Contest of Colonial Memories*, edited by Stefan Jonsson and Julia Willén, 161–181. New York: Routledge.

Guerrant, Edward. 1950. *Roosevelt's Good Neighbor Policy*. Albuquerque: University of New Mexico Press.

Guimarães, Lais de Barros Monteiro de. 1979. *História dos bairros de São Paulo—Liberdade*. São Paulo: Departamento do Patrimônio Histórico Divisão do Arquivo Histórico. Accessed November 13, 2017, at https://issuu.com/ahsp/docs/1979-hb-16-liberdade.

Guimarães Filho, Luis. 1925. *Samurais e mandarins*. Rio de Janeiro: Livraria Francisco Alves.

Gupta, Arun das. 1999. "The Maritime Trade in Indonesia, 1500–1800." In *India and the Indian Ocean, 1500–1800*, edited by Ashin das Gupta and M. N. Pearson, 91–125. New Delhi: Oxford University Press.

Halberstam, Judith. 2005. *In a Queer Time and Place: Transgender Bodies, Subcultural Lives*. New York: New York University Press.

Halbwachs, Maurice. 1992. *On Collective Memory*. Chicago: Chicago University Press.

Hall, Stuart. 1997a. "The Work of Representation." In *Representation: Cultural Representation and Signifying Practices*, edited by Stuart Hall, 13–75. London: Sage.

———. 1997b. "The Spectacle of the 'Other.'" In *Representation: Cultural Representation and Signifying Practices*, edited by Stuart Hall, 223–291. London: Sage.

Hampton, Timothy. 2009. *Literature and Diplomacy in Early Modern Europe*. Ithaca, NY: Cornell University Press.

Han, Xiaorong. 2005. *Chinese Discourse of the Peasant, 1900–1949*. New York: SUNY Press.

Hanke, Lewis. (1959) 1970. *Aristotle and the American Indian. A Study in Race Prejudice in the Modern World*. Bloomington: Indiana University Press.

Hansen, João Adolfo. 1995. "Teatro da memória: monumento barroco e retórica." *Revista do IFAC* 2:0–54.

———. 2001. "Artes seiscentistas e teologia política." In *Arte sacra colonial: Barroco memória viva*, edited by Percival Tirapeli, 180–189. São Paulo: UNESP/Imprensa Oficial do Estado.

———. 2006. *Alegoria: Construção e interpretação da metáfora*. São Paulo: Hedra Campinas, Editora da Unicamp.

Hansen, Jette Barnholt. 2012. "Danish Revue: Satire as Rhetorical Citizenship." In *Rhetorical Citizenship and Public Deliberation*, edited by Christian Kock and Lisa Villadsen, 249–264. Philadelphia: University of Pennsylvania Press.

Hart, Matthew. 2013. *Nations of Nothing but Poetry: Modernism, Transnationalism, and Synthetic Vernacular Writing.* Oxford: Oxford University Press.

Hartman, Saidiya. 1997. *Scenes of Subjection: Terror, Slavery, and Self-Making in Nineteenth Century America.* Oxford: Oxford University Press.

Hashimoto, Lica. 2009. "Imigração chinesa e japonesa nas crônicas de Machado de Assis (1839–1908)." PhD diss., University of São Paulo.

Hayot, Eric. 2009. *The Hypothetical Mandarin: Sympathy, Modernity, and Chinese Pain.* Oxford: Oxford University Press.

Hebrew Bible. (c. 1400) 2010. New York: Oxford University Press.

Helly, Denise. 1993. *The Cuban Commission Report: A Hidden History of the Chinese in Cuba. The Original English-Language Text of 1876.* Baltimore: Johns Hopkins University Press.

Hertzman, Marc. 2013. *Making Samba: A New History of Race and Music in Brazil.* Durham, NC: Duke University Press.

Hespanha, António Manuel. 1999. "O Orientalismo em Portugal (séculos XVI–XX)." Comissão Nacional para as Comemorações dos Descobrimentos Portugueses, coordinated by Ana Maria Rodrigues, 15–37. Lisboa: Inapa. Exhibition catalogue.

Hevia, James L. 1998. "The Archive State and the Fear of Pollution: From the Opium Wars to Fu Manchu." *Cultural Studies* 12, no. 2: 234–264.

Hilton, Stanley. 1981. "The United States, Brazil, and the Cold War, 1945–1960: End of the Special Relationship." *Journal of American History* 68, no. 3: 599–624.

Hirsch, Marianne. 2012. *The Generation of Postmemory: Writing and Visual Culture after the Holocaust.* New York: Columbia University Press.

Hochstrasser, Julie. 2010. "Remapping Dutch Art in Global Perspective: Other Points of View." In *Cultural Contact and the Making of European Art since the Age of Exploration,* edited by Mary D. Sheriff, 43–73. Chapel Hill: University of North Carolina Press.

Hoeller, Hildegard. 2005. "Racial Currency: Zora Neale Hurston's 'The Gilded Six-Bits' and the Gold-Standard Debate." *American Literature* 77, no. 4. 761–785.

Hoffecker, John, Scott Elias, and Dennis O'Rourke. 2014. "Out of Beringia?" *Science* 343, no. 6174: 979–980.

Holanda, Sergio Buarque de. 2012. *Roots of Brazil.* Notre Dame: University of Notre Dame.

Honour, Hugh. 1961. *The Vision of Cathay.* New York: Harper and Row.

hooks, bell. 1992. *Black Looks: Race and Representation.* New York: Routledge.

Horn, Maja. 2014. *Masculinity after Trujillo: The Politics of Gender in Dominican Literature.* Gainesville: University Press of Florida.

Hu-DeHart, Evelyn. 1992. "Chinese Coolie Labor in Cuba and Peru in the Nineteenth Century: Free Labor or Neoslavery." *Journal of Overseas Chinese* 2 (2): 149–182.

———. 1993a. "Latin America in Asia-Pacific Perspective." In *What Is in a Rim? Critical Perspectives on the Pacific Region Idea,* edited by Arif Dirlik, 251–282. Boulder, CO: Westview Press.

———. 1993b. "Chinese Coolie Labour in Cuba in the Nineteenth Century: Free Labour or Neo-Slavery?" *Slavery and Abolition* 14, no. 1: 67–83.

———. 2016. "Diaspora and Transnationalism through the Lens of Chinese Diaspora Worldwide." Paper presented at the 34rd Annual Meeting of the Latin American Studies Association, New York, May 27.

Hsu, Madeline. 2002. *Dreaming of Gold, Dreaming of Home: Transnationalism and Migration Between the United States and South China, 1882-1943.* Stanford: Stanford University Press.

———. 2004. "Qiaokan and the Transnational Community of Taishan County, Guangdong, 1882 - 1943." *China Review* (Spring). Accessed December 23, 2017, at http://ezproxy.cul.columbia.edu/login?url=https://search.proquest.com/docview/199502160?accountid=10226.

———. 2015. *The Good Immigrants: How the Yellow Peril Became a Model Minority.* Princeton: Princeton University Press.

Ide, Danilo Sergio. 2014. "Perambulações no bairro da Liberdade: Passeios ao vivo e em video com moradores locais." PhD diss., Univerdidade de São Paulo.

Imigração japonesa no Brasil. 2000. São Paulo: Memorial do Imigrante/Museu da Imigração. *Immigration Act of 1924 (The Johnson-Reed Act).* Office of the Historian, US Department of State. https://history.state.gov/milestones/1921-1936/immigration-act.

Irick, Robert L. 1982. *Ch'ing Policy toward the Coolie Trade: 1847–1878.* Taipei: Chinese Materials Center.

Isfahani-Hammond, Alexandra. 2008. *White Negritude: Race, Writing and Brazilian Cultural Identity.* New York: Palgrave Macmillan.

———. 2014. "Slave Barracks Aristocrats: Islam and the Orient in the Work of Gilberto Freyre." *The Middle East and Brazil: Perspectives on the New Global South,* edited by Paul Amar, 162-181. Bloomington: Indiana University Press.

Ishimatsu, Lorie. 1984. *The Poetry of Machado de Assis.* Valencia: Albatros Hispanofilia.

"John Chinaman." 2017. *Merriam-Webster.com.* Accessed March 15, 2017, at https://www.merriam-webster.com/dictionary/John%20Chinaman

Johnson, Randal. 1999. *Black Brazil: Culture, Identity, and Social Mobilization.* Los Angeles: University of California Press.

Jordon, Donald. 2001. *China's Trial by Fire: The Shanghai War of 1932.* Ann Arbor: University of Michigan Press.

Jung, Moon-Ho. 2009. *Coolies and Cane: Race, Labor and Sugar in the Age of Emancipation.* Baltimore, MD: Johns Hopkins University Press.

Kant, Immanuel. 1784. "What Is Enlightenment?" http://www.columbia.edu/ acis/ets/CCREAD/etscc/kant.html.

Karl, Rebecca. 2002. *Staging the World: Chinese Nationalism at the Turn of the Twentieth Century.* Durham, NC: Duke University Press.

Keevak, Michael. 2011. *Becoming Yellow: A Short History of Racial Thinking.* Princeton, NJ: Princeton University Press.

Kennedy, Robert. 2008. "The Chinese Question." *Harper's Weekly.* http://www.harpweek.com/09Cartoon/BrowseByDateCartoon. asp?Month=February&Date=18.

Kim, Elaine. *Asian American Literature: An Introduction to the Writings and their Social Context.* Philadelphia: Temple University Press.

Klein, Herbert, and Francisco Vidal Luna. 2010. *Slavery in Brazil.* Cambridge: Cambridge University Press.

Knowlton, Edgar. 1976. *Machado de Assis and His Lira Chinesa.* Macau: Imprensa Nacional.

Kondo, Dorinne K. 1990. "M. Butterfly: Orientalism, Gender, and a Critique of Essentialist Identity." *Cultural Critique,* no. 16 (Autumn): 5–29.

Kushigian, Julia. 1999. *Orientalism in the Hispanic Literary Tradition: In Dialogue with Borges, Paz and Sarduy.* Albuquerque: University of New Mexico Press.

Laërne, C. F. Van Delden. 1885. *Brazil and Java: Report on Coffee-Culture in America, Asia and Africa, to H.E. the Minister of the Colonies.* London: W. H. Allen.

Lai, Walton Look. 1993. *Indentured Labor, Caribbean Sugar: Chinese and Indian Migrants to the British West Indies, 1838–1918.* Baltimore, MD: Johns Hopkins University Press.

Lammardo, Clélia Person. 2016. "Será que você conhece São Paulo?" *Jornal Maturidades* (Pontifícia Universidade Católica de São Paulo). http://www.pucsp. br/maturidades/com_palavra_professor/sera_qvc_conhece_sp_42.html.

Landau, Iddo. 2005. "To Kill a Mandarin." *Philosophy and Literature* 29.

Lane, Jill. 2008. "ImpersoNation: Toward a Theory of Black-, Red-, and Yellow-face in the Americas." *PMLA* 123, no. 5.

Las Casas, Bartolomé. 1960. "Thirty Very Juridical Propositions." *Columbia College, Introduction to Contemporary Civilization in the Wes,* edited by Bernard Wishy, Marvin Harris, Sidney Morgenbesser, and Joseph Rothschild. New York: Columbia University Press.

Lean, Eugenia. 2015. "The Butterfly Mark: Chen Diexian, His Brand, and Cultural Entrepreneurism in Republican China." In *The Business of Culture: Cultural Entrepreneurs in China and Southeast Asia, 1900–65*, edited by Christopher Rea and Nicolai Volland, 62–92. Vancouver: UBC Press.

Lee, Ana Paulina. 2012. "The Afterlives of Chico Rei." *Transmodernity: Journal of Peripheral Cultural Production of the Luso-Hispanic World* 2, no. 1: 1–13.

———. 2014. "Luso-Hispanic Archipelagos: The Imaginary of Asia in Brazilian and Cuban Literary and Visual Cultures, 1847–2014." PhD diss., University of Southern California.

Lee, Erika. 2003. *At America's Gates: Chinese Immigration during the Exclusion Era, 1882–1943.* Chapel Hill: University of North Carolina Press.

———. 2007a. "The 'Yellow Peril' and Asian Exclusion in the Americas." *Pacific Historical Review* 76, no. 4: 537–562.

———. 2007b. "Hemispheric Orientalism and the 1907 Race Riots on the Pacific Coast." *Amerasia Journal* 33, no. 2: 19–47.

Lee, Hyunjung, and Younghan Cho. 2012. "Introduction: Colonial Modernity and Beyond in East Asian Contexts." *Cultural Studies* 26, no. 5: 601–616.

Lee, Robert. 1999. *Orientals: Asian Americans in Popular Culture.* Philadelphia: Temple University Press.

Lee-Loy, Anne-Marie. 2015. "An Antiphonal Announcement: Jamaica's Anti-Chinese Legislation in Transnational Context." *Journal of Asian American Studies* 18, no. 2: 141–164.

Leite, José Roberto Teixeira. 1999. *A China no Brasil.* Campinas: Unicamp.

Leite, Míriam Moreira. 1984. *A condição feminina no Rio de Janeiro século XIX: Antologia de textos de viajantes estrangeiros.* São Paulo: Hucitec.

Lesser, Jeffrey. 1995. "Neither Slave nor Free, Neither Black nor White: The Chinese in Early Nineteenth Century Brazil." *Estudios Interdisciplinarios de America Latina y el Caribe* 5, no. 2. http://www.tau.ac.il/eial/V_2/lesser.htm.

———. 1999. *Negotiating National Identity: Immigrants, Minorities, and the Struggle for Ethnicity in Brazil.* Durham, NC: Duke University Press.

———. 2002. "In Search of the Hyphen: Nikkei and the Struggle over National Brazilian Identity." In *New Worlds, New Lives. Globalization and People of Japanese Descent in the in the Americas and from Latin America in Japan*, edited by Lane Hirabayashi, Akemi Kikumura-Yano, and James Hirabayashi. Stanford: Stanford University Press.

———. 2007. *A Discontented Diaspora: Japanese Brazilians and the Meanings of Ethnic Militancy, 1960–1980.* Durham, NC: Duke University Press

———. 2013. *Immigration, Ethnicity and National Identity in Brazil, 1808 to the Present.* Cambridge: Cambridge University Press.

Lewis, Martin, and Kären Wigen. 1997. *The Myth of Continents: A Critique of Metageography.* Berkeley: University of California Press.

Liang Zhan. 2016. "Wenming, lixing yu zhongzu gailiang: yige Datong shijie de gouxiang [Civilization, rationality and racial improvement: The blueprint of a world of great unity]." In *Shijie zhixu yu wenming dengji* [World order and civilization hierarchy], edited by Lydia H. Liu, 101–162. Shanghai: Sanlian Chubanshe.

Lima, Ari. 2011. "Modernity, Agency, and Sexuality in the Pagode Baiano." In *Brazilian Popular Music and Citizenship,* edited by Idelber Avelar and Christopher Dunn, 267-277. Durham, NC: Duke University Press.

Lipsitz, George. 1998. *The Possessive Investment in Whiteness: How White People Profit from Identity Politics.* Philadelphia: Temple University Press.

Lisboa, Henrique Carlos Ribeiro. 1988. *A China e os chins: Recordações de viagem.* Montevideo: Typographia a vapor de A. Godel.

Lobato, Monteiro. 1917. *O Sacy-Pererê: Resultado de um inquérito.* São Paulo: Globo.

Locke, John. (1689) 1993. *Two Treatises on Government in Political Writings.* New York: Hackett.

Longobardi, Andrea Piazzaroi, and Patricia Viera de Souza. 2011. "Um dragão chinês presta votos a Nossa Senhora da Expectação do Parto: apontamentos a partir do maquinário visual da Capela de Nossa Senhora do Ó." *Revista Angelus Novu* 2: 81–109.

Louie, Andrea. 2004. *Chineseness across Borders: Renegotiating Chinese Identities in China and the United States.* Durham: Duke University Press.

Lopes, Antonio Herculano. 2001. "Auto-imagem nacional." In *Caderno Pensar o Estado de Minas.* http://www.casaruibarbosa.gov.br/dados/DOC/artigos/k-n/FCRB_AntonioHerculano_Lopes_Algumas_notas_sobre_o_mulato_a_mulata_ea_invencao_de_um_pais_sem_culpa.pdf.

López, Kathleen. 2013. *Chinese Cubans: A Transnational History.* Chapel Hill: University of North Carolina Press.

López-Calvo, Ignacio. 2008. *Imaging the Chinese in Cuban Literature and Culture.* Gainesville: University of Florida Press.

Loti, Pierre. 2006. *Madame Chrysanthème.* New York: BiblioBazar.

Lott, Eric. 1992. "Love and Theft: The Racial Unconscious of Blackface Minstrelsy." *Representations* 39: 23–50.

Loureiro, Rui. 2000. *Fidalgos, missionários e mandarins: Portugal e a China no século XVI.* Lisbon: Fundação Oriente.

Low, Kelvin. 2014. *Remembering the Samsui Women: Migration and Social Memory in Singapore and China.* Vancouver: University of British Columbia Press.

Lowe, Lisa. 2015. *Intimacies of Four Continents.* Durham, NC: Duke University Press.

Lui, Mary Ting Yi. 2007. *The Chinatown Trunk Mystery: Murder, Miscegenation, and Other Dangerous Encounters in Turn-of-the Century New York City.* Princeton: Princeton University Press.

Luca, Heloisa Helena Paiva de. 1998. Introduction to *Balas de Estalo de Machado de Assis: Edição completa e comentada.* São Paulo: Annablume.

Machado de Assis, Joaquim Maria. 1870. *Phalenas.* Rio de Janeiro: B. L. Garnier. http://www.brasiliana.usp.br/bbd/handle/1918/00210100#page/3/mode/1up.

———. 1873. "Notícia da atual literatura–Instinto de nacionalidade." *Novo Mundo,* March 24.

———. 1878. "Chinoiserie." *Revista Illustrada,* no. 115.

———. 1880. "Memórias Póstumas de Brás Cubas." *Revista Brazileira* 3.

———. 1896. *Não Consultes Médico.* Rio de Janeiro: Fundação Biblioteca Nacional. http://www.dominiopublico.gov.br/download/texto/bn000135.pdf.

———. 1994. *Obra Completa de Machado de Assis.* Rio de Janeiro: Nova Aguilar. http://www.machadodeassis.ufsc.br/obras/cronicas/CRONICA,%20A%20semana,%201892.htm.

———. 1998. *Balas de Estalo de Machado de Assis: Edição completa e comentada.* Compiled by Heloisa Helena Paiva de Luca. São Paulo: Annablume.

Machado, Sandra. 2014. "Chineses no Rio de Janeiro." In *MultiRio: A mídia educativa da cidade.* http://www.multirio.rj.gov.br/index.php/leia/reportagens-artigos/reportagens/795-os-chineses-no-rio-de-janeiro.

Madsen, Andrew D., and Carolyn L. White. 2011. *Chinese Export Porcelain.* Walnut Creek, CA: Left Coast Press.

Maher, Frances A., and Mary Kay Tetreault. 1993. "Frames of Positionality: Constructing Meaningful Dialogues about Gender and Race." *Anthropological Quarterly* 66, no. 3: 118–126.

Maldonado-Torres, Nelson. 2008. *Against War: Views from the Underside of Modernity.* Durham, NC: Duke University Press.

"Mandarin." 2008. *Merriam-Webster,* 11th ed. Springfield, MA: Merriam-Webster. Accessed June 8, 2017, at http://www.merriam-webster.com/dictionary/mandarin.

"Mandarin." 2016. *Oxford Dictionaries.* Oxford University Press. Accessed June 8, 2017, at http://www.oxforddictionaries.com/us/definition/american_english/mandarin.

Mantua, Simão de. [Pseud. Antônio Gomes Carmo]. 1923. *Cartas de um chinez do Brasil para a China.* São Paulo: Monteiro Lobato & Co.

Martínez, María Elena. 2008. *Genealogical Fictions: Limpieza de Sangre, Religion, and Gender in Colonial Mexico.* Stanford: Stanford University Press.

Mata, Maria Eugénia. 2007. "Interracial Marriage in the Last Portuguese Colonial Empire." *E-Journal of Portuguese History* 5: 1.

Matsusaka, Yoshihisa Tak. 2001. *The Making of Japanese Manchuria, 1904–1932.* Cambridge, MA: Harvard University Press.

McKeown, Adam. 2001. *Chinese Migrant Networks and Cultural Change: Peru, Chicago, Hawaii, 1900-1936.* Chicago and London: The University of Chicago Press.

McNeil, William, 1963. *The Rise of the West.* Chicago: University of Chicago Press.

Meagher, Arnold J. 2008. *The Coolie Trade: The Traffic in Chinese Laborers to Latin America.* Bloomington, IN: Xlibris Corporation.

Metzger, Sean. 2014. *Chinese Looks: Fashion, Performance, Race.* Bloomington: Indiana University Press.

Mignolo. Walter. 2001. "Coloniality at Large: The Western Hemisphere in the Colonial Horizon of Modernity." Translated by Michael Ennis. *New Centennial Review* 1, no. 2: 19–54.

———. 2005. *The Idea of Latin America.* Oxford: Blackwell.

———. 2008. *Coloniality at Large: Latin America and the Postcolonial Debate.* Durham, NC: Duke University Press.

———. 2014. "Looking for the Meaning of the Decolonial Gesture." In *Decolonial Gesture,* edited by Macarena Gómez-Barris with Jill Lane and Marcial Godoy Anativia. *e-misférica,* 11, 1. http://hemisphericinstitute.org/hemi/en/emisferica-111-decolonial-gesture/mignolo.

Mignolo, Walter.

Mill, John Stuart. 1991. *On Liberty and Other Essays.* Oxford: Oxford University Press.

Molloy, Silvia. 1998. "The Poetics of Posing." In *Hispanisms and Homosexualities,* edited by Sylvia Molloy and Robert McKee Irwin, 141–161. Durham, NC: Duke University Press.

Mónica, Maria Filomena. 2005. *Eça de Queiroz.* New York: Tamesis.

Montaldo, Graciela. 1994. *La sensibilidad amenazada: Fin de siglo y modernismo.* Rosario, ARG: Beatriz Viterbo Editora.

———. 1999. *Ficciones culturales y fábulas de identidade en América Latina.* Rosario, ARG: Beatriz Viterbo Editora.

———. 2014. "Dialogues in Theory: Emancipation and Emancipatory Acts." *Parallax* 20, no. 4: 334–344.

Monteiro, Maurício. 2008. *A construção do gosto: Música e sociedade na corte do Rio de Janeiro—1808–1821.* São Paulo: Ateliê Editorial.

Moog, Vianna. 1955. *Bandeirantes e pioneiros.* Globo: Rio de Janeiro.

Moon, Krystyn. 2005. *Yellowface: Creating the Chinese in American Popular Music and Performance, 1850s–1920s.* New Brunswick, NJ: Rutgers University Press.

Moriyama, Alan Takeo. 1985. *Imingaisha. Japanese Emigration Companies and Hawaii, 1894–1908.* Honolulu: University of Hawaii Press.

Moura, Carlos Francisco. 2011. *Liou She-Shun, Plenipotenciário do Império da China: Viagem ao Brasil em 1909.* Macau: Instituto Internacional de Macau.

Nabuco, Joaquim. (1879) 2010. *Joaquim Nabuco.* Brasília: Biblioteca Digital da Câmara dos Deputados.

Nakamaki, Hirochika. 2004. "Aliança Colony." *Japanese Overseas Migration Museum.* Yokohama: Japanese International Cooperation Agency. Museum exhibit.

Naylor, Celia. 2008. *African Cherokees in Indian Territory: From Chattel to Citizens.* Chapel Hill: University of North Carolina Press.

Neder, Alvaro. 2016. "About João de Barro." *MTVartists.* http://www.mtv.com/artists/joao-de-barro/biography/.

Neto, Luiz Costa-Lima. 2008. "O teatro das contradições: O negro nas atividades musicais nos palcos da corte imperial durante o século XIX." *Opus* 14, no. 2: 37–71.

Ngai, Mae. 2004. *Impossible Subjects: Illegal Aliens and the Making of Modern America.* Princeton, NJ: Princeton University Press.

———. 2015. "Chinese Gold Miners and the 'Chinese Question' in Nineteenth-Century California and Victoria." *Journal of American History* 101, no. 4: 1082–1105.

Nguyen, Viet Thanh. 2016. *Nothing Ever Dies: Vietnam and the Memory of War.* Cambridge, MA: Harvard University Press.

Nguyen, Viet Thanh, and Janet Hoskins. 2014. *Transpacific Studies: Framing and Emerging Field.* Honolulu: University of Hawaii Press.

Nietzsche, Friedrich. (1887) 1967. *On the Genealogy of Morals and Ecce Homo.* New York: Random House.

Nippo. 1999. "Crueldade marca início do bairro da Liberdade: No local eram enforcados criminosos e escravos no período colonial." Accessed December 1, 2015, at http://www.nippobrasil.com.br/especial/n027.php.

"O riso encontra eco." *Veja.* November 20, 1889. Accessed March 5, 2016, at http://veja.abril.com.br/historia/republica/teatro-fritzmac-Artur-aluisio-azevedo.shtml.

Okihiro, Gary. 2016. *Third World Studies: Theorizing Liberation.* Durham, NC: Duke University Press.

Olick, Jeffrey, and J. Robbins. 1998. "Social Memory Studies: From 'Collective Memory' to the Historical Sociology of Mnemonic Practices." *Annual Review of Sociology* 24: 105–140.

Oliva, Osmar Pereira. 2008. "Machado de Assis, Joaquim Nabuco, Eça de Queirós e a imigração chinesa–qual medo?" *Revista da ANPOLL* 2: 65–84.

Oliveira, Amurabi. 2013. "O Brasil e sua herança oriental na obra de Gilberto Freyre." *Revista Esboços* 20, no. 29: 177–183.

Omi, Michael, and Howard Winant. 1994. *Racial Formation in the United States: From the 1960s to the 1990s*. New York: Routledge.

Ortiz, Renato. 1985. *Cultura brasileira e identidade nacional*. São Paulo: Editora Brasiliense.

———. 1997. "Aluísio de Azevedo e o Japão: Uma apreciação crítica." *Tempo Social* 9, no. 2: 79–95.

Painter, Nell Irvin. 1997. *Sojourner Truth: A Life, a Symbol*. New York: Norton.

Palumbo-Liu, David. 1999. *Asian/American: Historical Crossings of a Racial Frontier*. Stanford: Stanford University Press.

Paranhos, Adalberto. 2011. "Dissonant Voices under a Regime of Order-Unity." In *Brazilian Popular Music and Citizenship*, edited by Idelber Avelar and Christopher Dunn, 28–43. Durham, NC: Duke University Press.

Peppercorn, Lisa. 1941. "Musical Education in Brazil." *Bulletin of the Pan American Union* 74. [July-December 1940.] US House, Document no. 531, pt. 7, 8, 9, 10, 11, 12.

Perrone, Charles, and Christopher Dunn. 2002. *Chiclete com Banana: Internationalization in Brazilian Music*. New York: Routledge.

Plante, Trevor. 1999. "U.S. Marines in the Boxer Rebellion." *Prologue Magazine* 31, no. 4. http://www.archives.gov/publications/prologue/1999/winter/boxer-rebellion-1.html.

Plato. (c. 380 BC) 1992. *Republic*. New York: Hackett.

Pratt, Mary Louis. 2007. *Imperial Eyes Travel Writing and Transculturation*. New York: Routledge.

Qi Yaolin. 1918. "Xunling: Jiangsu sheng zhanggongshu xunling di sanbaibashiyi hao *Jiangsu Sheng Gongbao* 1485 (January 19) [Order of Chief Executive Office of Jiangsu Province No. 381 *Gazette of Jiangsu Province*]. Translated by Wang Siwei.

Queiroz, Renato da Silva. 1987. *Um mito bem brasileiro: Estudo antropológico sobre o Saci*. São Paulo: Livraria Editora Polis.

Quijano, Aníbal. 1998. "La colonialidad del poder y la experiencia cultural latinoamericana." In *Pueblo, época y desarrollo: La sociología de América Latina*, edited by Roberto Briceño-León and Heinz R. Sonntag, 139–155. Caracas: Nueva Sociedad.

———. 2000. "Coloniality of Power and Eurocentrism in Latin America." *International Sociology* 15, no. 2: 215-232.

Quijano, Aníbal, and Immanuel Wallerstein. 1992. "Americanity as a Concept, or the Americas in the Modern World-System." *International Journal of Social Sciences* 134: 583–591.

Rancière, Jacques. 2004. *The Politics of Aesthetic.* Translated by Gabriel Rockhill. London: Continuum.

Rao, Anupama. 2009. *The Caste Question: Dalits and the Politics of Modern India.* Los Angeles: University of California Press.

Reid, Michael. 2014. *Brazil: The Troubled Rise of a Global Power.* New Haven, CT: Yale University Press.

Ribeiro, Darcy. 1995. *O povo brasileiro: A formação e o sentido do Brasil.* São Paulo: Campanhia das Letras.

Richardson, Joanna. 1986. *Judith Gautier: A Biography.* London: Quartet Books.

Ricoeur, Paul. 2004. *Memory, History, Forgetting.* Translated by Kathleen Blamey and David Pellauer. Chicago: University of Chicago Press.

Roach, Joseph R. 1996. *Cities of the Dead: Circum-Atlantic Performance.* New York: Columbia University Press.

Roberts, Brian Russell, and Michelle Ann Stephens. 2013. "Archipelagic American Studies and the Caribbean." *Journal of Transnational American Studies* 5, no. 1: 1–20. http://escholarship.org/uc/item/52f2966r.

Rodriguez, Helio Suêvo. 2004. *A formação das estradas de ferro no Rio de Janeiro: O resgateda sua memoria.* Rio de Janeiro: Sociedade de Pesquisa para Memória do Trem.

Rohmer, Sax [Arthur Ward]. (1913) 2008. *The Insidious Fu Manchu.* Project Gutenberg. EBook 173. http://www.gutenberg.org/files/173/173.txt.

Roncador, Sonia. 2016. "The 'Chinese Question' in Machado's Journalism." In *Emerging Dialogues on Machado de Assis,* edited by Lamonte Aidoo and Daniel Silva, 105–122. New York: Palgrave Macmillan.

Said, Edward. 1978. *Orientalism.* New York: Vintage.

Saito, Hiroshi. 1959. "Alguns aspectos da mobilidade dos japoneses no Brasil." *Kobe Economic and Business Review, 6th Annual Report* (49–59).

———. 1961. *O japonês no Brasil: Estudo de mobilidade e fixação.* São Paulo: Editora Sociologia e Política.

Saito, Hiroshi, and Takashi Maeyama, eds. 1973. *Assimilação e integração dos japoneses no Brasil.* São Paulo: Voces/EDUSP.

Sakai Naoki. 2016. "The West and the Tropics of Area Studies." *Asian Diasporic Visual Cultures and the Americas* 2, no. 2–1: 19–31.

Sakai Naoki, and Hyon Joo Yoo. 2012. *The Transpacific Imagination: Rethinking Boundary, Culture and Society.* Singapore: World Scientific Publishing.

Sakata, Yasuo. 2004. "Beginning of Overseas *Dekasegi*." Japanese Overseas Migration Museum. Yokohama: Japanese International Cooperation Agency. Exhibition catalogue.

"Salamaleque." 2015. *Priberam Dicionário*. Lisboa: Priberam Informática. Accessed October 7, 2015, at http://www.priberam.pt/dlpo/salamaleque.

Saranillio, Dean Itsujio. 2013. "Why Asian Settler Colonialism Matters: A Thought Piece on Critiques, Debates, and Indigenous Difference." *Settler Colonial Studies* 3, no. 3–4: 280–294.

Sawer, Marian. 1977. *Marxism and the Question of the Asiatic Mode of Production*. Dordrecht: Springer Netherlands.

Schmidt, Benjamin. 2015. *Inventing Exoticism: Geography, Globalism, and Europe's Early Modern World*. Philadelphia: University of Pennsylvania Press.

Schwarcz, Lilia Moritz. 2006. "Gilberto Freyre: Adaptação, mestiçagem, trópicos e privacidade em *Novo Mundo nos trópicos*." In *Gilberto Freyre e os estudos latino-americanos*, edited by Joshua Lund and Malcolm McNee, 305–334. Pittsburgh: University of Pittsburgh Press.

———. 2012. *Nem preto, nem branco, muito pelo contrário: Cor e raça na intimidade*. São Paulo: Editora Claro Enigma.

Schwarz, Roberto. 1987. *Que horas são?* São Paulo: Campanhia das Letras.

———. 1988. "Brazilian Culture: Nationalism by Elimination." *New Left Review* 1:167.

———. 2000. *Ao vencedor as batatas*. São Paulo. Livraria Duas Cidades.

———. 2001. *A Master on the Periphery of Capitalism*. Introduction by John Gledson. Durham, NC: Duke University Press.

Schwartz, Jorge. 1983. *Vanguarda e cosmopolitismo na década de 20: Oliveiro Girondo e Oswald de Andrade*. São Paulo: Perspectiva.

Scott, David. 2008. *China and the International System, 1840–1949*. New York: SUNY Press.

Seigel, Micol. 2009. *Uneven Encounters: Making Race and Nation in Brazil and the United States*. Durham, NC: Duke University Press.

Seijas, Tatiana 2014. *Asian Slaves in Colonial Mexico: From Chinos to Indians*. Cambridge: Cambridge University Press.

Sepulveda, Juan Ginés de. 1960. "Democrates Alter, Or, on the Just Causes for War against the Indians." *Introduction to Contemporary Civilization in the West*, edited by Bernard Wishy, Marvin Harris, Sidney Morgenbesser, and Joseph Rothschild. New York: Columbia University Press.

Shah, Nyan. 2011. *Stranger Intimacy: Contesting Race, Sexuality and the Law in the North American West*. Berkeley: University of California Press.

"Shanghai." 2017. *Dictionary.com Unabridged* (Random House, Dictionary.com). Accessed March 27, 2017, at http://www.dictionary.com/browse/shanghai.

"Shanghai." 2017. *Dictionary.com Unabridged* (Random House, Dictionary.com). Accessed May 1, 2017, at http://www.dictionary.com/browse/shanghai.

Shizuno, Elena Camargo. 2010. *Os imigrantes japoneses na segunda guerra mundial: Bandeirantes do Oriente ou perigo amarelo no Brasil.* Londrina: Eduel.

Shohat, Ella, and Robert Stam. 2014. "Tropical Orientalism: Brazil's Race Debates and the Sephardi-Moorish Atlantic." *The Middle East and Brazil: Perspectives on the New Global South*, edited by Paul Amar, 119-161. Bloomington: Indiana University Press.

———. 2016. "Genealogies of Orientalism and Occidentalism: Sephardi Jews, Muslims, and the Americas." *Studies in American Jewish Literature* 35, no. 1: 13–32.

Shouyi, Dong, and Wang Yanjing. 1995. "Chinese Investigative Missions Overseas, 1866–1907." In *China, 1895–1912 State-Sponsored Reforms and China's Late-Qing Revolution: Selected Essays from Zhongguo Jindai Shi—Modern Chinese History, 1840–1919*, edited by Douglas Reynolds, 15–35. New York: Routledge.

Silva, Beatriz Basto da. 1994. *Emigração dos culés: Dossier Macau, 1851–1894.* Macau: Fundação Oriente.

Silva, Denise Ferreira da. 2007. *Towards a Global Idea of Race.* Minneapolis: University of Minnesota Press.

———. 2014. "No-Bodies: Law, Raciality and Violence." *Meritum* 9, no. 1: 119–162.

Silva, Valéria Torres da Costa e. 2011. *Orientalisms brasileiros: Gilberto Freyre e a peleja entre Vênus e a Moura Encantada.* Recife: Carpe Diem Edições e Produções.

Simas, Mônica. 1999. "Um monóculo perdido em Lisboa: A cidade em Eça de Queirós." In *Semear: revista da Cátedra Padre Antônio Vieira de Estudos Portugueses.* Pontifícia Universidade Católica do Rio de Janeiro.

Siskind, Mariano. 2014. *Cosmopolitan Desires: Global Modernity and World Literature in Latin America.* Evanston, IL: Northwestern University Press.

Siu, Lok. 2005. *Memories of a Future Home: Diasporic Citizenship of Chinese in Panama.* Stanford: Stanford University Press.

———. 2012. "Serial Migration: Stories of Home and Belonging in Diaspora." In *New Routes for Diaspora Studies*, edited by Sukanya Banerjee, Aims McGuinness, and Steven Charles McKay, 143–173. Bloomington: Indiana University Press.

———. 2016. "Hemispheric Raciality: Yellowface and the Challenge of Transnational Critique." *Asian Diasporic Visual Cultures and the Americas* 2, no. 1–2: 163–179.

Siu, Lok, and Bettina Ng'weno. 2015. "Comparative Raciality of Afro and Asian Latin Americans." Paper presented at the 33rd Annual Meeting of the Latin American Studies Association, Puerto Rico.

Skidmore, Thomas. 1993. *Black into White: Race and Nationality in Brazilian Thought*. Durham: Duke University Press.

Slack Jr., Edward R. 2009. "The Chinos in New Spain: A Corrective Lens for a Distorted Image." *Journal of World History* 20, no. 1: 35–67.

Smith, Adam. (1759) 1790. *The Theory of Moral Sentiments*. London: A. Miller.

———. (1776) 2000. *The Wealth of Nations*. New York: Modern Library.

Sommer, Doris. 1991. *Foundational Fictions: The National Romances of Latin America*. Berkeley: University of California Press.

Spillers, Hortense. 1997. "Mama's Baby, Papa's Maybe: An American Grammar Book." In *Feminisms: An Anthology of Literary Theory and Criticism*, edited by Robyn Warhol and Diane Price Herndl, 384–406. New Brunswick, NJ: Rutgers University Press.

Stam, Robert. 2012. *Race in Translation: Culture Wars around the Postcolonial Atlantic*. New York: New York University Press.

Stephan, Nancy Leys. 1991. *The Hour of Eugenics: Race, Gender, and Nation in Latin America*. Ithaca, NY: Cornell University Press.

Suárez, José. 2015. "Eça de Queiroz: Defender of the Chinese Coolie." *Luso-Brazilian Review*, 52:1: 61–76.

Takeuchi, Marcia Yumi. 2009. "Entre gueixas e samurais: A imigração japonesa nas revistas ilustradas (1897–1945)." PhD diss., Universidade de São Paulo.

Tambling, Jeremy, and Louis Lo. 2009. *Walking Macao, Reading the Baroque*. Hong Kong: Hong Kong University Press.

Taylor, Diana. 2003. *The Archive and the Repertoire*. Durham, NC: Duke University Press.

Taylor, Paul. 2013. *Race: A Philosophical Introduction*. Malden, MA: Polity Press.

Tchen, John Kuo Wei. 2010. "Notes for a History of Paranoia: 'Yellow Peril' and the Long Twentieth Century." *Psychoanalytic Review* 97, no. 2: 263–283.

———. 2012. "'The Yellow Claw': The Optical Unconscious in Anglo-American Political Culture." In *The Oxford History of Popular Print Culture, 6,* edited by Christine Bold, 477–500. Oxford: Oxford University Press.

Teatros do Centro Histórico do Rio de Janeiro: Século XVIII ao Século XXI. 1997. Funarte: Rio de Janeiro. Accessed October 15, 2017, at http://www.ctac.gov.br/centrohistorico/TeatroXPeriodo.asp?cod=117&cdP=17.

Théo-Filho [pseud. of Freire Filho, Manuel Theotonio de Lacerda]. 2000. *Praia de Ipanema*. Preface by Ruy Castro. Rio de Janeiro: Dantes.

Tierney, Brian 2001. *The Idea of Natural Rights: Studies on Natural Rights, Natural Law, and Church Law, 1150–1625*. Grand Rapids, MI: Eerdmans.

Tinajero, Araceli. 2004. *Orientalismo en el modernismo hispanoamericano*. West Lafayette, IN: Purdue University Press.

Tinker, Hugh. 1974. *A New System of Slavery: The Export of Indian Labour Overseas, 1830–1920*. Oxford: Oxford University Press.

Tocqueville, Alexis de. 2003. *Democracy in America and Two Essays on America*. New York: Penguin Books.

Vejmelka, Marcel. 2013. "O Brasil no espelho de Amaterasu: *O Japão* de Aluísio Azevedo." *Brasiliana—Journal for Brazilian Studies* 2, no. 2.

Veneziano, Neyde. 1991. *O Teatro de Revista no Brasil*. São Paulo: Sesi-SP, 1991.

———. 1996. *Não Adianta Chorar: Teatro de Revista Brasileiro . . . Oba!* Campinas: Unicamp.

Veracini, Lorenzo. 2010. *Settler Colonialism: Theoretical Overview*. New York: Palgrave Macmillan.

Viana Filho, Luís. 1984. *A vida de Eça de Queiroz*. Lisbon: Editora Nova Fronteira.

Vieira, Francisca Isabel Schuring. 1973. *O japonês na frente de expansão paulista: O processo de absorção do japonês em Marília*. São Paulo: Pioneira.

Wallerstein, Immanuel. 2000. *The Essential Wallerstein*. New York: New Press.

Wang, Guanhua. 2001. *In Search of Justice: The 1905–1906 Chinese Anti-American Boycott*. Cambridge, MA: Harvard University Press.

Wang Siwei. 2016. "Transcontinental Revolutionary Imagination: Literary Translations between China and Brazil (1952–1964)." Master's thesis, Columbia University.

Weinstein, Barbara. 2015. *The Color of Modernity: São Paulo and the Making of Race and Nation in Brazil*. Durham, NC: Duke University Press.

Wimmer A., and N. Glick Schiller. 2002. "Methodological Nationalism and Beyond: Nation State Building, Migration and the Social Sciences." *Global Networks* 2, no. 4: 301–334.

Wills, John. 2010. *China and Maritime Europe, 1500–1800: Trade, Settlement, Diplomacy, and Missions*. Cambridge: Cambridge University Press.

Winant, Howard. 1994. *Racial Conditions: Politics, Theory, Comparisons*. Minneapolis: University of Minnesota Press.

Wolfe, Patrick. 2006. "Settler Colonialism and the Elimination of the Native." *Journal of Genocide Research* 8, no. 4: 387–409.

Wong, Edlie. 2015. *Racial Reconstruction: Black Inclusion, Chinese Exclusion, and the Fictions of Citizenship*. New York: New York University Press.

Wood, Amy Louise. 2009. *Lynching and Spectacle: Witnessing Racial Violence in America, 1890–1940*. Chapel Hill: University of North Carolina Press.

Yoneyama, Lisa. 1999. *Hiroshima Traces: Time, Space, and the Dialectics of Memory*. Berkeley: University of California Press.

Young, Elliott. 2014. *Alien Nation. Chinese Migration in the Americas from the Coolie Era through World War II*. Chapel Hill: University of North Carolina Press.

Yu, Pauline. 2007. "'Your Alabaster in This Porcelain': Judith Gautier's *Le livre de jade*." *PMLA* 122, no. 2: 464–482.

Yun, Lisa. 2008. *The Coolie Speaks*. Philadelphia: Temple University Press.

Zhang, Yi'ou. 1918. "Jiangsu sheng zhangguan gongshu gongshu xunling di 381 hao" [Order of Chief Executive Office of Jiangsu Province, no. 381], *Jiangsu Sheng Gongbao* (Jiangsu Communiqué) 1494: 11–13. Translated by Wang Siwei.

Zivin, Erin Graff. 2008. *The Wandering Signifier: Rhetoric of Jewishness in the Latin American Imaginary*. Durham, NC: Duke University Press.

Index

CPSIA information can be obtained
at www.ICGtesting.com
Printed in the USA
LVHW03s0707220818
587621LV00002B/18/P